CHOISEUL ISLAND SOCIAL STRUCTURE

HAROLD W. SCHEFFLER

CHOISEUL ISLAND SOCIAL STRUCTURE

1965

Berkeley and Los Angeles

UNIVERSITY OF CALIFORNIA PRESS

University of California Press
Berkeley and Los Angeles, California
Cambridge University Press
London, England
© 1965 by The Regents of the University of California
Library of Congress Catalog Card Number 65–16482
Printed in the United States of America

PREFACE

This study of the social structure of Choiseul Island, which lies in the northwest corner of the British Solomon Islands Protectorate (see map, Fig. 1), is based on data gathered during eighteen months of field work between November 1958 and April 1961. An interim period of one year was spent at the Australian National University. During that period the data were given initial formulation and later checked by a further three months of field work. The island has six major dialect areas, but extensive research was undertaken in only one of them, the Varisi area. Since many Choiseulese are multilingual, once I had acquired some knowledge of Varisi I was able to check information gathered in that area with informants from other areas. I found that the Choiseulese share a relatively uniform culture, and although this analysis pertains only to the Varisi area, it is probably valid in general terms for the island as a whole.

I began to learn Varisi soon after my arrival, but it was only after the eighth month that I used it exclusively. In the earlier stages systematic investigation was limited to a few informants who spoke Solomon's Pidgin or elementary English, and I usually had to work through an interpreter of limited facility when talking with older men. I did not become a fluent speaker of Varisi with strong command of idiom, but I could readily understand my informants and question or cross-examine them. In rapid conversation the Choiseulese could lose me if they wished.

The social structure described herein is in large part a "reconstruction," and the focus is primarily upon Choiseulese society as it was about 1900, and in some places until 1915 or 1920. I do not think it is necessary to justify this interest, since any anthropologist faced with a problem of social change—the larger context within which this study has been conceived—must of necessity construct some reasonably systematic picture of the "base line" from which he may make inferences about change. Chapter 1 discusses some aspects of the social and cultural changes that have taken place on the island during the past sixty or so years; but despite change there has been some continuity too, and, furthermore, what their ancestors did in the past continues to affect what the Choiseulese do today. Former activities, as "history" or as "custom," continue to affect choices and decisions in the present, so that to understand the present it is necessary to attempt to understand the past to the degree now possible. Attention has been given to the problem of possible differences between the situation as it was and as some Choiseulese would now like to believe it was. Very few of them, however, cherish any romantic illusions about their former way of life.

Information derived from present activities may also provide evidence about the past. Thus I use facts about the present to elucidate the operation of the society in the past. Of course, this procedure must be exercised with caution and is suited to generalizations rather than to concrete details. For instance, at one point I argue that conflict between kin groups was an essential element in the attainment and maintenance of their discreteness, and I show how the state of those groups today and the relations between them support this generalization. Statements about particular events or relations in the past are not important as particular truths but rather for what they may reveal of conditions and processes in general.

Dealing with the past and present at once, as I must often do, has resulted in some knotty problems in presentation of the data. Use of the historic present tense throughout would simplify presentation and perhaps comprehension, yet it would leave the reader in doubt about the nature of the present situation and also about the data upon which various statements are based. I have chosen to write of events and conditions during my residence on the island in the present tense and of conditions and statements about the past in the past tense. Where, to the best of my knowledge, statements apply to both periods, I use the present tense, and unless otherwise specified what is said about the present is to be understood of the past too. For the most part, I had to accept statements about past conditions in general as true, whether they were statements of norms or, of what people in general usually did under given circumstances. I attempted to check these statements against case histories wherever possible. However, rather than burden the general discussion with disjointed anecdotal material I have reserved for a later chapter the discussion of some lengthy case histories which illustrate many general points. Discrepancies do occur between general statements and presumably factual accounts of events in the past and the present. These seem to me to form an important body of data which should never be dismissed from an ethnographic statement and which need explanation in other than "normative" terms; nor are such discrepancies explainable simply in terms of "social change."

There is a further reason for choosing to focus upon a "reconstructed" social structure. Choiseulese society contains groups which have so-called ambilateral characteristics, and since field studies of such groups are rare and usually incomplete and the analysis of such societies is still beset by numerous problems, this study has been conceived in large part as an attempt to deal with some of those problems.

Choiseul was chosen for study precisely because meager data reported by Thurnwald (1912) suggested the presence of "ambilateral" kin groups. My earliest attempts to understand Choiseulese social structure were greatly facilitated by Firth's notable paper on descent groups in Polynesia (1957) and by an earlier draft of his more recent paper on "bilateral descent groups" (1963). Later, analysis of the data attempted to answer what might be called the "cognatic descent problem" as posed by J. D. Freeman:

> The difficulty posed by cognatic or non-unilineal descent is that collateral cognates (from first cousins onwards) belong to more than one cognatic stock. This means that cognatic stocks, at this level, overlap; and consequently, unless some criterion other than, and in addition to, descent be brought into operation, it is impossible to achieve the division of a society into discrete groupings. No account of a bilateral or non-unilineal system can be considered complete until the way in which this difficulty is solved has been demonstrated in detail; and this, in my view, has yet to be achieved for the ambilateral *hapu* of the New Zealand Maori, as for the "non-unilinear descent groups" postulated by Goodenough for the Gilbert Islands and other parts of Malayo-Polynesia (1961: 200).

This study attempts to answer the "problem" posed by Freeman (see also Goodenough 1955; Firth 1957, 1963; Fortes 1959), but in order to do this it has been necessary to reconsider much of the recent debate about "descent" and "descent groups."

Discussions about descent and descent groups have been needlessly obfuscated by a failure to distinguish between descent as a biophysical phenomenon, a cultural construct, and certain complex social processes within which concepts of descent may be utilized. All these, and other things too, have been labeled "descent." In this study "descent" refers to certain types of genealogical construct (see chap. 2), and I have had to reject those usages which would confine the word to the labeling of "the process whereby persons become members of corporate kin groups" or "the transmission of kin group membership," for such usages, however qualified they may be, only lead to the confusion of cultural constructs ("norms" in this case) with social processes. (See Scheffler [1964b] for a defense of this point of view.) Using descent as I do resolves some problems but at the same time creates or at least points to others. If descent is a phenomenon in the realm of ideology or culture, what is its significance in the realm of action? Systems of social grouping and social action, it seems to me, must be described, analyzed, and compared or contrasted both in terms of their formal organizational ideologies and the substantive interests and transactions or operations which those ideologies presumably regulate or somehow constrain. A major anthropological problem is to relate ideas to action, and this is what I have tried to do in this study. I return to this problem throughout the text and in the conclusions.

A number of terminological problems have had to be faced in attempting to describe Choiseulese social structure. Not only has it been necessary to redefine some terms but also to dispense with others which have been used in the discussion of similar social systems (again see Scheffler 1964b). I have avoided neologisms and used the minimum number of terms consistent with clarity of reference. Where it is particularly crucial to the analysis I explain the usage in the immediate text or a footnote. In earlier presentations of some of the Choiseulese material and also in a paper on Simbo Island social structure (1962) I used a somewhat different terminology, which should now be regarded as superseded.

ACKNOWLEDGEMENTS

This study has benefited from the knowledge, encouragement, and criticism of many persons who deserve my wholehearted thanks. Of course, they are not to be held accountable for the use I have made of their advice.

To the Tri-Institutional Pacific Program and its director, Dr. Alexander Spoehr, I am indebted for the funds and other forms of assistance which made the initial field work possible. The United States Educational Foundation in Australia generously supported the period of preliminary analysis at the Australian National University in 1960–1961 and then a further period of field work.

My professors at the University of Chicago, especially the late Dr. Robert Redfield, Dr. Fred Eggan, Dr. Julian Pitt-Rivers and Dr. Donald Horton, who tried to teach me some anthropology and sociology, may recognize some of their own ideas herein, but perhaps not so adequately expressed as they were communicated to me.

At the Australian National University I benefited greatly from the advice and instruction of Drs. J. A. Barnes, W. E. H. Stanner, and J. D. Freeman. The latter helped a confused novice to analyze the data gathered in the initial field-work period, formulate certain problems from it, and finally encouraged him to further field work. My debts to the others are apparent in my frequent references to their writings.

In addition to my dissertation supervisors, Drs. Fred Eggan and David M. Schneider, who have given generously of their time and thoughts, Drs. Raymond Firth, William Davenport, Floyd Lounsbury, J. A. Barnes, and Murray Groves have read portions of earlier drafts of the manuscript and offered useful suggestions which have substantially improved portions of the presentation and arguments.

The British Solomon Islands Protectorate government and its officers made available transportation between government stations and Choiseul and Simbo Islands and lent other forms of assistance when possible, without which field work could not have been done. Mr. J. Grover, director of the B.S.I.P. Geological Survey, offered generous hospitality and technical assistance, and on our way to the islands Drs. H. I. Hogbin and P. Coleman, of the University of Sydney, assisted in the preparations for field work and gave much useful advice about life in the islands.

To the staffs of the various Christian missions on Choiseul my wife and I are indebted for their many kindnesses and frequent insights into Choiseulese life. But most important were the contributions of the Choiseulese in general who were patient teachers and kind hosts. I am especially indebted to Levai Tanavalu, Assistant District Headman Tepazaka District, Boas Pitanapi, Assistant District Headman Varisi District, Anduru Ponggevolomo, David Paukubatu, Eliza Polosokesa, and Philip Mumugavere. To Paukubatu I am indebted above all, for without his profound knowledge of and even sociological insight into his own society and culture I doubt that this study could have been written, and certainly not in its present form.

H. W. S.

CONTENTS

TABLES

FIGURES

Chapter 1

The Island:
Its People
and Its History

This chapter sketches the physical and larger social environment within which Choiseulese society operated and to which it was to some extent an adaptive response. This is done only to provide a background to the few references made to this larger environment, and no systematic attempt is made to assess the "determinants" of the social structure. The state of Choiseulese society today and its more recent history are also sketched in order to place the material in the larger context within which it becomes more comprehensible.

THE ISLAND

Choiseul is the northwesternmost island in the British Solomon Islands Protectorate and the sixth largest land mass in the Solomon's chain. Its nearest neighbors are the Shortland Islands and Bougainville to the west, Santa Ysabel to the east, and Vella Lavella to the south, all of which are at least twenty-five to fifty miles distant from the nearest point on Choiseul. The island is about eighty miles long and eight to twenty miles across; it comprises a total area of approximately 1,140 square miles. The highest point, thirty-five hundred feet, is on Mt. Maitabe near the geographic center of the island. This is an exceptional elevation, for the island is more generally a mass of deep valleys and sharp ridges averaging between one and two thousand feet. There is little flat ground except for a few highland plateaus and a few

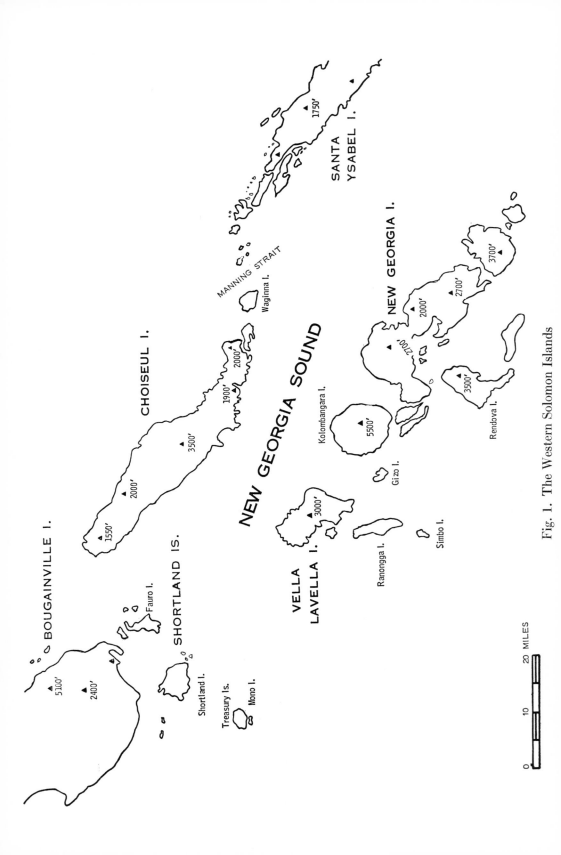

Fig. 1. The Western Solomon Islands

areas near river mouths along the coasts. The coasts are fringed by reefs making approach difficult by craft other than canoe or small launch.

The seasons are typical for the Southwest Pacific: a southeast from May to October with strong and steady breezes, only a little drier than the northwest from December to March. The island lies outside the hurricane belt so that winds are seldom destructive. Rainfall is estimated [1] at 100–200 inches per year with at least seven inches per month, and there is seldom a shortage of rainfall in either season. The climate is typically equatorial maritime. Mean maximum temperature (slightly warmer in the northwest season) varies between 86 and 91 degrees; the absolute maximum is 94 degrees. The temperature does not fall below 70 degrees even in the early hours of morning along the coasts, but it is considerably cooler inland at higher altitudes. The relative humidity is consistently between 75 and 85 per cent.

Except for small coconut plantations and garden areas, the whole island is covered with rain forest which forms a high overhead canopy. The undergrowth, however, is not dense except in areas of recent secondary growth, and the island may be traversed on foot without great difficulty. Numerous tracks exist throughout the interior, but only a few run right across the island. The Choiseulese cover all but the longest tracks in a single day or less.

Until about 1905 the people dwelled inland, dispersed in small hamlets along the numerous ridges. They seem to have preferred the coastal ranges, though many lived in the center of the island. Indeed, some of the principal settlements, that is, those of the strongest groups, were situated there. (Settlement pattern is discussed more extensively below pp. 25–27, 94.)

The island is netted with a vast number of streams and rivers, a few of considerable size and extent; except near the mouths of rivers, the water is uniformly safe for consumption. Although much of the island is volcanic in origin, there are no active volcanoes. Maitabe is an extinct volcano, and one of the few re-

---

[1] The geographical information presented derives from my own observations, which were not systematic on this subject, and from a World War II "Area Study" (1943). Much of the data in that document are inferential and derived from more complete information available for New Georgia Island to the south of Choiseul. Further geographical data are found in Allan (1957) and Belshaw (1950).

maining interior villages in 1961, Sarelata, is situated on its rim at the lowest point. The island is still geologically active, however, and it appears to be sinking into the sea at the rate of a few inches a year.

The results of limited soil surveys undertaken in the Protectorate, though none have yet been made on Choiseul, have not been encouraging (Allan 1957: 3). Soils are generally porous and particularly subject to erosion and leaching, and the luxurious vegetation is deceptive. However, the Choiseulese are aware of the differential productivity and suitability of different soils and locations and site their gardens accordingly. Other than technical factors also enter into the siting of gardens today; for instance, a site may be chosen not for its intrinsic value in gardening but because it will make a good coconut plantation after the garden has ceased to be productive.

The two seasons are recognized by the Choiseulese and named for their respective prevailing winds, but the seasons are defined also in terms of activities which were, in the past, affected somewhat indirectly by them. The principal crop, taro, could be planted and harvested at any time, little if at all affected by the minor seasonal variations in climate. Wetter periods affect ability to work in the gardens and also the growth of the crops through lack of sunlight, but, so far as my informants were aware, the seasonal variation in rainfall is not sufficient to make a marked difference in gardening activities or productivity. However, an important natural cycle for the Choiseulese was that of the *ngari* (canarium almond) which ripens in June–July. These nuts, together with taro, formed the principal ingredient in a pudding (*taoga*) which was traditionally served at all feasts associated with important transactions (see chap. 4). Gathering the nuts and preparing them for drying and storage was an activity of note in itself. There was no "feasting season," though feasts do seem to have been most frequent soon after the ripening of the *ngari*. The necessity for a large taro crop, numerous pigs, and peaceful local conditions also affected the timing of a feast, but if these conditions were met a feast was usually held as soon as the *ngari* were ready.

Animal life is sparse. Wild pig and opossum of several varieties formed a part of the diet but only as supplements and not as major items. Today the Choiseulese believe themselves to have little time for hunting except for a few men who periodically do so. Domestic pigs were kept at one time, but today few men have even one. Nevertheless, at least one pig is always killed at a feast of any note, though today's feasts are neither of the same scale nor given for the same reasons as those of the past.

Aquatic life is extensive in the sea and fresh-water streams and is taken by hook, line, and net. Seacow and turtle were taken by group action with large nets. The significance of these items in the diet in the past is difficult to estimate, but today it is minimal indeed; even fishing is only sporadic. I was surprised at the lack of attention given to gathering sea life today, but the Choiseulese, though they now live on the coasts, consider themselves a "bush people," and they do not look to the sea as a primary source of subsistence. Their ancestors did make lengthy voyages over the open sea to make war with the peoples of Vella Lavella or even New Georgia, but it is said that they made the voyages only reluctantly and then only when assured of good weather.

THE PEOPLE

The Choiseulese are not well known anthropologically. Capell (1943) summarized the available information in a short article in *Oceania*, and a fairly complete set of references is contained in his bibliography. However, those accounts are all sketchy and superficial and often simply erroneous in dealing with the ethnographic facts. Thurnwald (1912) offers the only data of any sociological interest, but it is interspersed with data on Buin (Bougainville) and difficult to use.

No systematic physical anthropology has been done on Choiseul, nor did I do any. It is generally conceded that the Choiseulese are "Melanesian," both physically and linguistically. They are, however, much darker in skin color than the Solomon Islanders to the south and east, and they are not of the "tall type found farther to the north" (Capell 1943: 20). Neither are the Choiseulese particularly short in stature. I did note that they seem to be of a more linear body form than, say, the peoples of New Georgia to the south who I thought were more often shorter and more robust in body form. Generalizations are complicated by the fact that there is much physical variety among the Choiseulese themselves.

The population of Choiseul is approximately 5,700.[2] This figure is derived from the World Health Organization Yaws Campaign of August–October 1956 during which 5,447 penicillin injections were given on the island and another 325 persons were estimated absent from the island as laborers, students, or for other reasons. With an estimated area of 1,140 square miles, this works out to a population density of about 5 per square mile. This figure is comparable to those for the other large islands in the Solomons, which vary from 4–7 persons per square mile (Allan 1957: 16–17). It must be added, however, that none of these figures is very realistic, for, with the exception of Malaita and Guadalcanal, no island has an appreciable number of inland or "bush" villages. The peoples are almost entirely concentrated on the coasts, and in most cases vast areas in the interior regions are seldom if ever used for any purpose other than an occasional wild-pig hunt or the gathering of house-building materials.

There can be little doubt that there was a considerable decline in total population during the late nineteenth and early twentieth centuries due to deadlier and perhaps more intensified warfare, "blackbirding," and new diseases such as influenza and measles. However, it is very difficult, if not impossible, to estimate the size of the "aboriginal" population. Warfare, even before its nineteenth-century "technological revolution," was a deadly affair and probably contributed to the maintenance of a low population density. There is no reliable evidence upon which to compile a pre-contact estimate, but I doubt that the population was ever near that of the present day Malaita (about 40,000), an island of comparable size.

Despite the inaccuracy of the available figures (1931—4,051; 1955—4,572; 1957—5,700), it is apparent that the population is now on the increase. The "depopulation" of Melanesia (cf. Rivers 1922), at least in this general area (cf. also Scheffler 1962: 137), has been arrested and even reversed.

Capell (1943: 21–22) states that the Choiseulese languages are "Melanesian, of one group, but that group is very different from the Melanesian of Florida and the southern islands" (of the Solomons). Furthermore, "the Melanesian content is smaller than in

---

[2] The Pacific Islands Year Book (1963: 428) gives a figure of 6,570, but this is probably only an estimate based on a recent census of the Solomons which did not sample Choiseul itself.

the more southerly languages, and it is clear that the main stream of Melanesian movements missed Choiseul." According to Murdock's (1964) interpretation of Dyen's recent lexicostatistical analysis of Oceanic languages, the Choiseulese languages form one of three related "closed composite groups" of the Solomons; most of the languages of the Solomons, including the Choiseulese, are classed by Murdock (on the basis of Dyen's data) as a "divergent" group which "is at least potentially an independent family coordinate with Malayo-Polynesian" (Murdock 1964: 119–120).[3]

The Choiseulese recognize some six major "languages" (or dialects?) spoken on their island. Superficially at least they seem more closely related to one another than to any other language in the general area. Within some of these linguistic units further differentiation is to be found, but these differences are minor and

TABLE 1

CHOISEUL LANGUAGES

Language	Speakers
Vagua	1,000
Varisi	1,000
Ririo	50
Babatana	1,600
Sisingga	1,200
Kirunggela	850

largely phonemic. Table 1 lists the major linguistic divisions and the approximate number of speakers of each language today; locations are indicated on the map in Figure 2.

Political administrative divisions established by the Protectorate Government in recent years correspond only roughly with the major linguistic divisions, but in aboriginal times there seem to

---

[3] All Choiseulese words contained herein are from the Varisi language. My orthography does not claim to be phonemic; the symbols used below are taken from Webster's "Guide to Pronunciation."

a: as in father, ä.   b: nazalized, mb.
e: French é, but occassionally   d: nazalized, nd.
    unaccented.   g: "Melanesian g."
i: as in machine, ē.   ng: as -ng in sing.
o: as in note, ō.   ngg: as -ng in finger.
u: as in lute, ū.   v: soft, difficult to distinguish
                                                       from the "Melanesian g."

have been no important cultural or social differences between the language divisions. Vagua-Varisi-Ririo seems to form a relatively distinctive linguistic unit in contrast to Babatana-Sisingga-Kirunggela, and these two large units differ in a few other relatively minor ways. The former peoples made pottery and stone repositories (monolithic) for the cremated remains of their deceased big-men; the latter peoples did not. There are also some systematic differences in the patterns of kinship terminology and conduct. The Choiseulese are little aware of or concerned about such differences and are prone to view their island as culturally uniform.

Fig. 2. Choiseul Island Languages

Attempts have been made to work out the cultural history of the Melanesian peoples, notably by Rivers (1914), but until much more complete ethnographic and archaeological information is available it seems unlikely that such attempts will be productive or generally acceptable. Insular Melanesia is noted for the variety of social and cultural forms which abound there, only a fraction of which have been described so far; and not much more of this variety is likely to be described because of the rate of cultural loss consequent to recent social changes in the area. Nor is local traditional "history" very helpful because for the most part there is none. Allan (1957: 11) states that he found that "any enquiry about land-tenure automatically evinces accounts of past migrations and movements, of peoples who lived there 'before,' and of how present interests are derived." There is some truth in these remarks, yet what Allan leaves unsaid is important too. If my own experiences with the Choiseulese and Simboese are in any way representative of the general situation in the Western Solomons, it would appear that "migrations and movements" can refer only to very recent and small-scale ones, such as from "bush" to "beach," and "other peoples" can be taken to mean only fairly recent ancestors of the present populations, not people of a different "kind." About their more remote "origins" the Choiseulese may be said to be totally ignorant, and, what is more, they do not evince much interest in such matters. So far as they are concerned, the island has been theirs and theirs alone since time immemorial. Unlike the Simboese to the south (Scheffler 1962: 137–138), they have no historical or mythological traditions concerning the whole population and very few concerning the origins of its lesser social units. Tales concerning particular local kin groups deal with ancestors only a few generations removed from the present, and these have a myth-like quality and sameness. In these respects the Choiseulese are like many other Melanesians.

Ecology

In the past the Choiseulese practiced subsistence horticulture with many varieties of taro (*mana*, the whole plant; *ngolo*, the tuber) as their principal crop. Their taro was apparently of the relatively nonstorable variety. In addition they planted yams (*inggama*), bananas (*songga*), sugar cane (*paraka*), and a few greens. They also gathered much from sea, stream, and forest, but it is now quite impossible to estimate more than very roughly the relative contribution of each of these items to the total diet or the relative amount of time devoted to each pursuit. Today, sweet potatoes, which are tended in ways quite different from those required in taro cultivation, are the principal dietary item along with polished rice and canned meat, which are acquired in exchange for copra from itinerant Chinese traders. Many men concern themselves almost entirely with copra production, depending upon how many palms they have, and only infrequently work in their gardens, which are left to the women except when new areas are needed a few times a year. Furthermore, the introduction of steel knives and axes has reduced considerably the amount of time men must spend in their gardening activities. Sweet potatoes and a few other food stuffs were introduced apparently in post-contact times, but by whom is unknown. However, they have become increasingly predominant, and since World War II they have been the staple for nearly all Choiseulese. Their relative ease of cultivation accounts for much of their popularity, but their cultivation has been forced upon the Choiseulese by a fungal blight which has progressively afflicted the taro and the land until today there are only a few small areas in which taro is or can be cultivated to an appreciable extent. Concomitantly, gardens have become a source of little interest or concern—economic competition has shifted to other realms—even though they are still economically more important than in some other areas of the Solomons.

Since gardening techniques have undergone extensive change, I rely largely upon generalized accounts of past practices, but in a few "bush" communities gardening is still practiced as I describe it, with important changes in the tools used. It is quite clear that taro production was the major subsistence concern in the past and that most other activities were adapted to that concern. In the absence of soil surveys and precise climatic data it is difficult to say why the Choiseulese concentrated on taro. It is true that they still prefer it as a food in contrast to all others, yet this is probably not the explanation; more likely, taro was the best crop available to them under the particular environmental conditions. Other things grew, but probably not so well; thus they concentrated from necessity on the most productive item. Choiseulese taro, in contrast to such crops as yams, is not storable for more than short periods of, say, a few days. It can be kept in the ground for perhaps a few weeks, but once removed it must be eaten. Therefore, unlike the situation among yam cultivators, no large surplus can be produced and then stored for a lengthy period. Taro must be planted and harvested year around to assure a ready supply at all times. Large quantities can be planted and then harvested at one time, and this was often done in preparation for large feasts (see chap. 4).

The Choiseulese practice swidden horticulture because of their technology and the crops available to them. A number of considerations make this unavoidable even today. They still have only hand tools which in the past were made of wood, stone, and shell; the stone axe was the principal tool, along with fire, for clearing bush for gardens. Thus clearing forest is a major task requiring the coöperation of several or many men. Garden areas cannot be thoroughly cleared of large timber, much of which must be left standing and only "topped" or felled and left lying once branches are trimmed off. The land itself, because of rapid leaching of nutrients, is never suitable for more than one planting (the Choiseulese seem never to have used any form of irrigation) after which it must be left to fallow for varying periods. Ten to twenty or more years may be required, or such were the estimates of my informants. Then, too, secondary growth comes in rapidly, and by the time the crop is mature it is difficult to control. All of this means, of course, that large areas of land are required per capita and that local groups must have at their disposal much larger areas than they can use at any one time. The population must be dispersed and of relatively low density.

Coöperative labor was and is a necessity in gardening. Not only is it more efficient and pleasurable than solitary labor, but it was also necessary for safety because of the intergroup conflict endemic in indigenous Choiseulese society. Typically, a number of men ready to make a garden at any one time worked together to clear a large area, perhaps fenced it (if pigs presented a problem), and then divided it into family plots which each family then separately planted and harvested. The teams for these "joint gardens" were formed strictly *ad hoc* and did not necessarily continue to make gardens together afterwards, nor were the teams formed in accordance with any particular principles of kinship. Since the families concerned varied in size and, therefore, rate of consumption, they used up their plots at differential rates. Not all members of the original gardening team were likely to be ready to start new gardens at the same time, and so one time partners allied with yet other men to form new teams and clear new plots. Men who were not yet ready to start new plots themselves nevertheless contributed their labor to those who were in the expectation of reciprocity in kind.

Informants estimated that in the past a man might need to start about five plots per year, but not all of these plots were necessarily segments of a larger joint garden, and today most men garden solitarily though still with the initial help of others. Solitary gardening was unsafe: women working in the gardens had to be guarded by several men lest they be sought out by other men for adulterous affairs or attacked by enemies of the group.

The use of land for gardening did not require formal title to it but only the permission of those with formal title. Such permission was ideally granted all kinsmen, consanguineal or affinal, who took this to be a privilege of kinship and one not lightly denied. It was not necessary that the user be a partipating member of the group holding title to the land, and men frequently planted on the lands of neighboring and friendly groups; but the possibility of so doing clearly depended upon the size of the holdings of the groups concerned and the proximity of their settlements to the lands of the adjoining groups. It is said that men would travel considerable distances to garden on the lands of other groups, or on their own lands which might have been some distance from their immediate residences, but again the possibility was conditioned by the presence or absence of peaceful conditions in the locality and the quality of relations between those individuals and groups.

It is tempting to consider the possibility of an "ecological explanation" for the presence of "nonunilineal descent groups." Raulet (1960) has argued that the pursuit of subsistence under such conditions leads men into a variety of allegiances of expediency rather than permanent alliances with persons of a specific kintype; men are led to stress all types of kinship connection and to ally with other individuals and groups on the basis of any kinship relation possible so long as the alliances serve their interests. I can accept this as a plausible assessment of the Choiseulese situation though certainly undemonstrated on the basis of the scant information presented here. However, the interests served by changes of primary segment [4] affiliation, whether on a temporary or permanent basis, were far more numerous and complex than subsistence interests. The indeterminant composition of primary segments; the interdependence of the members of different primary segments; the establishment of mutual obligation and aid on a "personal" basis rather than on the basis of any set

---

[4] I have borrowed this term from Sahlins (1961: 325) to describe the nucleated residential and proprietary units.

and specific type of kin tie—all of these seem more basically re-latable to some rather simple political facts of Choiseulese society. Ecologically, the Choiseulese certainly did not live in a vacuum, but many other factors should be considered as contributive to the relatively indeterminate composition of primary segments in terms of a specific kinship idiom. For instance, probably much weight needs to be given to the significance of intergroup conflict and to the fact that Choiseulese society was one without "law" in our naïve sense of the term.

With regard to the constraining effects of ecology, the remarks of Barnes in relation to New Guinea Highlands societies are relevant.

> Inheritance and the provision and distribution of bridewealth play a major part in African societies in determining the struc-ture of small lineage segments and in establishing their corpo-rate qualities. In New Guinea a man depends less on what he can hope to inherit from his father and pays less attention to the ill defined reversionary rights which he may perhaps have in the property of his agnatic cousins. In both areas a man looks first to his agnatic group for garden land, but it seems that in New Guinea he can turn with greater confidence to other groups as well. (Barnes 1962: 8.)

Barnes suggests that this situation in the Highlands is perhaps understandable in terms of the relative absence of long-lived tree crops or sites of particularly high fertility, "such as in Africa often form a substantial part of the collective capital of a lineage seg-ment." On Choiseul too the land seems to vary little in its relative productivity, and one large area seems to have been no more attractive than any other for subsistence concerns. Probably there would have been little to gain, and much to lose, for many, though not all, men by firm attachment to one and only one primary segment for land-holding and -using purposes. Here too, as in the Highlands, ". . . a man's capital resources consist largely in the obligations which he has imposed on his exchange partners and on his death these resources may be dissipated or disappear entirely. Hence to a greater extent than in Africa every man in the New Guinea Highlands starts from scratch and has to build up his own social position" (1962: 8). As shown in the course of this study, the Choiseulese have a concept of unilineal descent, but it cannot be understood simply as a criterion of eligibility to membership in kin groups, even though they may at times speak of some forms of entitlement in unilineal terms. For many purposes descent or kinship status within a local group was not, and is not now, brought into consideration. Members of local groups are kinsmen, and that is what matters. On the other hand, from the outside this kin group is seen as a descent group linked by genealogical ties to other descent groups, all of which (the number is widely various) are linked in an all-embracing pyramidal genealogical structure, similar to the situation in some African societies. However, although cognate descent groups were nominally obliged to render assistance to one another, alliances between them were contractual, just as were alliances between unrelated segments. The "big-man complex," so typical of Melanesian societies (see Sahlins 1963), existed here too. In many contexts, group membership consisted in allegiance to a prominent man and in assisting him in establishing relations with other prominent men in other groups, on the same basis as all men used to establish interpersonal relationships. The big-men served as focal points in intergroup relations and formed alliances with other big-men and their groups on a contractual basis, though some account could be taken of possible broader genealogical relations between the groups. The same thing—personal allegiance, though a kinship idiom could be used to declare it—that bound men to one another, bound them into groups and then regulated the relations between those groups.

KNOWN HISTORY

Here I attempt only to outline the general course of social change as it can be reconstructed from Choiseulese knowledge and historical documents. No attempt is made to be definitive nor to support each assertion in detail, for this is the subject of another study now in preparation.

The major changes in Choiseulese life during the past century are readily comprehended as consequences of pacification and integration into the European economy. Both occurred simultaneously, and neither would have been possible without the attractions of the other.

Choiseul first became known, but hardly significant, to Europeans when it was sighted and named San Marcos by the crew of the Spanish explorer Mendaña in April of 1568 (Amhurst and Thompson 1901: 35). Mendaña did not land on Choiseul, and his most extensive contacts were with the peoples of Santa Ysabel, just to the east. His relations with these people and his descriptions of their social life may be taken as typical of both the general Solomon Island indigenous social situation and the nature of islander-European relations for several hundred years afterwards.

After Mendaña's voyages, Choiseul, like the rest of the Solomons, was "lost" to Europeans for a little more than two hundred years. So far as is known it was next sighted by the French explorer Bougainville in June of 1768 (Bougainville 1772: 316), who made fleeting armed contact with about ten canoe loads of Choiseulese when they attacked his ship with bow and spear. His description of what he saw differs hardly from that of Mendaña or from later accounts dating into the twentieth century. It was Bougainville who conferred upon the island the name by which it is now known to Europeans. The people themselves call their island *Lauru*, and it is known to the peoples of nearby islands by that name or similar names (e.g., *Rauru*). Other adventurers may have sighted or landed on Choiseul, but we know nothing of such visits. In any event, none of the fleeting contacts of the explorers made a lasting impression upon the lives of the Choiseulese; their pattern of life remained apparently basically unaltered until regular visits were begun by Europeans in the nineteenth century.

To the early observers, perhaps the most outstanding feature of the social life of the Solomon Islanders was its seeming anarchy. Bougainville (1772: 322) concluded that these people "were from their manners . . . almost constantly at war with one another," and so they remained throughout the nineteenth century and, on parts of Choiseul, up to about 1925. Among European observers, the Solomon Islanders consistently had an unenviable reputation as ferocious savages. Interpersonal and intergroup relations were notable for their violence, much of which was quickly directed towards visiting Europeans, whose attitudes and actions were also important in initiating conflict. They could hardly have picked on a people more likely to take offense and to take reprisal seriously. Amhurst and Thompson (1901: xxiii) note in their introduction to the journals of the sixteenth-century Spanish explorers:

> For a parallel to the political *morcellement* of Melanesia, we may look the world through in vain. Every petty tribal unit inhabiting a few square miles spoke a dialect that was almost a different

language, and was at perpetual enmity with its neighbors. Every stranger was an enemy, whom it was a virtue to slay. Head-hunting canoes from other islands ranged the coast attacking all who were not strong enough to repel them.

The phrasing here is somewhat too strong, for it leaves unexplored other aspects of intergroup relations; the situation was surely not one of total anarchy, for the way of life in which these actions occurred did persist for several hundred years. Nevertheless, Spanish accounts abound with tales of viciousness, cannibalism, treachery, mobs of armed and hostile islanders, and frequent warfare. The Spanish did nothing, or very little, to convince the islanders that a different mode of intergroup relations was possible, and Mendaña himself did his own small part towards the depopulation of Melanesia. Everywhere he went he found the situation much the same: The Melanesians were almost always, though with some notable exceptions, initially hostile, seldom doing any real damage, but provoking the Spaniards to put on a show of force and to kill a few of them. This made the Melanesians somewhat more cautious but by no means submissive or pliant, and relations quickly went from bad to worse. Apparently, the islanders often wanted no more than to be left alone, and the pleasure of the sight of Mendaña's departure "we can well believe [was] dashed with no regrets for the parting guest" (Amhurst and Thompson 1901: xliii).

Those Europeans who came later found the situation identical in most respects.[5] The islanders had not changed, nor had their visitors, except in national origins. The traders of the nineteenth century were the first Europeans to have any continuing impact upon the life of the islanders. They were at first interested only in sandalwood, tortoiseshell, and *bêche-de-mer;* they did not attempt permanent settlement but established fairly regular trading relationships with certain groups and stimulated the desire for trade goods. The rapidity of social change here owes much to the Melanesian attraction to our worldly goods; it was one of the factors that led them to embrace Christianity in the futile expec-

---

[5] Mendaña may have found the islands much more populous in general, and in particular places, than they were in the eighteenth and nineteenth centuries or are today. Where he found many coastal villages, today there are none, and the more frequent and populous inland villages he noted do not seem to have been so frequent either at a later date. The accounts are, however, difficult to compare.

tation that they would thereby gain access to those goods, and it had much to do with their acceptance of the European imposition of generally peaceful conditions.

For their tortoiseshell and *bêche-de-mer* the islanders received, and apparently demanded, mostly "axes, adzes, blue cloth, straw hats, knives, fish hooks, gimlets, looking glasses, boxes, and, at Eddystone [Simbo], flint guns" (Cheyne 1852: 64). No information is available on the trade with Choiseul itself, and the Choiseulese of today have retained little memory of encounters with Europeans before the 1880's or 1890's. There seems to have been a sort of gentlemen's agreement for a ban on the trade of firearms to the islanders, but Cheyne was willing to trade them with people, like the Simboese, who he felt were "friendly to Europeans." The Germans, who took possession of Santa Ysabel and Choiseul in 1886, enforced the ban in their territories, but the English, who had control of the trade in the so-called southern Solomons including New Georgia and Vella Lavella even before the declaration of the area as a British protectorate, were ineffective in controlling this trade. For a time, then, some groups had firearms while others did not. This obviously gave the former a decided advantage in the intergroup conflicts of which the Europeans disapproved and which were probably accelerated or intensified by their presence (see Ivens 1930: 43–44; Sommerville 1896: 399), but the traders did not allow the sentiments of others to interfere with profiting from the situation.

The Choiseulese did manage to get arms by 1895 and probably even earlier, though not in large quantities (Morrell 1960: 343). They got them in trade with people from New Georgia or Vella Lavella and in exchange for "slaves," or persons to be adopted into the kin groups of the recipient party. Some of these "slaves" were destined to be victims in sacrificial rites, but the Choiseulese apparently desired guns strongly, and some big-men gained poor reputations among their own people for engaging in this trade. In some areas of the Solomons, the islanders coöperated with labor recruiters and "blackbirders" in their vicious practices in order to get firearms in exchange for their services (see Ivens 1930: 201 and Belshaw 1954: 34–36).

The establishment of sugar-cane plantations in Queensland and Fiji in the 1840's created a demand for cheap labor, which was met by labor recruiters and "blackbirders" (see Oliver 1961 and Belshaw 1954), a euphemism for slave traders. Sometimes islanders were recruited by gifts of trade goods, firearms, and liquor given to their kinsmen or big-man and by promise of more goods upon their return home, but often they were kidnapped or enticed by various nefarious and vicious means. The Choiseulese, however, were little bothered by this particular practice, for the island with its small population was not nearly as attractive as nearby Malaita. A few Choiseulese were taken to Queensland and Fiji, and fewer still returned home, but those who did figured prominently in the process of social and cultural change which soon followed.

"Blackbirding" did not reach the Solomons until the 1860's and attained its peak in the 1870's and 1880's, but by then several factors were combining to bring an end to the practice. The islanders were reacting with violence, which was often directed towards relatively innocent Europeans, such as resident traders, planters, and missionaries. There were protests against the trade both in England and Australia, but legal actions and patrols by the Royal Navy in an effort to suppress it were not very effective—except against the islanders: " . . . punitive expeditions punished murders of or attacks on Europeans with considerable frequence. Villages were burnt, canoes destroyed, and natives fined or hanged after summary enquiry" (Belshaw 1950: 50). The Choiseulese both gave and took in these encounters which did nothing to create good relationships with Europeans. Australia finally outlawed the importation of island labor in 1902 and, as a consequence of an emerging "White Australia" policy, the islanders were forcibly returned to their "homes." It is doubtful, however, that many of them got back to their native islands: some were simply deposited on strange islands and left to shift for themselves, which often meant death at the hands of the hostile inhabitants.

British policy until the middle of the nineteenth century had been one of minimum intervention—the result of the "supremacy of the Royal Navy, the ferocity of the inhabitants, the lack of obvious commercial resources and the disinterest of other powers" (Allan 1957: 33). So long as Europeans were not settled in the islands the hostility of the people remained only a serious inconvenience. The establishment of a copra industry, which apparently began to be developed in the 1870's or earlier (Allan 1957: 32), and intensive missionary activity brought the first permanent settlers, other than a few earlier and unsuccessful missionary attempts. Hostility on the part of the islanders then became increasingly intolerable. Demands for protection were made and further pressed by the New Zealand and Australian governments who also wished to secure the area from other colonial powers, such as Germany, which were beginning to take an interest in the area. A reluctant Britain established the protectorate in 1893, and Choiseul became a part of it in 1899 by treaty with the Germans who had acquired domain over Choiseul, along with Santa Ysabel and several more northerly Melanesian islands, by a treaty which portioned colonial interests in the islands in 1884 (Morrell 1960: 331-349). The post of resident commissioner was established and the occupant given the responsibility of establishing law and order. By this time "blackbirders" were not much a problem, but difficulty with the islanders continued unabated.

Before 1900 the Royal Navy was occasionally sent to shell a village of presumed trouble makers and thereby discourage raids on Europeans and other islanders. But these raids sometimes had just the opposite effect and promoted further conflict because the islanders always sought revenge. It is clear that for a time the British themselves participated in the indigenous system of vengeance and counter-vengeance, though unwittingly. The British thought they were establishing peace, but the Solomon Islanders understood the actions differently.

C. M. Woodford, who was later to become the first resident commissioner, visited New Georgia in 1886 and noted that, " . . . no less than forty heads, besides slaves, were brought back from Ysabel in the course of my stay of two weeks, and a similar state of affairs continued up to and after the declaration of the British Protectorate in 1893. Consequently one of the first duties of the administration was to put down head hunting with a strong hand" (1909: 510). Furthermore, according to a long-term resident of the islands in 1899, sixty-two white men and women had been killed by the islanders on Rendova Island alone within the preceding few years (see Brown 1908: 517).

The British felt that no life would be safe until the institutions of raiding and headhunting were put down once and for all. Woodford's choice, perhaps the only one open to him, was to fight fire with fire, just as his predecessors had done. A system of bringing "immediate retribution . . . upon offenders" (Belshaw 1950: 51) was adopted, and a body of Fijian police, later replaced by men from the more easterly and more settled Solomon Islands, and on occasion assisted by the Royal Navy, continued to carry out punitive measurers. "According to the testimony of old settlers in the islands, he enlisted the support of missionaries and settlers. The latter had to be armed and were allowed to take retributive action in case of need" (Belshaw 1950: 51). The measures taken were often just as devastating and merciless as indigenous warfare,[6] so that the islanders quickly learned that Europeans, for organizational and technological reasons, could play the game better than they could. Fear of loss of property, resources, and life helped to put a stop to the fighting, but the Choiseulese were among the most reluctant to give up old ways. The B.S.I.P. Annual Reports for the years from 1914 to 1918 reported that "on Choiseul where there has been incessant intertribal fighting . . . numbers of men, women and children have been killed," and "except on Choiseul, serious crime is of rare occurrence."

Violent coercion was only one of the reasons why internecine conflict came to an end; the islanders had their own reasons too. Quite aside from the fact that the vengeance system constituted a vicious cycle from which at least some men wanted to escape if only a way out could be found, the islanders could get the things they wanted from the Europeans only by engaging in trade with them. As copra became the principal item of barter, trade increasingly required settled conditions for its development. The desire for European trade goods was and remains insatiable, and it has had much to do with the Melanesian susceptibility to social and cultural change.

Christian missions, here as elsewhere, played an important role in establishing the conditions that would allow effective exploitation of the human and material resources the islands had to offer. It is obvious that missionary efforts were not undertaken with such intent—perhaps they were just "latent functions" of the missionary enterprise. Nevertheless, the methods used by the

---

[6] For a graphic and crusading account of administration measures see Burnett (1911: 145 ff.), and for a purportedly first-hand account of indigenous warfare see de Tolna (1903: 344–359). De Tolna should not be taken too seriously, however, for like so many Europeans of his time he was inclined to see a "cannibal" behind every bush and in every hut.

missionaries were often not notably different from those used by the honest labor recruiter (Belshaw 1954: 52).

The missionaries sought to reach the Melanesians most effectively through their children. The Bishop of Melanesia (Anglican) wrote after a visit to Guadalcanal in 1867 (quoted in Belshaw 1954: 51) that he told the people, in order to get them to let their young people go with him to a training school, "What have you tried to do for me that I should give you presents? I keep these things for those who are helping me and working with me." He commented, "The opportunity of acquiring hatchets, fishhooks, etc. is a tangible advantage, which they appreciate at once. By degrees, we trust they will be enabled to see more and more clearly the value of the message we bring."

Early converts and returned laborers were instrumental in getting resident missionaries established. Many laborers had been converted in their absence from the islands and urged the acceptance of mission services when they were offered. An important motivation on their part was, again, the desire for European goods and other advantages had by Europeans. Hogbin (1939) notes of such men on Malaita, that in Queensland they were cut off from all contact with home, and missionaries were the only white men to take a kindly interest in them. They saw the wealth of the white man who was a Christian, and they drew the inference that his wealth and religion were somehow related to one another. Most of those who returned to the islands reverted to paganism, but a few remained strongly Christian in their perspective. All of them spread tales of the wonders they had seen and stimulated locally the desire to travel and gain some knowledge and, perhaps, even some control over the outside world. Many thought that the only difference between themselves and Europeans was one of "education," the ability to read and write, to which only the missions, through their schools, offered access. Education, or becoming a Christian, which amounted to the same thing, would somehow lead to access to the coveted trade goods (Hogbin 1939: 179–180). Conversations with elderly Choiseulese who remember the early mission days indicated that such were Choiseulese motives and thoughts too. Perhaps not so neat an equation—between Christianity and the advantages of the European way of life—existed in the minds of the Solomon Islanders as in the minds of the New Guinea people reported by Lawrence

(1954), but the missionary promise of peace and prosperity did nothing to dispel any such equation that the Solomon Islander might have made.

The first missionaries (Australian Methodists) came to Choiseul in 1904 from New Georgia where they had also just begun to work (Luxton 1955: 69–91), and their methods were similar to those of the Melanesian Mission and its bishop. They began by placing Fijian preacher-teachers in villages, and after these secured their positions in a number of communities an Australian took over the operations for the whole island. There was considerable ambivalence to the presence of missionaries, and some Choiseulese were actively hostile, but no missionary, European or native, was ever murdered.

The protectorate government from the outset courted and favored the various missions. They were encouraged in the hope that they would help pacify the area, and the government later became dependent upon the missions, as it is today, for the bulk of educational and medical activities outside the main government centers. Thus the missions early became an important voice in governing the Solomons. Morrell (1960: 349) describes the Melanesian Mission, rather than the Western Pacific High Commission, as the "true architect" of the protectorate, and Burnett (1911: 140) felt "justified" in describing the government as a "missionary administration." The missionaries were influential with the government because they represented a large and organized body of public opinion in England and Australia and because they eventually came to have much influence with the islanders. The head of the Methodist Mission in the Western Solomons, Mr. Goldie, established a reputation as a champion of native land rights and native rights in general, and he usually spoke in their behalf, except when the mission itself was affected. Another source of mission power was the direct political influence missionaries and their followers acquired in village and inter-village affairs. The suppression of warfare had a devastating effect upon the operating sanctions available to local "managers" (as I will term the "chiefs" or "big-men" of local groups), and extensive damage was done to their powers to settle local disputes and conflicts. The mission encouraged its adherents to bypass these men and take their complaints to the local preacher-teacher. These men began to mete out minor punishments and to act as arbitrators in quarrels. Since the missionaries were interested in establishing peace as well as Christianity, they frequently took it upon themselves to interfere in local disputes. Their intrusion was not always resented, and demands were often received, or so it is said (Luxton 1955: 69; Goldie 1914: 577), for preacher-teachers from groups not yet contacted directly. In time the demand became so great that the Methodists could not meet it (Luxton 1955: 77), and Catholics and Seventh Day Adventists began to send men to fill the vacuum, but none of these reached Choiseul until the early 1920's (Watson 1926: 243).

The missionaries worked on the managers of various local groups and in time were able to persuade many of them to make peace with one another. There were neither "hereditary" enemies nor was there "feuding" on Choiseul, only isolated though sometimes protracted instances of vengeance in which "sides" were vaguely defined and transient (see chap. 4). These conflicts could be settled by negotiation conducted by related third parties, and the missionaries fitted themselves, unwittingly, into the system of negotiation and redress, though they conceived of their role somewhat differently; the persuasive and pacifying powers of the Christian doctrine and preaching were given credit for the peace established.

As in most of the Pacific, whole villages or kin groups are adherents of only one "mission" or another. "The monopoly of education and, until recently, of medical services, held by the missionaries was a powerful social weapon. Melanesians would become adherents of a mission which provided them with these all-important services" (Belshaw 1954: 54). Usually, in the Western Solomons, only one mission offered its services at any one time, but when the Roman Catholic and Seventh Day Adventist missions entered the area they too got requests from Choiseulese who had not yet been accommodated by the Methodists, and they got requests from some who had been but were dissatisfied with the service. Thus peoples like those at Voruvoru village, the first to take a Methodist teacher, were occasionally left without one during personnel shifts. When the Methodists did not fill the gap quickly, they sent to the Catholics for a teacher.

Despite the attractions, conversion was slow, partly because the missionaries were cautious of accepting what were obviously only superficial allegiances. The first Christians were not baptized until 1910, but by 1913 the Methodists claimed four hundred converts on Choiseul. Nevertheless, paganism lingered on here and there until shortly after World War II. Today a few old men remain stubbornly pagan, but the indigenous religion ceased long ago to be of any major social significance. The missionaries forbade all pagan practices, but the Choiseulese, of course, did not comply immediately; they wanted the best of both worlds. However, much of the indigenous religion soon became meaningless and fell from use, especially as it was related to intergroup conflict. As pacification proceeded and interest shifted to making copra, the social situation which made the old religious practices meaningful no longer existed. Young people have learned less and less of it as time has gone on, so that today only a few old men know much about those beliefs and practices. One or two avowed old pagans still occasionally "talk" to the "gods" and "ghosts" or "spirits", but these practices do not constitute active social forces for most Choiseulese.

Some functions of the indigenous religion have been given over to Christianity, and a certain amount of ideological syncretism has taken place. The Christian god is generally believed to act in the same capacity as the pagan beings, giving aid, comfort, and protection to his adherents. Good health is believed to be one of his primary blessings just as individual and group welfare was the primary concern of the pagan beings. The practice of giving "first-fruits" to managers controlling the land upon which gardens were planted, in order to assure the continued fertility of the gardens and the welfare of the people, was discouraged by the missionaries, and the people were urged to give first-fruits to the local preacher-teacher in return for a Christian prayer. But even this is rare today. The giving of first-fruits to a manager was important as an acknowledgement of his stewardship over the land, and the demise of this institution has been but one more inroad into the authority of the managers. Occasionally today when a man makes a new garden, and particularly one he is anxious to have succeed, he will invite the local preacher to come along during the clearing process and make a prayer for his success. Indigenous garden magic is seldom practiced today, and if so is little elaborated. Gardening captures little interest because men are most concerned with their copra, and the major crop on which most of the magic was centered, taro, is increasingly difficult to cultivate. For the sweet potato they have no magic, nor have they any magic to control the Chinese traders from whom they acquire their other staples, rice and canned meat.

Several factors, then, seem to stand out in the success of the missionary enterprise. There can be little doubt that the pattern of hostile intergroup relations was already well set when Europeans wandered onto the scene, but there were forms of social control in operation to restrain and resolve that conflict. Peace was always a possibility and often highly desirable so that people might get on with other activities of importance. But the increased deadliness of warfare and the attendant economic disadvantages of conflict after European contact made the fighting even less attractive than it had been in the past, because, although some men enjoyed and benefited from a fight, a price always had to be paid, which was often excessive. Governmental repression and the desire for peace to enable trade and orderly life were the most potent factors in pacification, and the mission with its Christian teachings gave a rationale for the termination of conflict as well as a promise of economic rewards. To the younger men not yet personally caught up in the vengeance system the mission offered a new mode of prestige and power, an *entrée* into and some control over the European world as they knew it, through schooling and the promise of the acquisition of European goods. Yet another factor may have been the fierce competition for prestige between managers of local groups that was characteristic of this society. It seems likely that as some groups took on teachers, gave up fighting, and turned to trade with Europeans, the managers of other groups began to note the advantages of so doing and began to want to do the same. This probably gave rise to a snow-balling effect upon mission adherence.

The acceptance of peaceful conditions proved the undoing of much of the indigenous culture and society. One far-reaching consequence was a change in settlement pattern. Formerly the Choiseulese had been distributed fairly evenly over their island.[7] Several nearby hamlets of a few families each, or perhaps at times

---

[7] However, the area around Manning Straits and Wagina Island at the extreme southeast tip of Choiseul was perhaps largely unoccupied at the turn of the century. The area is low-lying and difficult to defend, and the Choiseulese were kept out of it from fear of New Georgia raiders who often hunted turtle in the area (see Ribbe 1903 and the Lands Commission Report, 1925).

only a single family, were the prevalent form of residential and proprietary unit. These were situated near gardens and high on the ridges which stretch by the hundreds throughout the jungle. Villages of considerable size were to be found as aggregations of people who had been living in hamlets and would go back to them shortly. Hamlets came together to form villages on two occasions: at time of war or impending war for protection, in which case the village was fortified with trenches and a stockade or built on a naturally fortified site; or after a war when feasts and exchanges had to be made to settle debts acquired during the fighting. Goldie (1909: 25) claims to have counted fifty houses inside the stockade of such a village in the Kuboro (most southeasterly) region in 1906. The average house today contains six or seven persons, and this figure was probably higher in the past, for my informants insisted that there is a greater tendency today for the recently married to reside separately from their parents. Thus such a village would have had a population of from three to four hundred at a minimum, and this figure conforms to the highest estimates of my informants. Such villages were occupied for a few years at most, and it seems unlikely that the subsistence economy could have supported such large aggregates for a longer period, but this was long enough to plan and organize a large feast or for hostilities to be worked out.

Many hamlets and villages were on the ridges just above the coasts, and these seem to have been particularly desirable spots. They were no more accessible to attackers than interior settlements, except that a long walk was required to approach the latter, and they offered the advantage of a good view of the sea so that approaching enemies might be spotted more easily. Being closer to the sea, the women could readily go gathering on the reefs at low tide for small sea life to supplement the diet and to get sea water for making salt. Peoples from the interior did these things too, but rarely and with considerably more inconvenience and risk. There seems to have been a small but not highly specialized trade between coastal and inland settlements, though today there is little knowledge of it.

The people living closest to the coasts were, of course, the first to be contacted by Europeans, and those in the Babatana region had the advantage of being, for a time, the only ones visited with any regularity by European traders. They had an early monopoly on rifles too, and they were the first to be extensively influenced by the missionaries. In order to facilitate schooling and because of a shortage of personnel, the mission encouraged the people to aggregate into larger units and to settle permanently, wherever possible, on the coasts. The government also encouraged this process to facilitate administration, and movement between the new units was discouraged, though it is difficult, if not impossible, to control. The mission and government were often influential in obtaining agreements to amalgamation, for the coastal peoples were sometimes reluctant to consent to them, even though the incomers were always kinsmen, since this meant sharing resources, especially scarce land suitable for coconuts. Interior peoples were reluctant too, despite the attractions, for they wished neither to become dependent upon others, nor to become embroiled in disputes over property, nor to leave their own lands which they feared would mean surrendering them. Nevertheless, the process has gone on steadily, and today there are fewer than half a dozen villages on the whole of the island which might be described as "bush" villages. Only two are an appreciable distance from the sea by Choiseulese standards.

Thus, today most Choiseulese live in fairly large villages, in comparison with past conditions, and on the coast itself. Many live on land to which they have no title and as the "guests" of kinsmen. Where one's own land is near a large village and includes some beach land, a hamlet near that village is likely to arise. Residential units now range in size from hamlets of three persons to villages of more than one hundred. Several large villages have formed wherever there are mission stations with educational or medical facilities. The records of the Choiseul Council give the total number of villages variously between sixty and eighty, depending upon what the local reporter calls a village.

Living close together in villages breeds disputes which in the past would have resulted in changes of residence, but the Choiseulese must live in villages to get schooling and to be able to attend *lotu* (religious services) every morning and evening, and four times on Sunday if they are Methodists! They must live in villages, too, for the convenience of visiting government officials and copra traders. Modern villages are quite stable, and this is possible because of the vastly changed ecology. But peace is an important factor. Formerly, residential units were constantly disintegrating and reforming as a result of intergroup conflict and various other factors (see chap. 4), not the least of which was the competition between big-men, or managers, for the allegiances of other men. Today such competition does not exist, at least in the same form. Leadership was established and subsequently validated in activities directly and indirectly associated with intergroup conflict, but with the conflict suppressed and finally wholly outlawed, managers lost the sanctions available to them to control and maintain their followings, and they in turn became dependent upon the missionaries and the government.

The government has also been consistently short of personnel and, therefore, usually unable to take an active interest in island affairs except to apprehend trouble makers or to hear an occasional land dispute, especially those affecting Europeans. They came occasionally to collect the head tax, which most Choiseulese fled into the bush to avoid paying. It was some time before the Choiseulese realized that not every government visit was undertaken to inflict some punishment or to gather taxes—in the early years the sight of a government ship was sufficient to cause the bulk of the population to disappear in the bush for a few days. Even today some villages do not see a government official more than once a year, if that often. For the most part, then, and despite occasional policy differences, the government left the everyday governing of the island to the Choiseulese and the Methodist Mission.

Local preacher-teachers often took upon themselves extensive duties and powers. They were supposed to act in conjunction with local managers, but many teachers were men of unusually strong ambition and character and managed successfully to control the managers. It was generally assumed that the teachers had the full backing of the mission, which they did, and the Choiseulese were not sure how powerful the mission was in relation to the government.

The dwindling of the powers of the managers created a power vacuum which the teachers were ready and willing to fill. When quarrels arose they were generally consulted, and an attempt was made to obtain a "Christian" settlement. This often amounted to a compromise which was grudgingly accepted by both parties, but it did not often truly resolve anything. As coconut land became more valuable the incidence of quarreling over such land and land in general also rose for control over land is a symbol of and an actual source of power in Choiseulese society. A study of some current land-tenure disputes indicates that the details were often too complex and the fabric of lies associated with the cases of the litigants so tangled that the preacher-teacher often completely disregarded the merits of the respective cases and urged the compromise of sharing the land under dispute. Sometimes the disputants seemed to acquiesce, but as soon as one of them attempted to use the land the dispute came to life again. The land then went unused or the dispute would spring up time and time again; some disputes remain unsettled even today.

In the later 1930's the government began a program of local government with village and district headmen. These men were chosen by the people by an informal vote, and they were usually the local managers. Their governmental appointments conferred little power, and they served largely as liason men being responsible for reporting any "troubles." Choiseul was established as a "district" with several subdistricts, of which there are seven today. But serious development of this scheme had to await the reestablishment of orderly life in the area after World War II.

The British evacuated the area late in 1941, leaving only a few men to act as coast watchers who spied on Japanese movements and radioed information to American forces on Guadalcanal throughout 1942 and 1943. The islanders were advised to abandon their coastal villages, and most of them did so. There were some hardships, and considerable fright, as the battles raged nearby; the islanders nearest the two small Japanese concentrations on Choiseul had to abandon their gardens and villages from time to time, especially after the Japanese began to raid the gardens when their supply lines were cut late in 1943. Many Choiseulese worked with the coast watchers and thoroughly enjoyed their participation in the war in this respect. They also collaborated with the only Allied forces to land on the island, a small group of American Marines who harrassed the Japanese for a few days in October of 1943 before the Americans launched the main attack on Bougainville. They had further contact with a few Americans whose planes crashed on or near the island and whom they helped to rescue.

The war had wide-ranging effects on all Solomon Islanders. European plantations were extensively damaged and few were reactivated after the war, so that an important source of employment was partly closed.[8] Furthermore, the islanders became accustomed to larger sums of money than they had seen before. The liberality of servicemen with government property impressed them with what they presumed to be the personal wealth and liberality of all Americans, and it made some of them wonder why the British and Australians had not been so generous in the past. They applied to this situation modes of reasoning characteristic of their own society and concluded that the British and Australians were trying "to keep the natives down" by depriving them of any significant knowledge of how to satisfy their wants. The sharp business practices of the Chinese traders only reinforced this conclusion, and I sometimes heard it asserted that mission schools refused to teach English for many years for much the same reason.

The war brought increased knowledge of the larger world and its economic attractions but little understanding of its complexities and no means of satisfying new wants. The discontent that remains has erupted here and there in movements with some "cargo cult" characteristics, such as the "Marching Rule" movement on Malaita and neighboring islands which agitated for political independence (see Belshaw 1947, 1954: 126–129; Allan 1957). This movement was squelched and its sentiments diverted, to a degree, into formal political activity controlled by the protectorate government, but a "religious" movement with definite political aspects and implications arose in the Western Solomons in recent years. This movement, referred to locally as the "long lotu," consists in a highly militant and devoted church breaking away from the Methodist mission. It is led by a man who preaches a brand of Christianity more fundamentalist than that of his salvation-oriented Methodist teachers, but recently he is said to have begun to revive aspects of the pagan religion too, notably the magical and sorcerous. The activities of this movement, which until 1960 were largely confined to New Georgia, have now spread to other islands, though so far only one village on Choiseul has shown interest in active participation. European missionaries are troubled by these events, but so far as I know the government has yet to

---

[8] Only two small plantations have been resumed by European planters on Choiseul, and these provide no employment for the Choiseulese. Aside from the two planters and a few Methodist and Catholic missionaries, there are no Europeans or European enterprises on the island.

react. One reason may be that the principal leader, who has the distinction of being one of the few effective leaders in the area, has not preached defiance.

This movement is clearly symptomatic of a broader social problem, and I suspect that it succeeded as far as it has because it is a political movement in religious guise. The islanders clearly feel deprived of leadership and meaningful political expression, even though they now have the government-sponsored councils (see below), for the government appointees are ineffectual and the councils have hardly begun their work. Since some of these people have been mission adherents for as much as fifty years or more, much of their culture is now that of the mission or "of" the mission as understood by the islanders themselves. They simply know little else than what they have learned through the missionaries, sometimes at second or third hand. When they go mad today, the madness almost inevitably takes a religious form. It is not surprising that a leader succeeds precisely when he expresses his leadership in a religious idiom.

It took some time for the government to reorganize itself after the war, and it was at first concerned largely with getting the protectorate economically solvent once again. This is still one of the major problems, for the economy remains largely dependent upon the erratic copra market, and it will probably remain so for some time since efforts to introduce rice, cocoa, and other items have either failed or are far from fruition. Choiseul is one of the major producers of native copra in the Solomons, but it is of relatively low quality and is produced in small lots by individuals and families. Cash income is neither large nor regular. Few wage laborers earn more than a few pounds (Australian) a month, and not much of that ever returns to the villages. Some Choiseulese have almost no cash income and barely manage to scrape up enough for taxes or clothing. One has enough income to file protectorate income tax return (perhaps more than one thousand Australian pounds a year), but he pays no tax because of the size of his family. Income varies widely for any one man from time to time because of the variable productivity of the coconuts and the broad fluctuations in the price of copra. Certainly any Choiseulese who took in one hundred pounds a year would consider himself well off. A few may manage to save a little, but by and large it is all spent on rice, canned meat, clothing, and other domestic supplies. Men with higher incomes like to purchase corrugated iron sheeting for house roofs, and many have gone into debt with the Chinese traders in order to acquire things for reasons of prestige.

As an extension of its prewar attempts at the formation of meaningful local government, the protectorate sponsored the establishment of the Choiseul Council in 1948. It consists of several representatives from each of the seven subdistricts and is organized on strictly European lines: indigenous political forms, such as they were, were totally ignored, if they were even known. The council began to meet twice a year some time in the mid 1950's with the district commissioner to discuss its business. Its activities are financed by a head tax, which has climbed steadily to the current (1960) level of three Australian pounds per year for all able-bodied men. Additional income is derived from fines and fees collected in the native courts and interest on savings-bank deposits. The latter sum is considerable, for in 1959 the council had some 4,600 pounds on deposit. This after normal expenditures and the purchase of a twenty-five-foot workboat at a cost of several thousand pounds!

The council has given some attention to the development of social services on the island, such as coöperating with the mission schools in providing minor funds from time to time, and contributing in a small way to the maintenance of dressers (who administer simple but much-needed medicines) who are trained and appointed by the protectorate government. Small hospitals are maintained by the Methodist and Catholic missions, and the council has planned one on the north coast in coöperation with the government and appropriated funds for its construction. Lack of personnel and torpidity of decision on all sides has snagged plans at every turn, and so far as I know the hospital has yet to be built.

Native courts were organized at the time the council was established, and their principal officers are the assistant district headmen and several "justices" appointed by him. Each court is provided with a handbook which defines the cases it may try, the decisions that may be reached, and describes the court procedure. Decisions may be appealed to the court of the district headman and from there to the district commissioner and the high commissioner. The powers of the native courts are wide-ranging: they may try any offense which is punishable by a fine of up to twenty-five Australian pounds or six months in jail or any civil case with the same limitations or involving property of up to one hundred pounds in value. This means that the native courts can hear just about anything that comes their way except for homicide and divorce, unless the marriage has been "by custom." Land is always valued at less than one hundred pounds, regardless of its real value, and the cases are always tried by a native court at least in the first instance.

I could find no records of the actions of the courts before June of 1950, but between then and January of 1960 they had heard at least 590 cases of all sorts, though most of them have been concerned with minor issues, such as failure to perform public labor or disobedience to a headman. Assault cases, occasionally indecent, accounted for 67; use of abusive or indecent language in public (a breach of "custom") for 56; adultery for 39; slander for 31; disputes over ownership of coconuts, 23; and land-tenure disputes for 22. Although the courts are always open to the public, few people ever bother to attend unless directly affected. The remarkable exception to this is when an adultery case is being heard; adultery was and still is a grave offense, and the cases are always heard in the greatest personal detail, providing grist for the gossip mills for weeks afterwards. In 1961 the government revoked the power of the native courts to try adultery cases as such, but they may still be heard under a general regulation permitting consideration of cases which are generally considered in violation of "custom."

Although comparatively few in number, property disputes, especially over coconuts and land, take up most of the courts' time. Furthermore, most of these cases are appealed, perhaps several times, and often reach the court of the district commissioner, who seldom manages to satisfy the disputants either. But despite their malcontent with court findings, disputants seldom take matters into their own hands except, for instance, when adultery is involved, or when one party destroys coconuts or gardens which another has planted on land under dispute. There has not been a case of homicide on the island in many years.

The number of disputes about coconuts or land which are heard by the courts is not indicative of the general incidence of similar disputes. Many others have been going on for years but have yet to erupt into the judicial domain. Prosecution is threatening in some cases, but in others there is little talk of "making a court."

There is, however, some likelihood that many of these disputes will come to court in the near future.

In 1959 the protectorate introduced a new land regulation (*Land and Titles Ordinance, 1959*) which provides for the issuance of titles to "native land." The regulation declares the conditions under which the protectorate may declare certain lands as "waste" and arrange for occupation or exploitation by persons other than "natives." The Choiseulese are disturbed by this, even though, or perhaps precisely because, it is only vaguely understood by them. The district commissioner explained the regulation to the Choiseul council in 1959, but they understood little of what was told them except that the government had made provision for the confiscation of land without compensation wherever that land had not been used by the islanders within the twenty-five years before the enactment of the regulation. Needless to say, the protectorate has, as far as I know, no plans for the wholesale confiscation of native lands, and some government officers do entertain the noble aspiration that the regulation will in time put an end to land-tenure disputes in the area.

However, the Choiseulese have had unpleasant dealings with the government in matters of land considered "waste" in the past, and they feel they have reason to be suspicious. In the 1880's and 1890's Europeans traveled through the Solomons declaring "waste" and laying claim to vast areas of land which they purportedly took to be uninhabited. They had little appreciation of the land requirements of the native systems of horticulture, and they may well have believed the lands were waste. Titles were conferred to this land without the slightest attempt to ascertain its true nature, but as some of it was taken up and readied for planting, local inhabitants began to complain. Eventually a lands commission was appointed to investigate native claims in the 1920's, and its report was published in 1925. Noting the conditions under which the land had been acquired and the fact that very little of the land for which titles were issued was in fact being developed, while local inhabitants were being excluded from it, the commission recommended that much of the land be returned to the islanders. Morrell (1960: 427) notes that "by negotiations with the companies in Sydney . . . a satisfactory settlement of the claims" was reached. Be that as it may, to the best of my knowledge and to the knowledge of the islanders I spoke to, not an inch of the disputed land was returned to the local inhabitants, and even today three-quarters of the island of Kolobangara remains nearly deserted for that reason.

Notwithstanding their suspicions, the regulation could be of value to the Choiseulese, for it would allow them to establish titles to their lands and preclude strife in the future, and land that has been rendered useless might be put to use. The regulation makes specific provision for the recognition of "native systems of land tenure" and also makes provision for "estates for groups of persons," so that lands may be held legally by corporate kin groups. But although the Choiseulese may benefit from the regulation, should they attempt to obtain titles for their lands, litigation over land is likely to increase. The protectorate appreciates this fact, and in preparation undertook a survey of customary land tenure (Allan 1957). The ordinance of 1959 is an outcome of that survey. (It is my understanding that the "waste lands" provision of the regulation was rescinded in 1963.)

Thus the government is committed to a consideration of indigneous land-tenure systems. Yet to my knowledge no adequate study of the land-tenure system of any group of Solomon Islanders exists. To add to the difficulties, some government officers have studied anthropology in British universities, and their understanding of the indigenous societies is colored too much by African models, which may be misleading (see Barnes 1962). Allan's survey is far too superficial, though it is sometimes perceptive, to serve as a guide to understanding the issues in any particular case. Furthermore, it has incorporated some of the pseudo-historical constructions of the earlier land commissioner, Mr. Phillips, and has failed to see some indigenous and workable situations for what they are.

The land commissioner of 1925, like many men of his time, lacked an appreciation of the possibility of any workable indigenous social system other than one based on unilineal principles. Where he found departures from his own naïve ideal-type he attributed them to social change. In the New Georgia area he noted what he took to be remnants of a "matrilineal system" being replaced by "bilateral descent." That is, men were exerting claims to land on the basis of both matrilateral and patrilateral kin ties. Two things led Phillips to conclude that social change was taking place: His informants were not in perfect agreement ("I found a certain diversity of opinion among them as to what natives made up a group or line for proprietary purposes"); and neighboring peoples, such as those on Vella Lavella, preserved matrilineal systems intact. For the first argument, Phillips expected to find concord in his ideal-typical "savage society," as we no longer do, so that this diversity of opinion may now be viewed as a part of our data and not necessarily a pathological result of change. More importantly, however, we do not know from Phillips' account whether the disagreement was over principles or particular issues, and since he had to communicate through pidgin English he may not have been sure himself. As for the second argument, Phillips was apparently ignorant of the fact that, unlike the other peoples of the New Georgia area, the Vella Lavellans are a so-called Papuan enclave in the Western Solomons. But in any event there is no reason why the peoples of neighboring islands should not have different "descent" systems, and especially systems which differ only slightly but yet significantly from one another. Phillips' conclusions were based largely upon supposition and a naïve knowledge of social structure, and it is regretable that Allan has placed reliance upon them, for he too has been unable to entertain the possibility that the "bilateral descent" elements are indigenous and has urged that steps be taken to modify them either to patrilineal or matrilineal or, failing this, "ambilateral" principles. (What he actually suggests is a "utrolateral" arrangement in which a person may make claims either through his father or mother, but not both at the same time—see Allan 1957: 90.) In truth, however, these people already have "ambilateral" systems of "descent," though if a researcher works in pidgin English, and for brief periods, he is not likely to discern this.[9]

Once it is realized that "ambilaterality" is already present, it becomes easier to comprehend what Phillips and Allan took to be abuses of unilineal systems of "descent" of land-tenure interests. Since Phillips could not conceive of an orderly system other than a unilineal one, he could account for the seeming "disorder" he found only by postulating a "breakdown" of the unilineal principle. He "found difficulty in ascribing reasons for the change," however, and postulated a series of possibilities, though for none was he able to offer any evidence; a more developed comparative

---

[9] See, for instance, Scheffler (1962) on the so-called matrilineal systems of the New Georgia area.

ethnology now obviates them anyway. There is nothing to be gained by refuting his arguments in detail, and he does not appear to have taken them seriously either. There probably was a certain amount of disorder prevalent in the 1920's, even as there is today, yet what Phillips found can now be interpreted, to a degree at least, as part of an orderly system of behavior, though not a rigidly determinate one, for "ambilateral" principles contain a built-in abiguity in their application.

The Choiseulese of today, then, are a variety of Oceanic peasantry. The taro subsistence economy of the past has been replaced by a mixed horticulture and one-crop cash economy. In the past they were often embroiled in intergroup conflict or the feasts and exchanges that followed. Today they are peaceful, nominal Christians who have lost much of their indigenous culture as a result of pacification and missionization. Nevertheless, that traditional culture remains significant, for knowledge of it figures importantly in land-tenure matters. Land rights purportedly still derive from "custom," which may mean either from the "rules" by which land rights previously operated or from particular events in the past. That disputes over land are so common and so difficult to resolve may be traced to a number of factors. The most important factor is the nature of the social structure itself, and present-day problems arise as much from the circumstances which the indigenous system is called upon to deal with as from changing conceptions of property rights, or changing "customs." Recent social changes have resulted in such conditions as the ignorance of many men in regard to the historical facts relevant to their claims and in regard to "custom" itself. Thus claims may be made on the basis of a faulty understanding of historical facts or "custom" in the abstract. There is also no denying that many Choiseulese are opportunists and not indisposed to getting ahead through the ignorance and confusion of others. Some disputes, on the other hand, may arise through conflicting but honest misunderstandings of a particular situation.

Choiseulese society and land tenure are, I think, not difficult to comprehend, at least in general features, but an "organizational" rather than a rigid "structural" approach (see Firth 1954, 1955) is mandatory to their understanding. This study does not attempt to explore or to explain all of Choiseulese society or even the land-tenure system in detail; it concentrates rather on certain aspects of the social structure which seem to be crucial for the operation of land tenure and which at the same time are of more general relevance to the solution of a problem in social anthropology, namely, a better understanding of the operation of "ambilateral" systems of kin-group affiliation.

Chapter 2

Kin Categories
and Kin Groups:
The Ideological Structure

This chapter focuses on the ideas of the Choiseulese about their social structure, particularly in regard to the form of kin groups and the meaning of affiliation with them. The empirical referent of "social structure" is here taken to be that nonnormative and general constellation of social relationships which is the "outcome of multiple individual choices rather than a direct reflection of jural rules" (cf. Leach 1960: 124). Social structure has sometimes referred to "norms," or "home-made" or "conscious models" (Lévi-Strauss 1953: 526–527); in this discussion "ideology" serves that purpose, though it is not suggested that these ideas were formulated as systematic or conscious attempts at explanation. Ideology here refers to sets of ideas which receive verbal formulation, and it is not presumed that the sets form any sort of unitary system in and of themselves. Nor is it suggested that the Choiseulese segregate these ideas as a separate subsystem within their culture. These matters are taken up again in the introduction to Chapter 3.

THE IDEOLOGY

The most general term for kin group or category in Varisi is *sinangge*. Its exact reference varies according to the context but may be clarified, though usually it is not, by the addition of descriptive terms. Thus "my *sinangge*" (*sinangge rera*) may refer to any one of several social units, and even though they are not always distinguished terminologically it is necessary to distinguish them analytically. *Sinangge* is also used in the sense of "kind" or "type."

In its most extensive meaning *sinangge* refers to all persons with whom a person can trace cognatic connection and to whom he may, at least nominally, turn for support. This is his *sinangge lavata*, "big *sinangge*." Another reference is to a named "cognatic descent category" which consists, again nominally, of all descendants, through both males and females, of an apical ancestor known to have founded the unit. From the individual's point of view all cognatic descent categories to which he belongs converge upon him to form his *sinangge lavata*, or what we may term his "kinship circle." (See Fig. 3.)

Sinangge also, and most commonly, refers to a unilocal group (what I have heretofore called the primary segment). I call this unit a descent group, but not all persons resident with a particular local group are descendants of the apical ancestor known to have founded the group and its associated cognatic descent category; affines and many other "attached" kin of various sorts are commonly covered by this usage. As noted in the preceding chapter, in terms of its position within the larger society, the local group is conceived of as a descent group linked to one or more other groups of the same sort by ties of common ancestry. *Kapakapa* is also used in reference to the unilocal descent group, but it refers more specifically to the coresident descendants of its apical ancestor. Thus *sinangge Gabili* may refer to a cognatic descent category, a local group composed largely of persons appearing in the genealogy of that category, or, more specifically, to only those members of the local group who do appear in the genealogy of the category. *Kapakapa* refers to the latter only. The Choiseulese sometimes refer to the local group as a *sinangge sukasuka*, "small *sinangge*," and this distinguishes it most specifically from the *sinangge* as a "kinship circle." It is to the less rigidly bounded unit nominally built up around the *kapakapa* that I refer when I speak of a descent group. *Kapakapa* is translated here as "descent-group core."

Finally, *sinangge* may refer to any collection of kinsmen, such as a task group for gardening, fishing, or, in the past, warfare. In this context again affinal kin may be included, and so in general the term signifies that the persons referred to trace common cog-

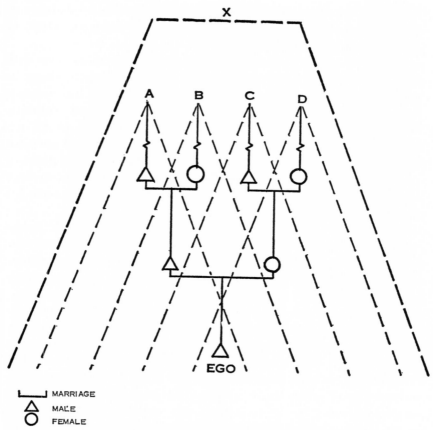

MARRIAGE
MALE
FEMALE

Fig. 3. Some Aspects of the *Sinangge*

natic or affinal connections of some sort and coöperate on the basis of a moral injunction which imposes an obligation to "help one another."

Kinship, aside from that imposed by affinal bonds, stems from common membership in cognatic descent categories. These categories also link descent groups to one another, for the members [1]

---

[1] "Member" throughout this discussion refers to social recognition or classification most commonly rendered by the use of a group name (cf. Firth 1957: 6). "Belongs" implies the same; one is spoken of or speaks of oneself as one of a group or category by application of the name of that unit to oneself.

of any one descent group belong to various and sometimes numerous cognatic descent categories. But the descent groups themselves are the most significant units of Choiseulese society, for it is around and through them that most social activities are organized. Task groups are recruited initially from them, although a task group may not include all members of any one or any several descent groups.

At this point, an extended terminological aside is necessary. All human beings have lengthy and bilateral ancestries because they reproduce bisexually. In the biological sense both descent (or ancestry) and kinship in general are universally bilateral; but in the cultural sense they are nothing of the sort. What is needed, then, is a terminology which can be used to describe other peoples' concepts about that realm of phenomena we call "kinship" in our own society and now conceive of as grounded in biogenetic relationships. As I use the term here, "descent" is a label for a subclass of such concepts, those which formulate genealogical continua; the nature of the continua as conceived by the peoples concerned is, of course, of interest though not critical for the recognition of descent constructs (see e.g., Leach 1961a: chap. 1). (See Scheffler 1964b for further discussion of "descent" and "descent groups.")

I would agree with Service (1962: 31) that "descent group" is profitably used as a label for any *group* which is understood by the people concerned as being composed of descendants of a common ancestor or pair. In other words, as understood here, a descent group is any *group* in relation to which a descent concept may be said to serve as one or more of the following: (1) a principle of recruitment (i.e., a criterion for membership); (2) a conceptualization of the unity of the group; (3) a statement of the actual or "proper" composition of the group; and (4) a statement of the nature of the group's relations with other such groups within the same set of groups (or society). Thus, to say of a group that it is a descent group is not to say much unless it is specified how a descent concept relates to it.

There remains the issue of what social units are to be called "groups." This hoary sociological problem cannot be resolved here, but since a wide variety of social forms have been called groups despite striking qualitative differences among them—so that the word is often deprived of meaning and utility when so broadly used as to encompass any transient aggregate of persons or units of persons only conceptually aggregated—it is important to take an at least heuristic stand on usage. I follow Goffman (1961: 9), who contrasts "groups" with "gatherings" or "encounters":

> A social group may be defined as a special type of social organization. Its elements are individuals [but cf. Goodenough 1961]: they perceive the organization as a distinct collective unit, a social entity, apart from the particular relationships the participants may have to one another; they perceive themselves as members who belong, identifying with the organization and receiving moral support from doing so; they sustain a sense of hostility [or at least "opposition"] to outgroups. A symbolization of the reality of the group and one's relation to it is also involved.

Goffman goes on to point out other features which are thereby entailed, e.g., "regulation of entering and leaving; capacity for collective action; division of labor, including leadership roles; . . . and latent and manifest social function in the environing society." He also cautions against confusing the "group" itself with gatherings of its members, noting that although it is true that at a gathering of group members "there is likely to be a correspondence between the realm of group life and the realm of face-to-face interaction process," nevertheless the "frequent empirical congruence between the structure of a group and the structure of a gathering of its members does not imply any invariant relationship between the two realms" (1961: 12, 13).

From Goffman's discussion it is clear that he conceives of groups as "solidary" social units with rather specific organizational features. He also notes that, "while the morale of the group and the solidarity of its members may increase with an increasing number of meetings, there are strong groups that rarely have focused gatherings containing all of their members and weak groups that have many" (1961: 13; on this topic see also Schneider 1961: 10–11; Firth 1963: 23–24). This suggests that crucial for the formation of groups and their degrees of solidarity are the kinds of operations, activities, or transactions upon which meetings or gatherings focus; it is the quality of encounters between members rather than their number or relative frequency that matters. It also suggests that a further crucial factor may be the number of different kinds of transactions or activities upon which gatherings of essentially the same persons focus.

It is probably not possible, at least at this point, to specify *a priori* for all societies the kinds of activities which are crucial in the generation of groups and their degrees of solidarity, for the generative powers of any particular type of activity must surely depend upon the broader social and cultural context of the activity as well as its own specific nature. However, in general, units which are multifunctional to the extent of being residential, proprietary, and productively strategic may be expected to bear the attributes of groups as defined here and to be fairly strongly solidary too. As the following discussion will show, the localized aggregates called *sinangge* by the Choiseulese meet the specifications for "groups" set forth by Goffman. They do so, though less so now than in the past, precisely because they are sustained gatherings focusing from time to time upon various and multiple activities which are crucial for the perpetuation of human life and welfare. They are in fact, and aside from the task groups which are formed from them, the only units in this society worthy of the label "groups." I call them descent groups because of Choiseulese ideology about them, but this is not to suggest that only such units may be called descent groups, for people do not have to associate in this particular way for groups, corporate groups, and even strongly solidary groups organized in some way by descent concepts, to be generated among them.

The Choiseulese conceive of kinship in biophysical terms; to them, parent-child relationships are grounded in common "blood" and are bilaterally equivalent in substance. They trace ascendant kinship in depth through successive filial ties and have a term by which to describe the process of tracing genealogies—*tutusi sinangge*. They also recognize both undifferentiated and more specific forms of continuous genealogical connection (descent); for instance, they have a formal concept of patrilineal descent—*popodo valeke*. But in this society at least, patrilineal descent is not wholly and solely a criterion of eligibility to membership in kin groups. (See below for further details.) In the terms of this discussion, the Choiseulese cognatic descent category is a descent unit, not a descent group. The residential entity also referred to as a *sinangge* is a descent group, and eligibility for membership in it is restricted nominally by a cognatic descent criterion. There are patrilineal descent units too, membership in which confers certain rights and duties vis-à-vis the *sinangge* as a descent group, but patrilineal descent units in this society do not themselves form corporate descent groups.

The whole island is divided into a large number of tracts of land of varying size and irregular shape; each is the principal corporate property of a descent group and bears its name, or, vice versa, it may be the tract of land from which the descent group derives its name. Most, but not all, tracts are further subdivided into units belonging to segments of the group. These segments, also named and known as "branch" (*panggarana*) *sinangge*, may form discrete descent groups which remain linked genealogically to the originating or "truncal" group. The truncal group or segment is variously known as the "straight part" (*tutuluna*), "trunk" (*tokamana*), or "base" (*kutamana*) of the *sinangge*. Independent "branches" arose through the segmentation of a descent group or, alternatively, grew up, as it were, outside of the truncal group through the accretion of cognates and affines to an influential man, or *batu*, who was a member of the truncal unit. "Branches" achieved distinctiveness from the original unit as well as other descent groups through participation in such activities as revenge, warfare, and gift exchanges (see chap. 4). For convenience, the larger *sinangge*, including branches, are here termed "major *sinangge*," and the segments, which were sometimes autonomous descent groups, "minor *sinangge*." Major and minor here refer only to genealogical status; they imply nothing about political or local status. A minor *sinangge* may be a descent group or merely a formally distinguished genealogical segment of a descent group.

In attempting to explain to me how *sinangge* are formed and operate and in talking about such things among themselves, the Choiseulese often asserted: "The important side is that of the father; we follow our fathers." But frequently it was added: "We keep two sides because it is not good to lose the mother's side." It is recognized that, by logical extension, one could be said to "keep" many *sinangge*. Thus it is said one may claim or "keep" any *sinangge* with which one can trace a consanguineal connection regardless of how far one may be removed spatially or genealogically from the descent group of that *sinangge*. The problem then became to discern how the "father's side" is "important" and what is meant by "keeps" in relation to a *sinangge*. The latter part of the problem appeared, at first, quite simple: When one wishes to say that he is in some sense a "member" of a particular *sinangge*, he says, "I am *sinangge* X." Now since they say this about many *sinangge*, including those with which they are not resident but in which they have kinsmen, it is clear that "keeps" does not necessarily refer to one's residence or descent-group membership. The speaker means that he appears, or should according to his understanding, in the genealogy of the *sinangge* to which he refers. Consequently, when it is said, "We belong to one *sinangge*," no more may be meant than "We are kinsmen." "Belonging" to *sinangge* is an idiom of broader kinship relations, a way of stating kinship. But we might ask, why choose this particular idiom, and how is the father's *sinangge* most important?

"Upon marriage, men do not go out or leave the descent group but women usually do," or, "Men abide but women marry and then go out." This is to say, through patri-virilocal residence the men of a cognatic descent category come to form the "core" (*kapakapa*) of a residential segment. Those who trace their descent from the apical ancestor of the descent group solely through males are said to be *popodo valeke*, "born of men," of agnatic status. These men are said to have primary rights and interests in the property and affairs of the group; they are "strong" within it. Primogeniture is said to determine precedence in the agnatic line and thereby who will be *batu*, or manager, of the people and their estate.

The statements quoted above are "normal" and not "normative" assertions; it is not said that women "must go out" upon marriage and that men "must stay" but merely that they generally do so. The Choiseulese realize that a local segment can never be composed solely of *popodo valeke* if only because many, if not most, men will marry women from "outside" and thereby bring in "alien" women. This is not to imply that women are wholly incorporated (jurally), into the descent groups of their husbands, but for many purposes they are regularly referred to as members of that group. There are also children born out of wedlock to be considered. If a girl has a child before marriage, the father of the child, if he is known, has no claim to the child because there was no marriage and because he did not pay a brideprice (*nanggisi*). The child thus belongs wholly and solely to his mother's *sinangge*, for, socially speaking, he has no father. However, there is also an alternative form of marriage (*busi tamazira*) in which no bride price is paid to the bride's father, and uxorilocal [2] residence is then required. The children of *tamazira* marriages are said to belong primarily to the descent group of their mother; it is their "strong side." Their father's group still retains an interest in them, however, and they are always welcome within it.

Anyone is said to be always welcome in any descent group of any *sinangge* with which he can trace a consanguineal connection, and many persons are in fact living with groups into which they were not born as a consequence of parental residence.

In several ways, then, persons who are not of agnatic status may come to reside with a descent group and claim membership in its *sinangge*. As cognatic, but not agnatic, descendants of its founder they are referred to as *popodo nggole*, "born of women." They form a class of "secondary" members who may exercise only limited rights and interests in relation to the group and its estate. Members "born of women" are "weak" and not "strong" or "active" like members "born of men." The former are said to "live under" the latter; they are "guests" who live on and use the group's estate, but only so long as they "live quietly and cause no trouble." Nevertheless, they "belong to" that *sinangge* and descent group, for they do trace cognatic connection with its founder and live on its estate. They are also members in the pragmatic sense that they are obliged to participate in and contribute to group activities, such as gardening and (in the past) vengeance and gift exchanges, and to render assistance to their fellow members in general. However, they are "weak" in terms of relative formal influence in group activities, and though they may voice an opinion and take the initiative on some occasions they must do so always with the understanding that it is the men of agnatic status who allow it.

Members of a cognatic descent category who do not reside with its descent group are its *sasanggi*, those "born of" the *sinangge*. At least one of their ancestors was a member of its descent group, and they too have rights in the group's estate, rights which cannot be refused; but their primary interests and rights lie else-

---

[2] Terminology of residence follows that of Hogbin and Wedgewood (1953) and Barnes (1960). Uxorilocal thus refers to the residence of a married couple with or near the parents of the bride.

where with the group in which they have agnatic status. They may become resident with a group to which they are only *sasanggi* and do so, it is said, simply by option or "choice," and again, according to the ideology, they are not to be refused this right. However, it is freely admitted that known trouble makers are seldom welcome. So long as *sasanggi* remain nonresident they are not obliged to, but they may, participate in the group's activities. They are expected to refrain from conflict (as in warfare) with active group members or, for that matter, any kinsman. The *sasanggi* are *sinangge* members only in the limited sense of belonging to its cognatic descent category. To descent-group members the *sasanggi* are kinsmen, and they may be close kinsmen; they are persons upon whom one may call for all sorts of assistance, and as kinsmen they should not decline. In the broadest sense, then, when it is said that one belongs to many *sinangge* it is meant that one has interests in the personnel and estates of many descent groups and, furthermore, the rights of access to and residence upon the estates of those groups.

The realities of social life are seldom so simple, for social life is necessarily more complex than the dogmas people espouse about it. But these dogmas are nevertheless more than merely statements of how things work out or how people "should" behave, something people try, perhaps unsuccessfully, to "live up to." They are more than mere "guides to action," and statements of them may be forms of social action in themselves. The "norms" described above are as much something that people know about as they are "values" to which people are personally committed. With these qualifications in mind we can now consider these dogmas in greater detail.

SINANGGE ESTATES

Land is and has probably always been one of the most important assets of the Choiseulese. Group estates are far more than simply a source of subsistence, though as a horticultural people the Choiseulese are, of course, heavily dependent upon the land. The estates provided the foodstuffs, such as taro and the canarium almond (*ngari*), which figured prominently in the feasts accompanying gift exchanges. Thus control over an estate was a source of power for a manager, an important element in his ability to handle his followers, because the estate was a significant resource for use in intergroup relations, the sphere from which, ultimately, the manager derived his powers. But not all men were managers in any meaningful sense (which is to say that many men wanted to be managers), and consequently land was not equally significant to all men. As shown below, many men had to be content with diverse and not very specific rights or privileges of usage rather than firm control. The importance to managers of land-holding is perhaps seen in the frequent reference to them by use of the names of their estates rather than by personal names, such as *batu Gabili*, "*the* Gabili man," or perhaps "Mr. Gabili."

The estates have sentimental attachments for the people with interests in them; to those born and reared upon them or whose significant (principally agnatic) ancestors came from them, the estates are *unu me pua*, "origin land." As noted above, the *sinangge* as social units often take their names from their estates. "*Sinangge* Gabili," for instance, may refer either to the tract of land or to the people who share interests in it; context usually makes the reference clear. In any event, the *sinangge* as a group or category of people and the *sinangge* as an estate always bear the same name.

Allan (1957: 66), presumably referring to local descent groups says that "in Choiseul, the people are divided into over one hundred lineages." This is, of course, only a rough estimate, for no one has attempted to determine the exact number of descent groups by a detailed census of the entire population. I conducted a sociological census which included six hundred persons belonging to at least sixteen major *sinangge*, and if these figures are representative of the population of Choiseul as a whole, the number of major *sinangge* extant today may be in the neighborhood of 150 (5,700/600 × 16). Several *sinangge* are known to have become extinct within the past fifty years, so that the total number of major *sinangge* in precontact times may have been greater still. But while depopulation and amalgamation of residential units have resulted in a reduction of the number of major *sinangge* operative as descent groups and the extinction of some even as cognatic descent categories, their estates still retain their identities and some persons retain interests in them. Even in precontact times, however, not every major *sinangge* was operative as a discrete group or groups at all times.

Major *sinangge* estates vary widely in size, just as do the

TABLE 2

SIZE OF SOME TEPAZAKA
SINANGGE ESTATES

Sinangge	Square miles
Gabili	8.0
Korasokana	7.0
Moriva	3.5
Singgotu	10.5

sinangge themselves. I plotted roughly the boundaries of four estates in the Tepazaka District and established the figures presented in Table 2. I have no way of knowing how representative these figures may be; there are some major *sinangge* estates which are much larger (for instance, Kesi in the interior of what are now the Tepazaka and Varisi districts, and Rogabatu in the Varisi District) and several on the Varisi coast which are smaller, perhaps only one or two square miles in area. The larger estates are subdivided into numerous smaller estates of minor *sinangge*, and these smaller estates approach the size of those noted in Table 2. As shown below, the minor *sinangge* to which these estates belong often had political status similar to other major *sinangge* even though the former were genealogically mere "branches."

Estate boundaries usually follow more or less well defined natural phenomena such as ridges, rivers, or streams. Sometimes, however, they run from one point to another between which there are no such natural markers. Particular notable trees or rock outcrops may then serve to mark points on the boundaries. Among such notable trees are the *rokoso* (banyan) and the *ngari* and *solu* (almond trees), the latter known collectively as *masarani*. The boundaries of estates are carefully remembered and passed on as "oral tradition" from one manager to the next. Other people may know the boundaries, but it is a particular duty of the manager to know and to protect them.

Concentrations of *masarani*, nut trees, which may include some *karamau*, ivory nut palms from which the thatch for building is obtained, are known as *nggungguani*, "groves." Each grove is the property of a particular segment of a descent group and sometimes of a single man. A grove was an essential property, and a group without groves was of "no account." A man without groves to which he had ready access could never hope to be a manager.

Physically "groves" consist of more than simply the trees; they comprise, too, the land in the general vicinity of the trees. Often *nggungguani* and *rigutu* (ridge) are used interchangeably, for most groves are in fact situated on ridges. Each grove has a name of its own and certain boundaries, which are known to its owners. Nevertheless, when describing the proprietary interests of recognized segments within a descent group, it is always insisted that the property of branches consists only in *nggungguani*, groves which have been set aside for their relatively exclusive use. The land itself is said to be inseparable from the major *sinangge:* "They do not divide the land, only the nut trees, only for eating." The land itself is not allotted to segments within the *sinangge*, but segments are allotted certain groves over which they may exercise certain limited and relatively exclusive rights and from which they may take their subsistence. Usage rights over the land which comprises the grove are theirs too, but the right of alienation remains vested in the major *sinangge* and is inseparable from it.

Nominally, one may make a garden on any land held by the major *sinangge* of which one is a member, and a minor *sinangge*, or branch, does not hold exclusive rights of usage over the land on which its grove is situated. In practice, however, minor *sinangge* may hold considerable power over the land. If, for instance, a member of a minor *sinangge* A wishes to garden on the land of minor *sinangge* B, both cognate branches of the same major *sinangge*, he "cannot be refused." However, neither can he simply assume that right. It is said that he must "tell" the manager of B what he desires, and he will not be refused. "After all," it is said, "they are of one *sinangge;* how can he refuse?" It is emphatically denied that "telling" amounts to "asking permission," but it is clearly understood that if one were to start gardening on the land of any group without first "telling" the manager, it would be regarded as an infringement on his rights and tantamount to proclaiming the land as one's own. In these circumstances the manager of the land is justified in taking the situation into his own hands and uprooting any crops the interloper may have planted. Gardening on the land of any group, including another segment of one's own major *sinangge*, required a token presentation of first-fruits to the manager of that group. He then offered the first-fruits to his deceased ancestors so that the garden would "grow well," but the presentation of first-fruits to the manager himself was important too, for it constituted recognition of his stewardship over the land.

Any simplistic statement of the rights of minor *sinangge* is subject to qualification because of the considerable variation in their political statuses. Many minor *sinangge* are not autonomous vis-à-vis the truncal segment from which they originated; residentially and politically branch and truncal segments may remain as one, and the situation outlined above then holds true. In other instances, however, a branch may have come to "stand alone," to be politically and residentially discrete. The manager of the branch then ceased to be only a "hand" of the manager of the truncal segment and came to be a man of considerable influence on his own. While nominally still limited, his powers over the land which comprised his "share" of the *sinangge* estate became as nearly absolute as anyone's powers could be. In short, it would seem that when a branch assumed political autonomy its rights over its estate became *de facto* equivalent to those of a major *sinangge;* but more of this later.

Before we turn to a discussion of the *sinangge* as operative social units, in contrast to the *sinangge* as estates, something might be said about *sinangge* names. As noted above, *sinangge* have the same names as the estates they possess, also *sinangge;* but for the most part the Choiseulese are not aware of how the *sinangge* got their names, and often the meaning of the name itself is unknown to them. Kesi, for instance, is of unknown meaning; it is "only a name." Eromo, the name of an important and independent branch of Kesi, means "to talk bravely," but although it is assumed that the name was acquired through some particular event in the past, that event itself is unknown today. A branch of Eromo is known as Solukurata, its name deriving from one of its groves in which a *solu* tree and a *kurata* tree grow side by side. The *solu* is branchless for a considerable distance from its base, but the *kurata* has many branches and serves as a "ladder" for climbing the *solu*. Solutorengge, yet another branch of Eromo minor *sinangge*, derives its name in a similar way. Baukolo, an autonomous minor *sinangge* deriving from Kesi, takes its name from the fact that at one time the people living there were warned by third parties of impending attacks or raids upon them. The branches of Baukolo are again known for certain of their physical character-istics: Nambokosi, "a flat valley flanked by hills"; Tokata, a variety of tree growing in great profusion there.

SINANGGE AS SOCIAL UNITS

I noted that *sinangge* has a range of meanings—cognatic descent category, kinship circle, descent group, and task group—and I indicated how these are related to one another through a cognatic kinship idiom. The structure of each of these units is now ex-amined in more detail.

Cognatic Descent Categories

The *sinangge* as a cognatic descent category is the largest unit of persons sharing interests in an estate. The category is nominally genealogically defined and consists of all those persons who can trace descent from, or simply cognatic connection with, the apical ancestor who is known to have founded that *sinangge*. Theoreti-cally, that is, according to the ideology, it makes no difference that some persons may trace their descent from the apical ances-tor solely through males, others solely through females, and yet others through some combination of males and females; one still belongs to the *sinangge*, at least as a cognatic descent category, regardless of one's genealogical status, and one's name, other things being equal, should appear in the genealogy along with the other descendants of the apical ancestor. Clearly though, "other things" are seldom equal, and the genealogy recited by the man-ager and other knowledgeable elders of the descent group does not in fact include everyone who is a genetic descendant of the apical ancestor. It includes, perhaps, all the *known* descendants of the apical ancestor, but the processes by which some remain "known" and others become "unknown" are complex and of considerable importance for this analysis. It should be noted too that the genealogical charters of the cognatic descent categories may also include (e.g. by virtue of adoption) persons who are not in fact "blood" descendants of the apical ancestor.

The Choiseulese know little about the founding of their *sinangge*. Purportedly they have been what they are since time immemorial, certainly with respect to the major *sinangge*. About the founding of the subdivisions more is known, and it is this knowledge that relates most closely to rights in land. Most segments were probably founded in the relatively recent past through political processes to be discussed below (see chap. 4). Some knowledge exists concerning the activities of the founders or apical ancestors (variously referred to as "origin person" or "manager who links us to one another"), but such knowledge has nothing to do with how the *sinangge* were founded. It tells how certain taboos came to be placed upon the apical ancestor and his followers. "Who were these 'followers' and where did they come from?" I asked. As might have been expected, the question struck a completely unresponsive chord. Some shrugged their shoulders in dismay, while others tried to answer by saying: "We don't know—we only know that they were his people. It was long ago, and we have forgotten such things." The question as to who are the present descendants of those "followers" was answerable only

TABLE 3

Cognatic Descent Categories

Sinangge	Number of branches, including trunk	Generational depth total	Generational depth to proliferation or branching	Present members (approximate)	Branches founded by females
			Tepazaka		
Barokasa	2	10	7	85	1
Gabili	1	9	6	100	0
Kesi	20+	12	7	600	1
Korasokana	6	9	8	110	1
Kubobangara	3	9	7	40	2
Kubongava	3(?)	8	7	70(?)	1(?)
Moriva	1	11	9	70	1
Singgotu	6	11	8	250	0
			Varisi		
Barisengga	10	12	9	230	0
Kalekubo	3	9	8	95	0
Korasa	6	8	7	145	0
Kuakae	1	11	7	150	0
Rogabatu	7	12	8	270	1
Sirobangara	1	7	6	55	0
Sisikua	8	10	8	190	3
Zevekana	6	9	7	170	1

by similar remarks: "They died out, so we don't know," or "Many went away long ago, so we've forgotten them and remember only the important ones"—that is, those who have remained always with the descent group.

Table 3 summarizes some of the data relating to the *sinangge* as cognatic descent categories as they appeared in 1959–1961. The significance of these data for statements of past conditions is, of course, problematic. I do not know whether the genealogies I recorded are representative of the genealogies one might have recorded in 1900 or before. Upon this issue, the opinions of informants were conflicting. Now that the Choiseulese can write, some say they are able to record their genealogies and could, therefore, remember more than they did in the past. Yet some of the recorded genealogies I saw were so confusingly executed that they baffled not only me but also their authors, and such genealogies are usually, though not always, limited to small segments of major *sinangge*. Other informants claimed that people today are not as good at remembering such things as people used to be. It was sometimes remarked that it was a pity I had not come a few years earlier, for many knowledgeable old men had recently died and much genealogical and other knowledge of the past had gone with them. Both types of statement are probably partly correct. Some Choiseulese have benefited from being able to record their genealogies, but the old men who had participated in the traditional culture when it still had much of its meaning had cause to know much more than their own personal genealogies. Such men, and there are a few left, know the genealogies of many nearby groups to which they are related but in which they do not necessarily have any important or active proprietary or political interests. I suspect that genealogical knowledge is diminishing, and this is probably related to diminishing reciprocity among kinsmen.

I began recording *sinangge* genealogies early in my stay on Choiseul. Partly this was my own choice, but partly it was imposed upon me by the Choiseulese. Before long it became widely known that I was recording genealogies, and men began to come from neighboring villages to ask me if I wanted to record theirs. Frequently large numbers of men came together to record genealogies. Sometimes they arranged to do so among themselves before consulting me, and on other occasions the assistant district headman encouraged them to come together in order that we might incorporate the combined knowledge of all persons with an interest in the *sinangge* and so that I might be spared the difficulties in completing genealogies that might have arisen otherwise. This was a common procedure wherever I recorded genealogies, and sometimes the men met together to "clarify" genealogies before reciting them to me. In any event, there was always much discussion about the genealogies as they were recorded. They always began with the apical ancestor, the man known to have founded the *sinangge*, and then proceeded to recite the names of his sons and daughters, their spouses, their sons and daughters, and so on until the present generation. I tried to record offspring in order of their birth, the reputed descent-group affiliation of all spouses, and the type of marriage if known. Working this way, I discovered that men usually know particularly well the segment or branch of the descent group to which they belong, or at least they seem to have it clear in their own minds. Some might know other segments fairly well, but quite often they become confused trying to recite them, and it is common, when dealing with the distant past, to confuse the children or spouse of a man with his siblings. Someone else would then intervene, offer a suggestion as to the correct relationships, and a discussion would follow among several men. They would agree as to what should be recorded or finally admit that either they just did not know the relationships or that "One says it is one way and one another, but no one can be sure." If it had been a particularly long and trying session and the hour was particularly late, they might become exasperated and say, "A says it is this way, and B says it is that way; you write whatever you like." I simply made note of the confusion.

The Choiseulese explicitly formulate the distinction I make between the *sinangge* as a cognatic descent category and a descent group, not only in qualifying terms, but also in the way in which genealogical knowledge is maintained. For instance, I was sometimes asked if I were interested in recording only those "born of men," or if I wanted "everyone who belongs to the *sinangge*," but even if reciting only "those born of men" they would find occasions upon which it was necessary to make reference to some persons who were "born of women." This was when such persons formed a significant segment within the modern descent group; for the genealogies have as one of their primary functions the relating and organizing of descent group members, and the actual composition of the group influences the shape taken by the cognatic descent category of its *sinangge*. The distinction is also implicit in the way that the descent group is sometimes viewed as those of the *sinangge* who have, literally translating, "stayed put" as opposed to those who have "gone out."

The Choiseulese were always interested in recording genealogies, and a number of factors were responsible for this interest. Probably the most important is that genealogies are charters or titles to land rights, since all persons appearing in the genealogy of a cognatic descent category are said to have interests in its estate and claims upon other members, though not always an interest equal to that of all others. This means, of course, that genealogies are liable to be manipulated to suit the interests of those reciting them, and I found sufficient evidence that this was done. (Thus, I do not assume that these genealogies represent the simple genetic facts.) Another source of interest was, I am sure, that many Choiseulese believed that everything recorded would eventually be published, and their versions of genealogies would then be fixed forever in print as the "truth." Some were not above trying to use me in this way to further their own ends by establishing as "fact" what others regarded as dubious. However, some were concerned merely with getting the thing on paper and in print so that the knowledge would not be lost. (There were the usual numerous demands for copies of the genealogies once they were recorded.) The protectorate government has also furthered this interest in recording genealogies—not much encouragement was needed—by insisting that elaborate genealogies constitute part of the evidence in all land-tenure disputes.

The figures presented in Table 3 required some explanation. The first column, "Number of branches (including trunk)," reports the number of named segments within the major *sinangge*. This total includes branches and sub-branches, and the totals, where small, are probably erroneous. I tried to get informants to specify as many branches as they could, but despite this I sometimes found others later. In some cases, however, even a small figure is correct (e.g., Gabili). The truncal segment is neither necessarily larger nor politically more important than any or all of the branches, but it is sometimes both. According to Choiseulese dogmas, the truncal segment of the *sinangge* is the most "important" one, and its manager is also the manager of the major *sinangge* as a whole. Branches are said to be founded usually by younger sons and their descendants who are allotted their "shares" in the *sinangge* estate. Suffice to note at this point that things seldom worked out so neatly.

The second column, "Generational depth total," refers to the number of generations elapsed from the apical ancestor to the youngest member of the *sinangge* alive today. "Generational depth to proliferation or branching" refers to the number of generations between the youngest member alive today and the point at which the descending genealogy begins to ramify from a single male (in rare instances, a female) who was one of the reputed descendants of the apical ancestor. In some cases this ramification occurs simultaneously with the purported founding of branches, in other cases branches have yet to form. What I attempt to convey here is that most genealogies begin with an apical ancestor and then record only one person per generation for the next several generations (usually two or three but occasionally four or five). Since the three or four more recent generations are represented by living persons, at most five and usually only two or three generations separate some living persons from the point at which segmentation purportedly took place. As I show later, there is reason to regard these aspects of the genealogies as other than accurate historical records, even though some segmentation was still going on in the grandparental or great-grandparental generations of the genealogically eldest persons alive today.

It should be noted here that a major *sinangge* is not necessarily internally differentiated into formal segments. There may be only the "truncal" segment (as in the cases of Gabili, Moriva, Kuakae, and Sirobangara). Two or three levels of formal segmentation are common, and I doubt that more than four ever occurs.

"Present membership (approximate)" refers to the total number of persons alive today who can trace cognatic connection with the apical ancestor or who may have it claimed for them by others. These figures are, most decidedly, only approximate, and the true totals are probably in every case somewhat higher than those appearing here. After the initial recording of a genealogy, I would occasionally come across another person, living or dead, claiming, or having claimed for him or her, membership in that cognatic descent category. Checking with my original informants, I usually found that they had some knowledge of that person and could relate him or her to the genealogy previously given. Sometimes, however, they could not, for the kinsman through whom he was connected to the *sinangge* either "went away" from its estate or residential center so long ago or so far that meaningful social interaction with him or his descendants had long ceased and, therefore, accurate knowledge, or any knowledge, of the genealogical connection had been lost. This, of course, is one of the major reasons why not all descendants of an apical ancestor appear in a particular genealogy, nor would it be realistic to expect that they should. For one reason or another, then, the accuracy of these figures is variable. I note them only to demonstrate the wide range of variation in *sinangge* (cognatic descent category) size, and they probably do that accurately enough. None of the figures should be taken as definitive, although in some cases they are, I believe, probably as nearly complete as possible. In the case of *sinangge* Kesi, for instance, most people claiming a connection with it reside still in either the Tepazaka or Varisi districts, so I am fairly certain that I did manage to locate most of them. In other cases, such as Zevekana, Moriva, and others my informants knew of individuals several generations removed from the present who had gone to reside in distant areas for various reasons and whose descendants are now numerous and still living in those areas. The informants know of those descendants and even know the names of a few, but the exact connections and numbers are lost to them. Thus Kesi is perhaps not as exceptional in size as it might seem, but it is still by far the largest *sinangge* I know. However, the truncal segment of Kesi, but not some of its branches, exists only as a cognatic descent category at the present time.

Another problem which affects this "membership" figure is that of multiple membership or, simply, the appearance of the same person in the genealogy of more than one *sinangge* or perhaps several times in the genealogy of a single major *sinangge*. This happens simply because these genealogies are maintained cognatically and because *sinangge* per se, regardless of their genealogical or political status, are agamous so that there is marriage within and between cognate branches. Furthermore, there is a stated and practiced preference for such marriages. In computing the sizes of the major *sinangge* (cognatic descent categories) I attempted to compensate for this multiplicity of membership in branches of the same *sinangge* and counted each person only once, but I may have counted some twice, or more often, inadvertently.

It should be noted here that the total population of the two "regions" from which the data in Table 3 derive is only just over six hundred, but the total for those cognatic descent categories is two to three times that number. This is, again, because of multiple memberships and because many members of these categories live in other districts or in neighboring villages not included in the census. There is a preference, again both stated and practiced, for marriage between proximate descent groups. Thus, cognatic descent categories whose estates border upon or lie near one another frequently "overlap" in membership, and when the overlap is particularly great they are said to *vari kapakapa, vari* being the form indicating a reciprocal relationship, and *kapakapa* the word for the localized "core" of the cognatic descent category. *Vari kapakapa* thus refers to the fact that a large part of the membership of one cognatic descent category resides with the descent group of the other and vice versa. Such a situation does, of course, affect the activation of the rights associated with *sinangge* affiliation, but this is more readily discussed later in relation to the structure of the descent group.

Finally, the column "Branches founded by females" must not be taken too literally. Here I refer to the fact that some branches are said to have originated when a woman of the group, usually a "favorite" daughter or sister of the manager, married a man who came to live (*tamazira* marriage) with the manager, and this couple was given, to hold in trust for their offspring, a portion of the group's estate. Such portions are sometimes spoken of as that woman's "share" or may even be referred to as the property of her husband. Although this is perhaps no more than a convenient way of expressing his temporary stewardship over that land, he may as a result of that stewardship come to exercise considerable influence in descent-group affairs. This portion then forms the estate of a branch, and the woman affected connects the branch genealogically with the remainder of the *sinangge* (as a descent group or category). She is the "founder" then, but only in a limited sense. (All of this is discussed in greater detail below, p. 104.)

Although I have alluded to it, thus far I have made no attempt to analyze the genealogical process—how genealogies are formed and maintained—for this is a complex issue more profitably discussed in relation to the formation and operation of descent groups. I have, so far, attempted only to characterize the genealogies of cognatic descent categories, not to account for them. The characteristics, in very general terms, are these: The genealogy begins with an apical ancestor, and all descendants, whether male or female or tracing their descent from him through males or females or both, are said to belong to that *sinangge*. The apical ancestor is usually connected with a sibling-set, one to five descending generations distant. Occasionally, though not often, a female may form one of the intervening generations. Also, sometimes the apical ancestor or one of his immediate descendants had no children of his own, at least none who survived to continue the *sinangge*, and it is recognized that he adopted one or more persons for that purpose. At the sibling-set, ramification of the *sinangge* into a trunk and several branches may take place, and these branches may later ramify again.

At its most dogmatic, the indigenous ideology asserts that the "trunk" of the major *sinangge* is maintained and ordered largely by patrilineal descent and primogeniture, the branches being formed by younger siblings and their descendants, some of whom may be females. The cognatic descent categories vary in size from fewer than forty persons to more than six hundred. Total genealogical depth does not exceed twelve generations; nine to ten generations is more typical. Elaboration within the genealogies is usually about eight generations in depth, varying between six and nine generations. Of these six to nine generations, three to four are represented by living persons. The number of branches within a major *sinangge* varies between none and fifteen, or perhaps even more if we count every recognized segment that has separately defined but limited proprietary interests in a portion of the estate but is otherwise of little significance. The number of branches within a major *sinangge* appears to be only roughly correlated with the size of the major *sinangge*, but depopulation in the recent past has probably complicated this relationship. Furthermore, not all branches are of the same general social significance. Some are autonomous descent groups, others are merely separate and limited interest groups within a descent group.

Branches are sometimes, though not frequently, linked to the major genealogy through a female. In the present sample only one in every six or seven branches is so linked. More often, however, subunits within the estate of the major *sinangge* have passed through the hands of females, but women more often are the connecting links for those who are *sasanggi*, "born of" the *sinangge* but not members of its descent group. Again, at their most dogmatic, the Choiseulese do insist that all women and their descendants are retained in the genealogies of the *sinangge* as cognatic descent categories. Actually, of course, not all descendants, whether male or female, of the apical ancestor are retained in the genealogy, although there is a tendency, of which the Choiseulese are clearly aware, to "lose" women and their descendants more so than men and their descendants. Theoretically, sex status per se should not affect retention within the genealogy. Indirectly, however, it does, for given the tendency for patri-virilocal postmarital residence, women do tend to "marry out" of the *sinangge* (as a descent group) more so than do men, and this may come to affect genealogical knowledge about them and their descendants.

Thus *sinangge* genealogies, as cognatic descent categories, record lines of cognatic connection between living persons and apical ancestors, and those lines need be neither patrilineal nor matrilineal: the nature of the lines themselves is nominally insignificant, at least concerning inclusion in the cognatic descent category. I have found it both appropriate and necessary to speak of cognatic descent in this context, for I cannot think of a better term to describe the fact that the Choiseulese do retain an extensive knowledge of successive genealogical links and conceptualize this knowledge as *tutusi sinangge*. Cognatic descent places persons in nondiscrete descent categories and also entitles them to membership in descent groups. It has also been noted that a more restricted descent conception (*popodo valeke*) validates certain privileges in relation to descent groups. It is worthwhile to emphasize that the cognatic descent idiom itself gives form only to *categories* of persons of common cognatic connection, and these categories remain nondiscrete and only vaguely bounded. The formation of discrete and operative units (descent groups) is only facilitated by genealogical closure or nonrecognition of membership in cognatic descent categories. Recognition of membership in such categories is on occasion denied to some persons who claim to be descendants of the founder, but it is not their descent status that closes descent groups to them through this device; closure of the possibility of descent group membership to such persons comes about largely as a result of diminishing frequency, intensity, and quality of interaction, and these are conditioned largely by one's residence. Since residence [3] is an important factor in the shaping of genealogies and in giving them their significance, this whole process is again more meaningfully discussed in relation to the formation of descent groups (see below, especially chap. 3).

The Kinship Circle

From the point of view of the individual, all cognatic descent categories to which he belongs converge upon him to form his *sinangge lavata*, "big *sinangge*" or "kinship circle." The kinship circle thus consists of all those persons with whom any Ego can trace cognatic connection. Logically, this might amount to a truly large number of persons, but just as the cognatic descent category does not in fact contain all descendants of the apical ancestor, so the genealogical knowledge of the individual does not encompass all members of all cognatic descent categories to which he belongs.

Since one's kinship circle is formed by the intersection of numerous cognatic descent categories, it is perhaps inappropriate to speak of it as one's "personal kindred." [4] There are, however, structural and functional similarities between the "kinship circle" and the "personal kindred." For instance, in both cases "cognatic ties provide a continuing network of relationships from which . . . action groups may arise" (Freeman 1961: 203). Here I discuss only the form of the network of relationships; the actions of task groups which arise from that network are discussed in Chapters 3 and 4.

If any Ego does not know all members of all cognatic descent categories to which he may belong, how much genealogically, does he know? This is difficult to measure, for there are degrees of

---

[3] I am making a distinction between "domicile" and "residence." Following Leach (1958: 125), domicile refers to where one has his "legal residence"; while residence refers to where one is actually situated at any particular time.

[4] Freeman (1961: 205) argues that the personal kindred is formed by the intersection of all *cognatic stocks* to which any Ego belongs. Although they are similar to cognatic stocks, cognatic descent categories are not the same thing, for they do not consist of *all* descendants of the apical or founding ancestor and they are also recognized named units, relatively few as compared to cognatic stocks. Furthermore, the cognatic-descent-category concept is not an ideal-type analytical structure, as is the concept of cognatic stock; the former is an indigenous cultural construct.

knowledge just as there are degrees of kinship. There are, for instance, those kinsmen of whom one is fully aware in every sense, with whom one interacts regularly and with whom the genealogical connections are well known. It is not surprising that these two characteristics should go together; one is usually most closely related genealogically to those with whom one is coresident and regularly interacting, and even if he is not, knowledge of such connection as exists can be quickly acquired and remembered.

Kinship and its degrees are expressible in various ways, but kin are most generally referred to either as one's *sinangge* (this may include "affines," *tamazira*) or one's *onotona* (excluding "affines"). Two persons who are kin to one another are said to *vari tongovi*, "have one another," and close kin, say within first- or second-cousin range, are sometimes referred to as *parasanggu*, "of my blood." "Close" and "distant" are not definable in terms of genealogical distance alone, however. Those with whom one is coresident, say in the same hamlet or village, and to whom one is related quite closely, again usually within first- or second-cousin range, are one's *onotona dakisi*, just as two sticks lying against one another are *dakisi*, "close together." But *onotona dakisi* has no exact genealogical reference; definition of a relationship as *dakisi* depends upon the intensity with which the relationship is exercised as much as it does upon genealogical nearness. First and second cousins who are active members of another descent group are not *onotona dakisi* but rather *onotona kavakava*, kinsmen "across" *sinangge* boundaries, *sinangge* here being understood as the descent group. Even closer than one's *onotona dakisi* are one's *onotona soku*, one's parents, siblings, and parents' siblings. First cousins with whom one is on particularly intimate terms may also be referred to as *onotona soku*. The definition of *soku*, like that of *dakisi*, is only partly genealogical, partly "spatial." The quality of the interpersonal relationship itself is also important, so that genealogically close kinsmen who are not on good terms may prefer not to view one another as *onotona soku* or *dakisi*. However, in relation to the regulation of marriage these terms have fairly clear reference to the narrower genealogical limits—*onotona soku* to parents, siblings, and parents' siblings, *onotona dakisi* to first cousins, all of whom are neither legitimate mates nor sexual partners.

Onotona refers to those kinsmen with whom a cognatic connection is known to exist, and there is usually some knowledge, though perhaps incomplete, of the nature of that tie. Many are members of other descent groups with whom one is familiar but not particularly intimate. These are one's *onotona kavakava*. They may not be immediately knowledgeable of the genealogical connection, but usually two so related can work out the person in whom their genealogies meet. This is commonly done with reference to particular named descent categories, one party rummaging through his genealogical knowledge until he finds an ancestor who is also recognized as an ancestor by the other party. This may be done with relative ease by men of the same "region" (see below, p. 88), especially since others may be able to help them.

Another class of kin, not thoroughly separable from one's *onotona*, are one's *turana*, persons known as kin but with whom a genealogical connection is merely assumed. These are most often persons resident in another region and who, or whose parents, were addressed by one's own parents by a kin term, most often that for "brother." Some *turana* are clearly fictive kin, persons with whom a political or economic relationship has been established and maintained and then sanctioned with a kin term. In any event, interaction with *turana*, who are commonly rather far removed spatially, is infrequent, but it may be important from time to time. *Turana* is also translatable as "friend."

The Choiseulese clearly recognize the general correlation between spatial and genealogical separation; distant kin genealogically are usually resident at a distance as well. But since no group or category, except very close kin, is either exogamous or endogamous by cultural prescription, the correlation can never be complete. Close kin may reside in distant places, a fact that may be of some advantage to an individual. On the other hand, kinsmen who reside nearby may find themselves defined as "distant kin" if there is some advantage to be gained (see the discussion below of the cognatic kinship sentiment, pp. 85 ff.).

Genealogical knowledge is conditioned primarily by descent group affiliation. The genealogy one knows best is usually that of the cognatic descent category associated with one's own descent group, and within that knowledge is best about one's own branch. It follows then that a person who is affiliated with his father's descent group knows its genealogical charter better than that of any other, and, similarly, a person who is affiliated with the descent group of his mother is likely to know that genealogical charter best. But this is not always true. Since some people do change their descent group affiliations, or have them changed for them when their parents make a move, one may attain membership in a descent group about which one knows comparatively little genealogically; and a person occupying no especially significant position within a descent group is sometimes content to know, perhaps imperfectly, only the basis of his affiliation with it.

Because of the extensive residential and affiliation realignments that took place upon pacification and missionization, a complex relationship between individual descent group affiliation and individual genealogical knowledge exists today. In some cases depopulation has been important too. The estates of those descent categories that have "died out," and of many that are nearly extinct or at least no longer organized as operating groups, have passed into the hands of only one or a few persons, and those persons have taken on the responsibility of maintaining the genealogical charter of the *sinangge*. They have done so partly to protect their own interests in the land, partly to keep track of kinsmen for various reasons, and partly because it allows them an inflated self-image by assuming themselves to be managers even in this restricted sense. Nevertheless, the same persons are knowledgeable of the genealogical charters of the groups with which they are actually affiliated today.

It might be assumed that because the "father's side" is said to be the "important" one that genealogical knowledge of patrilineal or perhaps patrilateral kin would be most extensive. Since most Choiseulese are affiliated with a descent group with which their fathers were affiliated, the latter is true, but it would be a mistake to conclude that genealogical knowledge would then be patrilineal; one's father may have been affiliated with a descent group other than that to which he was agnatically related. Furthermore, although agnatic status in a descent group or category may have certain advantages, informants did not always stress agnatic genealogies. Some were clearly indifferent to their agnatic status in relation to a particular descent group even though there might have been some advantage in stressing it. They were indifferent because, as will become apparent, agnatic status does not operate in a vacuum and can be compromised (see chap. 3).

It is difficult, then, to generalize about which genealogies people are most knowledgeable, for this varies from individual to individual depending upon his and his parents' descent-group affiliations and also upon how stable those affiliations have been. Furthermore, individuals differ greatly in the extent to which they are concerned about genealogies. There are men of little ambition, with little interest in or concern about those things, such as prestige and power, which other men value and seek to obtain. Genealogical knowledge is valuable to an ambitious man for the uses to which he may put it. It is relatively useless to the unambitious, and they do not make much effort to obtain or remember it. For the ambitious, knowing kin far and wide was essential, and still is though to a lesser degree, because it was through kinsmen that one built and maintained a following or attained one's interests. Managers and those with managerial ambitions are, therefore, the most knowledgeable individuals. Not only must they know their kin and be able to manipulate them skillfully, but they must also be responsible to their kin, close and distant; a part of that responsibility consists in maintaining the genealogical charter of a descent group and being able to substantiate its validity with certain kinds of information about those ancestors who appear in it. Managers and the ambitious took (and sometimes still do take) considerable interest in the affairs of neighboring descent groups with whom they most often coöperated. Knowledge of the affairs of one's own group, of significant events that it had participated in, often required knowledge of the affairs of other groups and their managers and genealogies. Knowledge of the genealogies of neighboring groups, even though one may have had no proprietary interests in them, allowed a man to make common cause with those groups, to give moral support or rationalize other forms of assistance. Such knowledge could also facilitate justification of an uncoöperative or aggressive position, for it could entail crucial historical facts.

It follows that the range of personal genealogical knowledge is highly variable. Men of high status or ambition know more than other men. Those belonging to large major *sinangge* or large branches may have a greater range of kinsmen to be knowledgeable about than members of small groups. Most men are fairly competent genealogically within the range of second to third cousins; they may not know the names of the younger offspring of second and third cousins, but they at least know of their existence and numbers. Fourth and fifth cousins fall into that class of *onotona* with whom connection is known and can be reconstructed with some effort should it be necessary. This is not to say that everyone knows all his second or third cousins or that his knowledge is equilateral. Again, how much one knows of his patrilateral as against his matrilateral kin depends in large part upon his residence and its stability. If one's mother's kinsmen live some distance away, chances are that one is unlikely to see them very often. Hear of them one may, but one is not likely to find extensive knowledge of them and their interrelations very useful. Thus one's mother's kin become effectively "lost" not because they are one's mother's kin but simply because interaction with them is largely precluded. Where one's father has married *tamazira* and assumed uxorilocal residence the situation may work out similarly except that it is knowledge of one's "father's side" that is effectively "lost."

The total number of kinsmen known to any one adult must vary widely from person to person. Indeed, it would be almost impossible to compute the average accurately unless an inordinate amount of time and travel were devoted to the task. Yet, I did attempt to compute a figure for several men. In one instance, an adult male manager about fifty years old, knew approximately 250 living kinsmen, all within third-cousin range. This required a knowledge of more than 250 persons in some ways and less in others. That is, a large number of deceased men and women serve to link those 250 living kinsmen, but many of the living kinsmen are children of whom comparatively little is known, often only that they exist. He knew approximately their numbers and ages, but he had to call upon his son for their names. On the other hand, the figure does not include his many affinal kin (many of whom are also distant cognates) nor does it include the large number of persons for whom he knows and uses a kin term but knows little of the basis of their kinship with him. All in all, I would say that 250 known kin is a conservative estimate. Two or three very knowledgeable and curious elderly men that I knew well certainly knew more personal kin than the man discussed here. On the other hand, the number of kinsmen with whom active relationships are maintained is considerably less than 250 for any one man and less still for any one woman.

To summarize, genealogical knowledge is neither always nor

often perfectly equilateral, exactly the same for "mother's side" as for "father's side," although the Choiseulese emphasize the importance of "keeping two sides," of "not losing either the father's or the mother's side." But where knowledge is not equilateral this is because of residential or spatial factors affecting interaction and the immediate value of the genealogical knowledge rather than any relative lack of value placed upon a certain type of kin tie. The "father's side" is or may be, "most important," but that importance is limited and does not make the "mother's side" unimportant. In this society one depends upon all sorts of kin, not only patrikin, and those patrikin upon whom one may be most dependent are not necessarily those to whom one is also agnatically related. However, although it is not certain for any one individual what form his genealogical knowledge will take, for the "society as a whole," or from an over-all view, presumably there is a bias or tendency toward more extensive genealogical knowledge of patrikin. But again, this is not the same as agnatic kin.

KIN CLASSES AND THEIR NORMS   The kinship terminology of the Varisi dialect has only twelve basic vocative and referential categories, and lineality is not a distinctive feature of any of the classes. The twelve classes combine into nine sets of reciprocals for each of which there is an "aggregate" term (Table 4). Table 4 lists only the primary kintypes and a few of their combinations which are included in each class, but since the Choiseulese place no formal limit upon the genealogical range of kinship the terms are applied more broadly than indicated there or in Figures 4 and 5. *Mamae*, for instance, given as F, FB, FZH, and so on, is applied to FFBS, FFZS, FFFBSDH, and so on as well.

For the purposes of a componential analysis (see Goodenough 1956; Wallace and Atkins 1960; Lounsbury 1964) we will consider only terms used in face-to-face interaction by Ego to address an alter when no other relative is present. The following dimensions of contrast are relevant:

(1) Kind of relationship:
K: "Kin" (*onotona*)
  a. Descendants of a common ancestor; b. Spouses of one's senior kinsmen and, reciprocally, spouse's junior kinsmen.
A: "Affinal" (*tamazira*)
  Spouses of one's own generation and junior kinsmen and, re-

ciprocally, spouse's kinsmen of his or her own or senior generation.

(2) Generational removal:

G-0: Same generation as Ego. G1: One generation removed.
G2: Two or more generations removed.

(3) Relative sex:

X: "Cross"; opposite-sex relationship. ∥: "Parallel"; same-sex relationship.

(4) Sex of alter:

M: Male. F: Female.

(5) Sex of ego:

Em: Male Ego. Ef: Female Ego.

(6) Relative age of alter:

Sr: Older. Jr: Younger.

The ten *onotona* terms, as they apply to consanguineals only (indicated by "C"), may be defined componentially as:

vavae	:	$M \cdot Sr \cdot G2 \cdot C$
nggonggoe	:	$F \cdot Sr \cdot G2 \cdot C$
kanae	:	$F \cdot Sr \cdot G1 \cdot C$
mamae	:	$M \cdot Sr \cdot G1 \cdot \| \cdot C$
bubue	:	$M \cdot Sr \cdot G1 \cdot X \cdot C$
kakae	:	$Sr \cdot G\text{-}0 \cdot \| \cdot C$
kaenggu	:	$Jr \cdot G\text{-}0 \cdot \| \cdot C$
vavaninggu	:	$G\text{-}0 \cdot X \cdot C$
tunggu	:	$Em \cdot Jr \cdot G1 \cdot \| \cdot C$
		$Ef \cdot Jr \cdot G1 \cdot C$
babazunggu	:	$Em \cdot Jr \cdot G1 \cdot X \cdot C$
		$Jr \cdot G2 \cdot C$

The terms *tunggu* and *babazunggu* provide instances of polysemy; that is, they have somewhat, though not totally, different meanings for males and females. The validity of formulating two componential definitions for both terms is confirmed by their reciprocals and the aggregate sets in which they occur (they take multiple reciprocals and occur in several aggregate sets—see Table 4).

Most component dimensions and definitions pose no problem, but the "relative sex" dimension does require some comment. This dimension could be listed as three separate dimensions but they are reduceable to one following Lounsbury's example in his

TABLE 4

VARISI KINSHIP TERMINOLOGY

Vocative	Referential	Aggregate
Onotona		
mamae: F,FB,FZH,MZH, etc.	*tamana* [a]	*tatamana*
kanae: M,MZ,MBW,FZ,FBW, etc.	*sinana*	*tamasina*
tunggu: S,D	*tuna*	*tatamana* or
BS,BD (m.s.)		*tamasina*
BS,BD,ZS,ZD (f.s.)		
WyZ,WeZS,WeZD		
HyB,HeBS, HeBD,HZS,HZD		
kakae: eB, FBeS, FZeS, MZeS, MBeS (m.s.)	*togana*	*tamakena*
eZ,FBeD,FZeD,MZeD,MBeD (f.S.) etc.		
kaenggu: yB, FByS, FZyS, MZyS, MByS (m.s.)	*kaena*	*tamakena*
yZ,FByD,FZyD,MZyD,MByD (f.s.) etc.		
vavaninggu: Z,FBD,FZD,MBD,MZD,WBW (m.s.)	*vavanina*	*tamavavanina*
B,FBS,FZS,MBS,MZS,HZH (f.s.) etc.		
bubue: MB,MFBS,MFZS, etc.	*tuetana*	*tamatuetana*
babazunggu: ZS, ZD (m.s.), etc.	*babazuna*	*tamatuetana*
SS,SD,DS,DD,SSS,SSD, etc.		*tamasinggole*
WyZS, WyZD, WBS, WBD, Hy BS, etc.		or
		tamakuzake
vavae: FF,FFB,FMB	*tunazake*	*tamakuzake*
MF,MFB,MMB, etc.		
FFF,FFFB,MFF, etc.		
nggonggoe: FM,FFZ,FMZ	*sinananggole*	*tamasinggole*
MM,MFZ,MMZ, etc.		
FFM,FFMZ,MMM, etc.		
Tamazira		
ivanggu: ZH,WB (m.s.), etc.	*ivana*	*tamaivana*
BW,HZ, (f.s.), etc.		
ravanggu: WF,WM,HF,HM,SW,DH,BSW,BDH,	*ravana*	*tamaravana*
ZSW,ZDH,WeZ,HeB,WZH,HBW, etc.		

[a] The form given here is the third person singular with the personal possessive suffix incorporated (-na). The personal possessive suffixes (singular) are: *-nggu* (my), *-mu* (your), *-na* (his, her, its).

analysis of Seneca kinship terminology (1964). In Ego's own generation the three terms for consanguineals are readily glossable as "opposite-" and "same-sex kinsman of my own generation," the latter being further differentiated on the basis of age relative to Ego. The critical comparison is sex of Ego versus sex of alter, and the two possibilities are here designated "cross" and "parallel." For the designation of alters in the first descending generation (Jr·G1), a relative sex comparison is again made; this time sex of Ego versus sex of linking parent of alter, but the comparison is made by male Ego only. In other words, a male Ego continues to make the relative sex distinction he makes for own generation alters while a female Ego does not. Thus, for a male Ego there are two classes of kinsmen in the first descending generation (*tunggu* and *babazunggu*), but for a female Ego there is only one (*tunggu*). The distinction between *mamae* and *bubue*, for both male and female Ego, in the first ascending generation is but the converse

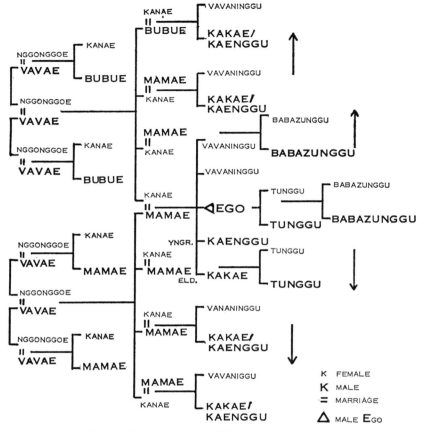

Fig. 4. Consanguineal Kinship Terminology

of the conditioned relative sex contrast made for first descending generation alters; it is sex of linking parent of Ego vs sex of alter, and it is made for male alters only. Thus for alters in each of these three generations a relative sex comparison is made, but the particular kintypes contrasted depend upon or are conditioned by features of alter and Ego in each instance.

The componential definitions noted above need but slight revision in order to fit those nonconsanguineal relatives also designated by *onotona* terms.

Spouses of senior consanguineals are addressed by the consanguineal term appropriate to their sex and generation standing, the latter taken from the consanguineals to whom they are mar-

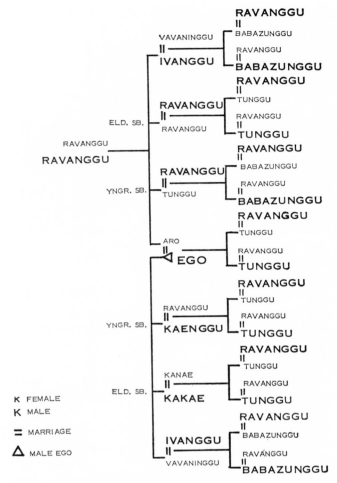

Fig. 5. Affinal Terminology

ried. Reciprocally, junior consanguineals of one's spouse are addressed by the consanguineal term appropriate to their generation standing relative to one's spouse (these terms are not sex-specific). As the Choiseulese put it, "a man follows his wife and a woman her husband," and the relevant relative sex and age comparisons are those made by Ego's spouse. Figure 5 shows that spouses of same-sex siblings (and cousins) are designated variously as *ravanggu*—an affinal term—or by the parent term appropriate to their sex, the former designation applying to spouses of junior same-sex siblings (and cousins) and the latter to spouses of senior same-sex siblings. These designations derive from the fact that a senior same-sex sibling is said to be "like a parent" and a junior same-sex sibling "like a child" to Ego. Even though he does not address them respectively as "parent" or "child," jurally at least Ego is expected to be generally subordinate to senior same-sex siblings and superordinate to junior same-sex siblings; and it is from the jural relations between Ego and his same-sex siblings that spouses of the latter take their generation standing relative to Ego. Reciprocally, since Ego "follows" his spouse in these matters, spouse's senior same-sex sibling, "like a parent" to one's spouse, is an "in-law" to Ego, and spouse's junior same-sex sibling, "like a child" to one's spouse, is a "child" to Ego. Designation of other junior kinsmen of the spouse requires some minor adjustments, however. For instance, spouse's junior same-sex sibling's children are classed as *babazunggu*, even though they are *tunggu* to one's spouse, because their parents are already *tunggu* to Ego. A woman calls her brother's children *tunggu* but her husband cannot "follow" this classification because to him WBW is *vavaninggu* and the children of a *vavaninggu* are *babazunggu* to him.

Vavaninggu ("opposite-sex sibling") is the only same-generation term which applies to nonconsanguineals, and the only non-consanguineals to whom it applies are spouses' opposite-sex siblings' spouses (WBW, HZH). Any attempt to understand this classification in componential terms would be unnecessarily complex; the operant principle is simply that anyone called *ivanggu* by one's spouse is one's own *vavaninggu*, and designation of WBW, for instance, as *vavaninggu* is simply an extension of that principle beyond one's own consanguineals.

The only nonconsanguineal kintype which cannot be handled by the component definitions stated above is MZH, who is classed as *mamae* ("father"). If we attempt to classify MZH by the distinctive features of the kintype he would be *bubue*, that is, a male first ascending generation kinsmen, opposite-sex of the linking parent. But the relative sex comparison applies, as we have seen, only between consanguineals, and the designation of MZH as *mamae* is because of that relative's marriage to a senior consanguineal who is designated by a parent term. *Mamae* is thus a complex class consisting of the "true father" plus some consan-

guineals who are not the "true father" but who share some significant features with him and, finally, spouses of female consanguineals designated as *kanae* ("mother").

The necessity of a disjunctive (nonunitary) definition of the
total *mamae* class is indicated by a distinction rarely, if ever, made
in the context of face-to-face interaction. The terms *mamae*, *kanae*
and *tunggu* may take the qualifier *lavata*, "big," as an affix in some
contexts, but this qualifier is never applicable to the kintypes F,
M, S and D. It is used referentially when Ego wishes to make the
point that the alter referred to is a "kinsman" but not the "true"
one of the type specified. The *lavata* qualifier is not a means of
separating "lineals" from "nonlineals" or "consanguineals" from
"nonconsanguineals"; its function is to isolate one's parento-filial
kinsmen from the rest of one's kinship universe, and the qualifier
is not necessary (it would be redundant) in any context other than
mamae, *kanae* or *tunggu* since the kintypes designated by the other
onotona terms are not parento-filial types. The qualifier, by
making a negative notation, "marks" the use of the root term as
a metaphorical extension. In the context of face-to-face interaction
the terms are used in a super-class sense, and the classes have
"marked" and "unmarked" members (see Lounsbury 1964:
1085). The relation between the "parent" and "parent + *lavata*"
kintypes may be diagramed as, for instance,

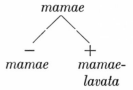

The "unmarked" member of the general *mamae* class (indicated
by —) is the "true father," the man by whom one was begotten
and the only man to whom the optional designation *lavata* cannot
apply. That *mamae* denotes true father in the biological sense
("blood" in Choiseulese terms) is further attested to by the fact
that subsequent husbands of the mother (step-fathers), even
though they may say that Ego is "just like a true son," are
nevertheless always qualified for the *lavata* designation whereas
the "true" parent never is even if he is not acting as a "social"
parent. The Choiseulese cannot know with absolute certainty,
anymore than we can, that a particular man is indeed a "true"

father, but they think they can with reasonable assurity, and that is what matters here.

Mamae lavata is, then, a residual class consisting of first ascending generation males who are neither one's true father nor called "opposite-sex sibling" by one's mother. A componential definition of the *mamae* superclass may be established by introducing the distinction parental vs non-parental kinsman, and this would be necessary if we were to include the rarely used *lavata* qualifier in the terminological system under analysis. The definition of the *mamae* class would then be as follows (where K indicates kinsman and $\overline{\text{X}}$ indicates not-cross)

$$mamae \begin{cases} mamae & : \quad \text{M} \cdot \text{Sr} \cdot \text{G1} \cdot \text{parental} \cdot \text{K} \\ mamae\ lavata & : \quad \text{M} \cdot \text{Sr} \cdot \text{G1} \cdot \text{non-parental} + \overline{\text{X}}\ \text{K} \end{cases}$$

At this point, it is more economical to omit the *lavata* qualifier from consideration and to write the *mamae* definition as:

$$mamae \quad : \quad (\text{M} \cdot \text{Sr} \cdot \text{G1} \cdot \| \cdot \text{K}) + (\text{M} \cdot \text{Sr} \cdot \text{G1} \cdot \overline{\text{X}} \cdot \text{K})$$

In either instance, we are left with a disjunctive definition in the system. Since the distinction between "cross" and "parallel" is not made for female alters in the first ascending generation there is no necessity for a disjunctive definition of the *kanae* ("mother") class, though again there would be if we were to include consideration of the parental vs non-parental distinction.

Componential definitions of the ten *onotona* terms, as they apply to both consanguineals and non-consanguineals, may be written as:

vavae	:	M $\cdot$ Sr $\cdot$ G2 $\cdot$ K
nggonggoe	:	F $\cdot$ Sr $\cdot$ G2 $\cdot$ K
kanae	:	F $\cdot$ Sr $\cdot$ G1 $\cdot$ K
mamae	:	(M $\cdot$ Sr $\cdot$ G1 $\cdot \| \cdot$ K) + (M $\cdot$ Sr $\cdot$ G1 $\cdot \overline{\text{X}} \cdot$ K)
bubue	:	M $\cdot$ Sr $\cdot$ G1 $\cdot$ X $\cdot$ K
kakae	:	Sr $\cdot$ G-0 $\cdot \| \cdot$ K
kaenggu	:	Jr $\cdot$ G-0 $\cdot \| \cdot$ K
vavaninggu	:	G-0 $\cdot$ X $\cdot$ K
tunggu	:	Em $\cdot$ Jr $\cdot$ G1 $\cdot \| \cdot$ K
		Ef $\cdot$ Jr $\cdot$ G1 $\cdot$ K

$$babazunggu \quad : \quad \text{Em} \cdot \text{Jr} \cdot \text{G1} \cdot \text{X} \cdot \text{K}$$
$$\text{Jr} \cdot \text{G2} \cdot \text{K}$$

We may now consider the two "affinal" (*tamazira*) classes, *ravanggu* and *ivanggu*. These comprise with a few exceptions those kintypes which speakers of American-English (or at least most of them) would call "in-laws." The exceptions are: (1) the Choiseu-lese use of these affinal terms is broader than ours (extends over a wider genealogical range); and (2) the introduction of generational displacement into the system by way of the contrast between junior and senior for same-sex, same-generation kinsmen means that there are, in effect, no opposite-sex siblings in-law in this system. This indicates that it would be mistaken to gloss *ivanggu* as "same-sex sibling in-law." Generational displacement leaves spouse's opposite-sex siblings as the only kinsmen in spouse's own generation, and it is therefore possible to define "affines" in this system as "spouse's same-generation and senior kinsmen and, reciprocally, one's own same-generation and junior kinsmen's spouses." The *tamazira* sub-classes may be defined componen-tially as:

$$ivanggu \quad : \quad \text{G-0} \cdot \text{A}$$
$$ravanggu \quad : \quad \text{G-}\overline{0} \cdot \text{A}$$

Or: *ivanggu*, "affine of my own generation," *ravanggu*, "affine not of my own generation."

Relatively few distinctions are made in regard to specific forms of behavior to be accorded to specific types of kinsmen. There is a blanket mutual obligation of assistance and friendliness and the general deference owed to all senior kinsmen. Some important distinctions are made, however, within one's own generation on the basis of relative age and opposite-sex relationships.

We have already seen that same-sex siblings (and cousins) are differentiated on the basis of age relative to Ego, that elder ones are "like parents" and younger ones "like children" in respect of jural status. Behaviorally, this means that the elder party in each of the pairs is entitled to deference and obedience and owes the younger care and protection. The eldest sibling in each sibling set is "most like a parent" and the jural "likeness" to a parent holds most strongly for the eldest male in a sibling set.

Opposite-sex siblings (and cousins) are highly *tabo* to one another. The Choiseulese use *tabo* to describe the relationship, and the word may be translated as "sacred" in the Durkheimian sense. Infringement of the strictures on interpersonal behavior between opposite-sex siblings is said to render the offended party "ordinary" or "profane" (*mabe*), and a fine of shell valuables must be paid to render him or her *tabo* again. The fine, which is paid to the offended party, is said to "buy" or "throw away" the "shame" or embarrassment caused by the villation. Many specific restrictions are imposed between opposite-sex siblings, and in particular any interaction is forbidden that might have even the slightest sexual connotation. They may not touch one another nor should they touch or come into contact with the other's personal possessions or sleeping places. A woman should never lie down in her brother's presence. A man may talk to his sister, but he should avoid extended conversations and especially those in which sexual references might arise. He should never be alone with her, especially inside a house. They are forbidden to hear from third parties tales of one another's activities, especially sexual, and should they inadvertently do so the party who communicated the information must pay a fine to the offended parties. Mature males may not sleep in the same house with their sisters, and when they reached puberty the boys slept regularly in the men's house where men gathered to talk or discuss local affairs. (These men's houses often do not exist today and seldom are used regularly by young boys. Most families now have dwelling houses and cook houses, and the girls usually sleep in the former and the boys in the latter.) It is also necessary for boys to sleep elsewhere because their sisters might have visitors during the night—"creeping" is a favorite nighttime sport for young men—and the situation could prove embarrassing for all concerned if a brother were present.

The force of the restrictions and shame diminishes with genealogical distance and spatial separation. The relationship between true siblings is "very *tabo*," and it may be the same between first cousins, especially if they reside in the same or adjacent villages or hamlets. But beyond these limits people begin to feel less ashamed, and others are less likely to feel that a moral wrong has been committed should infringements occur. After all, it is noted, they are only "distant siblings." But even such "distant" opposite-sex "siblings" feel ashamed in a "public" context. In 1960 one assistant district headman was required to hear (in a local court) an adultery case involving one of his female third cousins living in an adjacent hamlet. Reluctantly he presided over the hearing, but he paid a fine of several shillings to the girl immediately afterwards.

Of course, the range and intensity of the recognition of *tabo* relations vary with the particular individuals concerned. Nearly everyone feels that true siblings and first cousins are very *tabo*, and a few feel that second cousins are too. More generally, however, a second-cousin relationship is not felt to be an impediment to sexual intercourse or to marriage. It is said that, in the past, if true siblings or first cousins had sexual relations with one another their kinsmen would have had to kill them out of shame. Astute informants noted that exile would have been the more likely outcome, and in the case of first cousins a noisy protest might have been made but no serious action taken. I found instances of first-cousin marriage in genealogies, and these aroused no comment until I prompted it. Even then the matches were not viewed with derision, nor did these instances arouse community wrath in the past—or so my informants said. However, an incident of sexual relations between second cousins during 1960 created an unpleasant, though not long-lasting, relationship between their parents, and in this case it seems that there were other objections to this dalliance and more particularly to the marriage that might have resulted.

The Choiseulese do, in fact, delight in "illicit" sexual relations with women they call *vavaninggu*, but they usually indulge themselves safely with those beyond second-cousin range. A line of one lament popular with the women of Varisi goes: "I call you 'brother' but you crossed the mats and came to me at night." The suggestion of illicitness contained in "brother" in this context makes the affair all the more intriguing.

Same-sex "siblings" have ideally a relationship characterized by solidarity. They should "help" and "take care of" one another. They should work together and make liberal use of one another's property. They should not quarrel, and a younger brother should defer to the leadership of an elder brother. Nevertheless, I heard little positive sentiment expressed about relations between brothers, and the hostility between them is well recognized. Younger brothers are often jealous of and quarrelsome with elder brothers. This jealousy is generated by the control that elder brothers have over the property in which all brothers have an interest, and younger brothers often feel, sometimes justifiably, that they are being deprived of their rights. Thus they sometimes quarrel, but such quarreling was and is seldom violent nor does it often lead to an open and permanent breach in the relationship, probably because younger brothers remain dependent upon the common property and do not wish to renounce interest in it. It is recognized that such quarrels used to motivate the formation of branches within a descent group. For instance, it is said of Bose, one of the prominent ancestors of *sinangge* Kesi: "The old man of Kesi wanted his children not to quarrel among themselves, so he divided the land among them. 'You eat here, and you eat there,' he said." Nevertheless, at least one of Bose's sons was not satisfied with his share and went off to marry *tamazira* into another group some distance away. Choiseulese take their property interests seriously, and quarrels are common over them. Therefore the injunction placed upon kinsmen not to quarrel is difficult to follow, and it is precisely kinsmen who are most likely to quarrel, at least about some issues.

Again, it is clearly recognized that the obligations between "brothers" diminish with genealogical and spatial separation. "Siblings born together," those with the same mother and father, are theoretically most obligated to one another. Those with "different mothers" are less so, and especially if they have established different descent group affiliations. *Tamakena dakisi* ("close siblings"), usually first or second cousins with the same descent group affiliation, are supposed to coöperate closely and support one another, but if they do so it is probably as descent group mates with similar interests on particular occasions. The relations between "distant siblings" are subject to wide variation. Every man has many others to whom he is a "distant sibling," and it is simply impossible to relate to all of them in the same way. What is done, of course, is to define the relationship as important and "close" when it is of some utility and to define it as "distant" and unimportant, of no binding quality, when it is of no utility or of some advantage to deny the validity of claims and obligations.

While the "same-" versus "opposite-sex sibling" terminological dichotomy has extensive correlates in behavior, the same cannot be said for the *mamae* ("father") versus *bubue* ("mother's brother") distinction and the social significance of the distinction is no more apparent to the Choiseulese than it is to their ethnographer. *Bubue* are treated deferentially and should be obeyed, but the same is true for all elder kinsmen. *Bubue* have no special obligations toward their alters that differ from those towards their brothers' or their own children (except, of course, in degree in the latter instance). The Choiseulese could offer no explanation for the distinction.

One significant difference between *bubue* and all other males in the same generation is that the others are either the genitor or his legitimate substitute as mother's spouse, whereas *bubue*, as *vavanina* to one's mother, are "forbidden" to her. But if this could be demonstrated to be the basis of the distinction, it would still remain a problem why FZ is not distinguished from MZ following the same reasoning.

The distinction may perhaps be that one's *bubue* would be, according to the dogma of group formation and operation, one's closest kinsman in one's mother's natal descent group. However, only some *bubue* belong nominally to one's mother's natal descent group, but many men of that group would be *bubue*, and the *bubue ogoto* ("true mother's brother") would probably be an active member of that group. As one's closest kinsman in it, he would be one's "natural ally" and the promoter and protector of one's interests in its estate, and it would be in his particular share of that estate that one's strongest interests would lie. It is to him that one would most likely turn for assistance in recruiting aid from that group, and he or one of his "brothers" should be the one most likely to offer unsolicited aid. If one's parents chose to reside patri-uxorilocally, one's father's brothers would occupy an analogous position. Where one's parents reside with his *bubue* one consistently falls under his authority and is heavily dependent upon him economically just as one falls directly under the authority of his father's brothers and is dependent upon them when one's parents reside patri-virilocally. In other words, the roles played by father's brothers and mother's brothers are similar and complementary, and the difference in terminology, therefore, cannot reflect consistent behavioral differences because none exist.

(In the portion of Choiseul from the Babatana and Ririo regions to the southeastern tip, MB is addressed by the "grandfather" term and a male Ego addresses his sister's children as "grandchildren," as is done in the Varisi area. There are no special referential or aggregate terms for the mother's brother-sister's child relationship.)

Among affines, too, particular emphasis is placed upon opposite-sex relationships. Although all *tamaravana* relationships are *tabo*, this quality applies most strictly only between those of opposite sex. *Tamaravana valeke* (men) or *tamaravana nggole* (women) are *tabo* relationships but mostly as a matter of respect, though there are some sexual overtones even here. Two men who are *ravanggu* to one another should not expose themselves, but should it happen it would be of little consequence. Nor is it considered quite proper to make reference to one another's sexual activities.

The relationship between affines of opposite sex (these can only be those in a *tamaravana* relationship) is characterized ideally by respect, avoidance, and shame. As between "opposite-sex siblings," the opposite-sex affinal relationship is sanctioned by shame and the payment of fines when its strictures are violated and one of the parties rendered "profane." Furthermore, it is believed that if this and other *tabo* relationships are not observed one's gardens will not grow well and one's pigs and children will sicken and die; but if they are observed one will "live well" or "prosper." Opposite-sex affines are forbidden to touch each other or to hand food or other objects directly to one another; passing of any object must be done through a third party, or the object placed upon the ground or floor before the other can take it. Exposure of sexual organs is strictly forbidden, and any talk of a sexual nature proscribed. In fact, it is best to avoid one's opposite-sex affines where practicable, but this does not mean that all interaction must be avoided. One must be circumspect; opposite-sex affines may converse, but they should not hold general conversations; they should state their business and depart, and they should never converse in private. If one's opposite-sex affine is in a house alone and one wishes to speak with him or her, one remains outside to do so. The use of the names of all affines, other than *ivana*, is strictly forbidden, and if one has a *ravana* whose name contains a common noun, rigorous avoidance of the use of that noun is to be practiced at all times. Opposite-sex affines may sleep in the same house, but small barricades of mats are erected around the sleeping places of the females, especially unmarried girls, so that they may have privacy.

Again, the ideal strength of the various avoidances diminishes with genealogical distance so that those who are *ravana* to one another through other than primary kin are generally regarded as somewhat less *tabo*. The restrictions still hold in principle, but there is less concern if they are violated and they are interpreted somewhat more liberally if distant kin are affected.

Since most people who marry are already kinsmen to one another, many of Ego's affines may also be his cognates, and the problem arises whether he will continue to use cognatic or change to affinal terms. There are no explicit rules to cover such situations, and each one must be worked out on its own merits. Because of the personal and terminological difficulties implicit in the creation of a *tabo* relationship, there is a recognized tendency to avoid it wherever possible. The possibility depends largely upon the degree of "closeness" of the previous relationship and upon how strongly each party to the relationship feels about the *tabo* relationship that might henceforth exist between them. Nevertheless, the primary affines (e.g., WM, WF, HM, HF and SW, DH), and especially those who are of opposite sex, are always addressed as *ravanggu*. The spouses of siblings' children are technically speaking one's *ravana* too, and the term may be used but the restrictions on interaction hardly observed. Today the restrictions go largely unobserved by many people, but others still feel the *tabo* strongly and continue to observe them, especially within the immediate family. The spouses of siblings' children are now frequently addressed by the same term as the sibling's child. It is said that they know they are *tamaravana*, but they want to make each other "happy" so they do not use the term. In the Babatana and Ririo areas today, as in the past, people use parent and child terms between affines who could be called *ravanggu*. It is said again, that they know they are *tamaravana* but they do not like to use the term or to impose the restrictions. In the Babatana area the most *tabo* affinal relationship is that between a man and his wife's elder same-sex sibling or between a woman and her husband's elder same-sex sibling. This is a very strong *tabo* relationship in the Varisi area too, and the strength of it seems to be related to the jealousy between brothers. If the strength of the *tabo*

diminishes the possibility of adultery it has nevertheless sometimes been ineffective in this respect, and some of the most violent
quarrels between brothers have occurred over just such issues, or
so it is said.

The strongest "oaths" are those involving *tabo* kinsmen. To
ododo midiki is to swear upon the name of one opposite-sex sibling
and this may be done, for instance, to proclaim innocence when
accused of a disreputable act. One may also *vese midiki* by using
the name of one's *vavanina;* that is, to forbid others from using
some object (for instance, groves, coconuts, canoe, path, or door-
way) one may say that those who would use that object commit an
offense tantamount to accusing the swearer of having had sexual
relations with his *vavanina*, or one may imply that by so doing the
offender has eaten the feces of one's *vavanina*. Reference to one's
ravana may also be made in such oaths, but *vavanina* is more common. Anyone who commits an offense that such an oath is designed to prevent must pay a fine of shell valuables to its author,
and if this were not done in the past, further and more effective
sanctions were available (see pp. 206–207).

The *tamaivana* relationship is also *tabo*, but being a same-sex
relationship it is *tabo* mostly in the sense that it is important or
significant. The *ivana* relationship between males is foremost in
Choiseulese thought. Ideally this relationship is comparable to
that between two brothers, one of mutual obligation and allegiance. But there is a "saying" about the relationship of *ivana* that
I did not hear used in reference to brothers: "The *kapisi* says,
'When my *ivanggu* dies I will die with him.' " The *kapisi* is a small
black insect that is difficult to remove from the banana, for it runs
around the banana, always evading its pursuer. Thus when a
banana goes into a fire to cook, the *kapisi* usually goes with it. The
saying expresses the ideal strength of the solidarity of the *ivana*
relationship, especially between males. The *ivana* relationship is
said to be *tabo* "because" one of the men is married to the other's
"sister." Thus it is not quite proper for *ivana* to make sexual jokes,
especially with personal references, in each other's company. Nor,
for the same reason, should *ivana* expose their sexual organs to one
another. Because their relationship is *tabo* they should never
quarrel, another aspect of the ideal solidarity that exists between
them. One's *ivana* should come to one's aid in time of difficulty,
and if one is gardening or making a feast one's *ivana* should lend a

hand or help provide food, especially pig. Managers were particularly dependent upon their *ivana* for assistance in making feasts. *Ivana* have a legitimate but limited claim upon the resources of one another and should be allowed to plant gardens freely upon one another's land. Their limited privileges in regard to the estate of one's descent group derive from the rights of the women they have married. Managers, who were frequently polygynous, deliberately chose wives from among the "sisters" or "daughters" of other important men so as to establish a claim upon the services and resources of those men.

THE IMPORTANCE OF KINSHIP   It is evident from all this that the Choiseulese reckon "kinship," *onotona* or *sinangge*, cognatically. Lineal kinship, whether patrilineal or matrilineal, does not establish special relationships between two or more persons as individuals, nor is laterality a significant criterion in this respect, even in the mother's brother-sister's child distinction for male speakers. Being an agnatic descendant of the apical ancestor of a particular *sinangge* (cognatic descent category or descent group) may well affect one's status within that unit and do so necessarily in relation to other persons. But being related to others agnatically does in no way establish special relations between any two kinsmen such that they are distinguished terminologically or behaviorally as a class from all others. That is, the relationship between two kinsmen, even if they both have agnatic status in the same *sinangge*, in whatever sense, derives theoretically from common cognatic connection and not from the specific type of genealogical tie between them. It is true that two men with agnatic status in the same descent group may coöperate against those without it, but they do so as members of the same group with similar interests and not because they are obliged to do so as agnatic kin. "Born of men" is in fact a purportedly privileged status conferring rights over property and in relation to other persons, but it does not confer special relationships between individuals as such.

As noted earlier, the use of *sinangge* generally implies that the persons referred to trace common cognatic connection of some sort and that they coöperate on the basis of a general injunction obliging them to "help one another." The use of a kin term implies the same.

The obligation to help and care for one's kinsmen extends into every area of activity. To mention only a few, kinsmen share their

land with one another, help one another with gardening, the building of houses, the provision of food, and, until recently, the making
of feasts through provision of taro, pig, nuts, and so on. They look
after the children of deceased kin and provide for the needs of
elderly and incapacitated kinsmen. When traveling, kinsmen provide hospitality and protection. A good wife, as a matter of course,
regularly sent small gifts of food to her own and her husband's
kinsmen, especially when the family had something unusual such
as a good catch of wild pig, possum, or fish. Such gifts were not
obligatory nor were they given only to certain classes of kin. They
were given by "good kin" as tokens of recognition of kinship and,
purportedly, "remembrance" and affection. Direct and immediate
reciprocation was not required, but it was certainly expected that
it would occur, and comment was forthcoming if the gift was not
eventually acknowledged by a return. It was not that people
valued the objects given; they valued rather the recognition of
kinship and the acknowledgement of mutual obligation signified
by such exchanges. To give small gifts of food is to *nganga rove*,
literally "eat" and "know," and it may be translated figuratively
as "to eat wisely." Those who did not give such gifts were said to
nganga siko, literally "eat" and "steal," with the connotation that
they were depriving others of food. One informant viewed these
gifts as a "great tangle of exchanges" with people giving food "all
about" in no particular pattern. These small prestations were not
confined to one's hamlet or village; they were sent to relatives in
nearby hamlets or villages as well. In a similar way managers occasionally made small gifts of food to one another as tokens of
respect and allegiance. (These exchanges are almost entirely
defunct today. They take place only on special occasions, such as
Christmas, or when one has killed a wild pig or caught many fish.
It was on a Christmas Day that they first came to my attention.)

Tutusi, genealogical knowledge, is said to be "something important," because knowing one's relatives enables one to avoid
conflict with them or perhaps killing them inadvertently. *Tutusi*
also tells one whom to ask for help. Just as kinsmen are not to
quarrel, neither were they to participate in warfare or revenge
activities against one another. If a man of group A had kinsmen in
group B, and A and B went to war, ideally he should have stayed
out of the affair. He would stay at home and then close his house
to the warriors upon their return; they had to give him a single

ziku (a small ring worn as a bracelet on the upper arm, called *siroro* in this context) before he could open his house to them. This had to be done or the man would have had "bad luck" (*situ*) in the form of *marava*, a kind of sickness which causes one's teeth to fall out.

Now it should be self-evident that kinsmen do not live in some "mystical concord"; to the contrary, they do quarrel and they used to make war against one another, but fighting among kin was the most reprehensible form of conflict, and it was also the most readily settled. Furthermore, it was shaped by the fact that it was kinsmen who were disputing and not mere strangers. Thus, while it was precisely kinsmen who quarreled most, at least over certain issues because they shared similar interests in the same property, they also came less often to violence, not simply because they were kinsmen but because they were part of a social network that restrained their conflicts (see chap. 4).

Kinship obligations exhibit a gradation from *soku* to *dakisi* to *kavakava*, from *onotona* to *turana*, but there is no point at which kinship obligations can be said to terminate absolutely; so long and far as the connection can be traced the obligation persists. When it is said that kinsmen should help one another qualifiers are seldom added, but it is nonetheless clearly recognized that some kinsmen are *onotona volomo*, "kin of no significance." One could not legitimately be expected to expend energies and resources upon them. Although I am not dealing here with "personal kindreds" in Freeman's sense, his comments on the Iban are again relevant:

> . . . in the absence of arbitrary demarcation it is merely the cessation of inter-communication, for whatever reasons, that tends to terminate kindred relations and the moral obligations associated with them. It is, in other words, a *de facto* and not a *de jure* termination. Indeed, it is always possible, where circumstances make it advantageous, for a dormant relationship to be revived if those concerned are ready to recognize it (1961: 210).

It is possible, then, for each man to some extent to accentuate some of his many kinship ties as he pleases, or as suits his special interests. But his choice is by no means entirely free, for membership in social groups and categories is more or less constraining. To be a member of a particular descent group, for instance, is to accept obligations to fellow members as more important than obligations to other kinsmen. Thus kinship obligations are shaped by group membership, but they are shaped very little by the type of kin tie.

Within the range of "close" kin one must choose to accentuate some relationships and to ignore, at least temporarily, the remainder. The same is true within the range of "distant" kin. The closest and most binding relationships are usually between descent-group mates or members of proximate groups; the most distant and least binding are usually between members of widely separated and infrequently interacting groups. Between these two extremes lie the groups of one "region," those composed of persons speaking one dialect. "Region" describes an important unit of Choiseulese society; it is not the same as the modern district, for the latter is in a sense an artificial unit imposed upon the Choiseulese by the protectorate. However, modern districts usually do include the whole of an aboriginal region and usually include several closely related regions (see map, Fig. 6). A region is composed of several intermarrying and, therefore, interrelated descent groups, all speaking the same dialect and closely coöperating with one another. The exact number of groups forming a region varies. In the Tepazaka region there are eight descent groups today, and in the past there were more or less the same number (see map, Fig. 7). These people speak a dialect of the Varisi language which has some affinities to the Babatana language too. The modern Varisi District on the north side of Choiseul is composed of several regions. A census of one of them showed seven descent groups now operative there; again, more or less that number were operative in the past. The Varisi spoken in this region differs little from that of the other Varisi District regions. Today these descent groups are not always separate from one another residentially, but in the past they normally would have occupied sites upon their own estates, coming together in larger units only on special occasions. It was from its region that a group drew most of its assistance in the days when intergroup alliances were crucial and frequent; but it is from his own region that any individual also draws most of his assistance since it is from neighboring groups within his own region that he selects those kinsmen with whom he will coöperate most closely.

The Choiseulese say that the people of one region are "one big *sinangge*" since almost everyone is kin to everyone else within it. That a region contains a large and complex network of kinship ties

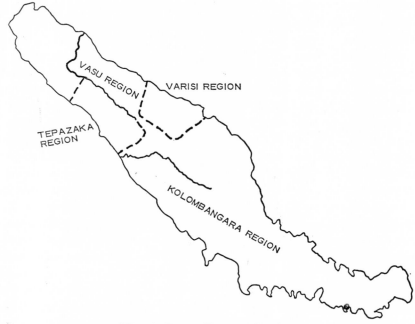

Fig. 6. Some Choiseul Regions

is attributed to the preference for marriage within or between neighboring descent groups and their cognatic descent categories. Because everyone within the region is kin to everyone else, the region is the area within which one may travel most freely, within which one feels most secure. Kinsmen owe one another hospitality whether they live in the same region or in different regions, and one is always most comfortable with kinsmen. A Choiseulese in the company of non-kin is a miserable fellow. One of the principal reasons for this is fear of sorcery (*sukita*). Non-kin are generally feared and suspect. They need no particular reason to practice sorcery, but it may be that they harbor some grudge, of which one is not aware, from the distant past. Because of this fear of strangers many Choiseulese refrain from traveling even today.

Just as one region is "one big *sinangge*" so too is the whole of the island when compared with another island. Choiseulese should coöperate with one another against the inhabitants of other islands, but there is no formal obligation in this respect and the sentiment seems to stem largely from modern conditions. In the

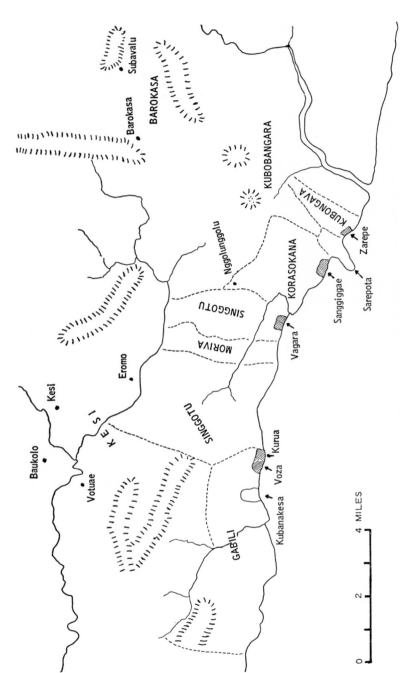

Fig. 7. Tepazaka Region

past Choiseul was hardly a solidary unit against outsiders even though once in a while some—never all—Choiseulese seem to have organized as such to war against, say, the Vella Lavellans. More frequent, however, were alliances between some Choiseulese and some Vella Lavellans against other groups of Choiseulese.

One further aspect of kinship needs mention here. It has already been noted that marriages are often between kinsmen, and a person may then have both cognatic and affinal ties with his or her spouse's kinsmen. Some mention has been made of the ways in which the terminological problem is resolved, but by the same token a person is often related in more than one way to many of his cognatic kinsmen, and this is especially true of those who live in the same region. It is important to note how these "tangles" are resolved terminologically, for we might find some indication of a preference for, say, use of the term indicated by possible patrilateral or patrilineal connections in consonance with the dogma that "the father's side is most important." Nevertheless, there are no cultural "rules" governing which term should be chosen from among several possibilities. "They do not choose which side will be strong; the two sides are the same," at least in this context. It is added: "We do not throw away one side or the other," and both terms are remembered though only one might be used consistently. Clearly, neither the "father's side" nor the "mother's side" is given preference. It might be, that in practice one "side" is consistently chosen in preference to the other, but the instances I examined do not indicate this, and, since most terms are "bilateral" in their application only a relatively few cases could give evidence to test this supposition—for instance, a situation in which someone is both "father's brother" and "mother's brother" to a person and in the same degree.

"Closeness" of relationship is, again, given as the principal basis of choice of which kinship term will be used. One's parents are seldom equally closely related to a particular person, and one generally "follows" the terminology of the "closer" parent. Anomalies of age are noticed and thought inappropriate and, if possible, avoided. For instance, if one can call a woman *nggonggoe*, "grandmother," or *vavaninggu*, "sister," and she is of nearly the same age as oneself, she will probably be called *vavaninggu*, even though it may be the more distant relationship. Two men of similar age may prefer to relate as "elder" and "younger brother" rather than "father"-"son" (*kakae-kaenggu, mamae-tunggu*). Whether one "follows" one's father or one's mother may depend upon their residence. If one's father and mother are residing uxorilocally, for instance, and one's father is related as a cognate to some of one's mother's kinsmen, one will probably "follow" his mother's terminology, and vice versa. In an intragroup marriage, when both parents are already closely related, complications arise and people have a difficult time knowing what to do. Terminology is then a complete tangle, and people try to accommodate in any way that makes the other party happy or content. It is said that people sometimes get angry because of the terms others try to use, but such situations usually arise only when one party favors a *tabo* relationship the other "does not want."

In any event, the choice is not particularly crucial, for frequently kinship terms are not used and personal names are far more common in address and reference, and even as terms of reference for close kinsmen, such as one's parents' siblings. The kin term is used when one wishes to make it clear that the reference is for some reason to kinship itself. One informant remarked that kin terms are used "only when we want something of that person," to emphasize kinship and the obligations involved the kinship terms are used. They are commonly used also by parents when reprimanding their children and again to indicate respect when one is addressing parents or someone of advanced age or higher social status, such as a manager.

Descent Groups

The most common reference of *sinangge* is to the descent group. The local groups called *sinangge* include persons other than members of a particular cognatic descent category, for instance, wives and husbands of members, and to distinguish them I refer to members of a particular cognatic descent category living with its descent group as the "core" of that group. "Core" is equivalent to the Varisi word *kapakapa*. Descent groups may be described as the "primary residential-proprietary segments" of Choiseulese society, for everyone lives in some form of association with a descent group, and descent groups jurally [5] and effectively (in the past

---

[5] "Jural" is used here "to cover a mixture of law and morality . . ." (Firth 1955: 5). It refers to *explicit* rules and norms, but I beg the question of whether Choiseulese society had "law."

more so than now) control the properties about which the Choiseulese are so concerned. It was only through a descent group that
a man could gain prestige or renown, become a *batu*, or manager,
and it was only through allegiance to such a group that security
could be obtained. The descent-group core was the basic unit of
organization and coöperation in most significant activities. Task
groups of many varieties arose from it but included operation-
ally those members of the group who were not members of its
core and sometimes included members of other groups too. However, a descent-group core was usually the nucleus of a task group,
and task groups are referred to as *sinangge* on that basis as well
as because they were composed of kinsmen coöperating with one
another.

Ideally a descent group resides on its estate, but there were
times when this was not possible, as when security needs demanded that several friendly and usually adjacent and closely
related groups unite to form a larger unit for the common defense. Then, too, it was sometimes decided that avoidance of conflict was the wiser course, and the group disbanded temporarily.
Individuals or families or sets of families sought refuge (*bori*), protection, and shelter elsewhere with close or distant kin and a
powerful manager whose prestige guaranteed their safety. The
descent group was usually reorganized at a later date. As noted
earlier, the reorganization imposed by changing settlement patterns in recent years brought an end to many *sinangge* as descent
groups. They no longer have any residential solidarity or only a
minimal amount, and solidarity as action groups is extremely rare.
These conditions of minimal solidarity obtain where a group divided into several smaller units, each of which settled among other
groups according to the attractiveness and availability of kin ties
with those groups.[6] These smaller units are sometimes referred to
as *sinangge* in more than a simple categorical sense, but their personnel also see themselves more often, or at least as much, as
members of the groups among which they have settled. This system of group membership tolerates varying definitions of membership with comparative ease. As might be expected, these now
isolated segments of once unitary descent groups act as solidary

---

[6] See pp. 25–28 for a statement of recent events which have brought about
many such divisions of once solidary descent groups.

units or seek some active identity with the other segments only when their shared land interests are threatened.

To say that a descent group usually resided on its estate is not to imply a large and compact residential unit such as a permanent village. Small hamlets dispersed throughout the estate and perched on ridges near groves and gardens were probably the more typical residential unit. Hamlets are referred to as branches of the *sinangge* and are sometimes called "branch settlements" (*panggarana komala*), implying that they were offshoots of the "original" or "base settlement" which was the residence of the "truncal" segment. However, some hamlets were the residences of branches with political autonomy whereas others were merely the separate residences of a family or a few closely related families constituting a branch of dependent status and with no more than relatively exclusive rights of usage to a portion of the estate. More often than the former, the latter adjoined one another, stretching out along a single ridge where the "original settlement" was. However, even cognate branches of autonomous political status sometimes joined temporarily to form a large hamlet or village. In short, there was no simple correlation between the genealogical, political, and residential status of the branches of a major *sinangge*. Each branch might have been a discrete descent group or it might not, and several cognate groups might have formed a large residential unit—usually only temporarily—or they might have been dispersed on adjoining estates.

"Descent group" here refers to a politically autonomous local and residential entity. A number of independent but cognate descent groups, or perhaps only one such unit, constitute a "major *sinangge*," and when it is necessary to refer to a segment of such a major *sinangge* I term that part a "minor descent group" (see Fig. 8). But a minor descent group may have a number of recognized segments within it which are distinguishable not only genealogically but also residentially in that the houses of their members form clusters noticeably, though perhaps barely, separate from all others. These, too, are "branches" in Choiseulese parlance. I call them "descent group segments." Such distinctions are difficult to maintain "on the ground," and it is important to remember that they are mine and not wholly indigenous. The Choiseulese sometimes use *komala* and *sinangge* interchangeably.

Descent groups were in part built up around a *batu* or manager who attained his status partly through an ascribed criterion and partly through achievement. The achievement criteria were prowess in organizing warfare, vengeance, and gift exchanges, which amounted to competition with similarly ambitious men. Mortality in warfare and vengeance activities was high, and there was a correspondingly high rate of mobility to avoid these conflicts. Consequently, the composition of local groups was fluid, and their fates varied. Cognatic and affinal ties were widely used to obtain shelter and protection among close or distant kinsmen and with a powerful manager. Despite these intergroup conflicts, there were extended periods of peace, at least within limited areas, allowing groups some degree of stability, and unless nearly annihilated in

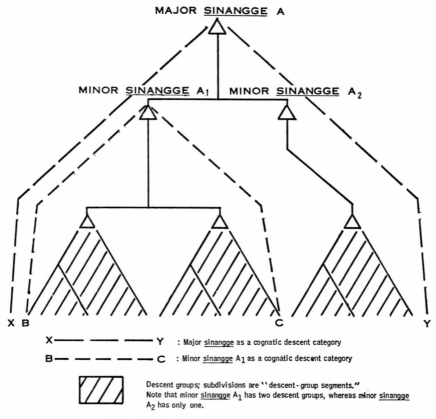

X———— ———— ———Y   : Major sinangge as a cognatic descent category

B— — — — — — C   : Minor sinangge A₁ as a cognatic descent category

Descent groups; subdivisions are "descent-group segments." Note that minor sinangge A₁ has two descent groups, whereas minor sinangge A₂ has only one.

Fig. 8. Simplified Model of a Major *Sinangge*

warfare a descent group usually maintained at least a portion of its members resident on its estate. This general situation encouraged the recruitment of potential members to descent groups if for no other reason than to increase military potential and ability to perform gift exchanges. However, the ecological situation— poor land, limited technology, and taro cultivation—imposed decided limits upon the size of local groups, and ecological considerations were not the only ones which limited group size. As I show later, the complex system of revenge and reconciliation in intergroup relations effectively prevented enduring alliances and larger social units than already existed, and although nonresident kin were sometimes recruited to descent groups there were also considerations limiting the extent of such recruitment. There is nominally considerable freedom for change of descent-group affiliation, and in the past there was a great deal of residential mobility, but frequent and enduring changes of group affiliation have their disadvantages for individuals and groups, and such disadvantages impose some constraint upon such changes.

KINSHIP CRITERIA FOR DESCENT GROUP AFFILIATION   Since the Choiseulese think of their primary segments as kin and descent groups, it is best to begin by considering the kinship criteria involved in affiliation with them. It is important to remember here that descent groups are localized and political as well as kin groups and that, therefore, kinship criteria alone cannot account for their formation as, say, a genealogical criterion might account for the formation of certain conceptual aggregates or socially significant categories. People make choices and decisions which result in their own affiliations or the affiliations of others with certain groups, and kinship or genealogical criteria are important considerations in those choices; however, the processes through which choices and decisions are made are as important in the formation of the groups as the genealogical criteria themselves.

For the moment at least I assume a descent group already formed by the political processes to be discussed later (chap. 4). I now discuss how it is said that new members are recruited to such groups and others lost from them at least partly on the basis of kinship or genealogical considerations.

Anyone becomes a member of a *sinangge*, or rather of several *sinangge*, simply by being the child of his or her parents, but it is clear that here we speak of the *sinangge* as a cognatic descent category. Because cognatic descent categories are maintained, so far as the genealogical criterion is definitive, by the continual recognition of the offspring of members, regardless of the sex of the members or their offspring, I call the genealogical criterion of cognatic descent category membership "cognatic descent." However, for any particular individual his retention in cognatic descent categories is contingent on his residence in relation to the spatial distribution of the cognatic descent categories to which he could belong and the frequency and intensity of his interaction with other members of those categories.

Recognition as a member of a descent group is a complex process, or at least it may be. Initially it usually is not: an individual's natal descent group membership is not a matter of "choice" for him, for he becomes a member of that group simply by being born (or adopted) into it as the child of his parent (or parents if theirs has been an intragroup union)—or in short, by the process of "filiation." Persons are *born into* descent groups and become identified with them by parental connection, and "filiation" here refers to the process, not to any indigenous organizational principle. Though this process may be recognized as a principle elsewhere,[7] this is not the case in Choiseulese society, so that my usage here is analytical and not meant to be a translation of an indigenous concept.

---

[7] My use of "filiation" derives from, but is not identical to, that of Freeman (1958: 51) who uses it in relation to the Iban of Borneo to refer to "the system whereby an individual establishes membership of a structurally continuing group by virtue of birth (or adoption), and with reference to one of his (or her) parents." Among the Iban, filiation is "utrolateral"; a child is born into either his mother's or his father's *bilek* family and his birth in one excludes him from the other. The choice, made by his parents at the time of their marriage, to affiliate with one of their *bilek* families automatically excludes their offspring from the other. This is the *process* of utrolateral filiation, but the Iban apparently codify it as a principle of organization too. Filiation has also been used by Fortes (1953: 33; 1959: 206–207) to refer to the parent-child relationship, the universal "fact of life" which various societies may use or culturally recognize in different ways. For Fortes it appears to be an analytical concept. Barnes (1962: 6) has also used filiation in a way similar to my usage. In relation to New Guinea Highland societies he distinguishes between "filiation as a *mechanism* of recruitment to social groups and to ascribed relationships and descent as a sanctioned and morally evaluated principle of belief." It is recognized that confusion may result from these varied usages, and while this would be regrettable it also seems to me unavoidable at the moment.

If the child's parent (or parents) somehow change their descent-group affiliation and he goes with them, his affiliation changes too. A child, then, is subject to the decisions made by the parents, and his initial descent-group affiliation is a simple product of their affiliation. For instance:

If a child's father is a member of group A and his mother of B, and if his parents domicile with A, then he is *de facto* a member of A.

Similarly, if his parents domicile with B, then he is *de facto* a member of B.

The child of an unmarried mother, is a member of his mother's descent group, though this is not necessarily her father's descent group.

The domicile of the child's parents, then, is the crucial issue, and not their actual residence. Thus, for instance, if they were fleeing a war and had taken refuge with a group to which one of them was more or less closely related at the time of the child's birth, this should have no influence upon the child's identity as a member of one of their natal, or at least premarital, groups of origin.

A child is defined simply as a member of the group with which his parents (or parent) are most closely and continously identified, and unless the status of his parents is the subject of dispute, the social classification of children offers few problems—or at least few varieties of problem. Purportedly, the payment or non-payment of the brideprice (*nanggisi*) settles with finality the affiliation of children. If a brideprice is paid the woman is supposed to leave the group with which she is affiliated and take up residence with her husband in the group with which he is immediately affiliated. If a brideprice is not paid (*tamazira* marriage), the husband is supposed to take up residence with the wife in her group. In the former instance the kinsmen of the husband proclaim any children who may be born to be of their *sinangge*, and in the latter instance the kinsmen of the wife proclaim any children to be of their *sinangge*. (What happens after this depends largely upon the quality of the relations that continue to exist between the kinsmen of the wife and husband. This despite the "rules" about how things should go!)

When it is said that a child belongs to one *sinangge* rather than, or to the exclusion of, another it is meant that the speakers consider the primary interests of the child to lie within their own descent group. They feel that the child is primarily obligated to them, and they admit a primary obligation to that child. They profess to assume full responsibility for his welfare. They do not say that other descent groups have no interests in him, but only that any interests the others may have must be considered secondary and that he should continue to reside with his father's group if the brideprice has been paid or with his mother's group if it has not.

According to the ideology, then, if a brideprice is paid children become resident members of their father's descent group and should always remain such. The mother's descent group is admitted to retain, and usually does profess, an interest in the welfare of the child. The child is referred to by his mother's descent group of origin as their *babazuna* ("sister's child"), and he is purportedly welcome among them at any time as a visitor or as a permanent resident. In the past, had any harm come to him, his mother's group might have come to his aid without being solicited and, if he met death as the result of some act that could be construed as negligence on the part of his father's descent group, his mother's group had the right to demand compensation (*toka*). A similar situation exists with regard to a child who has become affiliated with his mother's group through a *tamazira* marriage: to his father's descent group he is their "child" (*tuna*) in whom an interest and great concern are again professed. They too welcome him as a visitor or permanent resident and may offer unsolicited aid in his behalf and could claim compensation. (The latter is no longer practiced.)

There is more to be said about the establishment of descent group membership and about the process of changing affiliation, but before going into this it is important to note in greater detail how rights and duties in descent groups are jurally distributed. However, let it be noted again that initial membership in descent groups is not simply by virtue of a descent criterion or "principle." It is, in a sense, "ascribed," but through a complex social process and not simply by a genealogically phrased principle or rule. Ascription of descent-group membership is in part the resultant of choices made by one's parents, and those choices may be relatively binding upon oneself. If they are, this again is not because of any "principle" but rather, as the following chapter shows, because of situational factors pertaining to the nature of descent-group membership.

JURAL DISTRIBUTION OF RIGHTS   Descent groups are composed of several classes of persons and those classes are defined in genealogical terms. Each class has certain rights in respect of the property of the group and its affairs, but rights differ from one class to another, not so much in kind as in degree. Implicitly, the Choiseulese recognize three classes of persons and three corresponding degrees of right over and interest in descent-group property and affairs. I call them "primary," "secondary," and "contingent."

Persons with primary rights and membership are, according to the indigenous dogma, the *popodo valeke*, agnatic descendants of the *sinangge* founder. One of their number, purportedly determined by primogeniture, is the manager of the group (see chaps. 3 and 4). It is his right and duty to serve as custodian or steward of all group resources—land, *kesa* (shell valuables; see pp. 200 ff.), and persons. He maintains the genealogical charter with the help of descent-group elders, and he is the principal organizer and executor of all groups affairs; his control over group property, and especially *kesa*, enabled him to provide protection and security for his allies. The manager is in a sense only the first among equals, and others with agnatic status share with him primary rights and interests which are purportedly inalienable under any circumstances. Even if in the recent or distant past one's agnatic ancestors left the group and became members of another, one looks upon the former group as one's *kutamana* or *ununa*, one's "bottom" or "origin" *sinangge*. Sometimes knowledge of one's *kutamana* becomes lost, but it is always recognized that one has an "origin" *sinangge* in which one should be a primary member had the dogmas of descent-group affiliation always been followed.

The notion of primary interests is expressed, for instance, in the contentions that one's interests are "strong" or "active," that one may "talk strong" or "take an active voice" in group affairs, such as land, *kesa*, groves, and formerly vengeance and gift exchanges. It is the manager who has the strongest voice, and others of agnatic status may "talk strong" too, but, like all other group members, they are said to be "covered" by the manager and subservient to him; they are "like his hands" and ready to do his bidding. But while agnatic members are also "under" their manager, they are always "first" in contrast to those who are "born of women," who are always "second." The latter are said to "live under" the former. Whether they became members of the group by filiation or by other means is, technically speaking, irrelevant, and they remain secondary members regardless of how primary members may have become such. Secondary status obliges them to "keep their peace," which is to say that they must abide by the decisions of primary members and never become obtrusive in group affairs. Only so long as they do so are they welcome in the group. One who becomes presumptuous—and many do—many be reminded of his status, be told to keep quiet or made to feel unwelcome.

Under certain circumstances, secondary members may take over primary interests in the descent group either temporarily or permanently. In the past when descent groups sometimes had to disband and primary members went elsewhere, presumably temporarily, they sometimes left secondary members to "care for" the estate. The latter then became in effect primary interest holders. The agnatic line may die out, as when a manager has no brothers or sons or when it was wiped out in a war. Then, of course, secondary members were left with the strongest title and became by default the primary interest holders. Since branches were sometimes founded through women, there may be segments of a *sinangge* in which the primary interest holders are only secondary members of the major *sinangge*. The Choiseulese pass this off by noting that "the major *sinangge* is the important thing," and those secondary members "only eat," that is, take their subsistence, from their segment of the estate. (I will return to this subject in the next chapter.)

Adoption and fosterage are very common; approximately 41 per cent of the adult married males in my census of 1959–60 had some history of adoption or fosterage. This figure may be higher than what one might have found some years ago, for the high death rate of the contact period may have had a profound influence upon such matters. However, if it did, the *sinangge* system has accommodated to the situation without pronounced difficulties. On the other hand, mortality was high in the past and life expectancy must have been shorter too, because of vengeance and warfare and poorer nutrition, so that orphanage was common then too. As in many Melanesian societies (cf. Oliver 1955), the heroes of Choiseulese folklore are usually orphans.

Only some adoptions result in a change of descent-group affiliation, and many adoptions result in an addition of possible affiliations. In general, a child is adopted only when "there is no one to care for it," and this usually means that one or both parents are dead. Ideally, orphaned children remain with the immediate kinsmen of the father or mother, and ideally those of the father. But they can be adopted by others if those with first claim are not interested. If someone other than his immediate kin adopts a child and effectively assumes the role of "parent" then the child purportedly acquires secondary membership in the adoptor's descent group. He does not thereby lose the right of membership in any other group to which he is related consanguineally. Under some circumstances (to be discussed more fully in the next chapter), young men may leave their parents and become associated with another man, usually the "mother's brother."

Similar to adoptees in respect of jural status were persons who had become descent-group members as *sake* or *mate bangara*. *Sake* is commonly rendered in Pidgin as "slave," but it is more accurately translated as "captive." A *sake* was someone taken captive in war or in a raid arranged specifically to acquire him. He was adopted into his captor's group as his "child." *Mate bangara* were also "captives" but were taken from another group specifically to "replace" a particular person, frequently a manager who had recently died. The *mate bangara* is said to have "replaced" (*soka*) the deceased manager, but he took the manager's place only in a limited sense, for although he sometimes assumed the manager's name, he was not captured to become a manager himself. *Mate bangara* were usually very young children. Indeed, sometimes they were intended sacrificial victims, their blood to be spilled upon a new war canoe or the repository of the manager's ashes, but a woman of the group could offer to adopt the child and thereby save his life. *Sake* and *mate bangara*, regardless of the status of their "sponsor," were technically only secondary members. Sometimes, however, they were taken by a childless man specifically to continue his line of descent. When the adoptor was a manager his *sake* or *mate bangara* could in time succeed him and, by delegation, come to hold primary interests in a descent group. *Sake* and *mate bangara* and their descendants were some of the persons who might lose all knowledge of the descent groups in which they had agnatic status.

So much for secondary members. Everyone else resident with a descent group is ascribed a similar role in its affairs, but those persons described above as secondary members are part of the descent group "core" by cognatic descent or a fiction thereof and are thereby accorded somewhat higher status and are somewhat more privileged that those who are not part of the "core." Those who are neither primary nor secondary members may, therefore, be described as a residual class, and I refer to their rights and interests as "contingent." They are contingent for many reasons but primarily because they are usually solely dependent upon close kinship or personal relationships with primary or secondary members, and if those connections cease to exist so do rights and interests based upon them. Those with contingent rights include, for instance, persons who have become associated with the group by marrying one of its primary or secondary members. They are referred to by group members and by outsiders as members of the descent group, for they are members of it at least as a local group and an active collectivity and do take part in its activities; their very presence in the local group implicates them in descent-group affairs. They acquire in their spouses' groups limited interests which are contingent on the affinal bond, and in time they become interested in the affairs of those groups as parents of primary or secondary members; but such interests, though they may be admitted to exist, are *de facto* and not *de jure*. In-marrying spouses retain fully their interests in their groups of premarital origin, or so it is said. A woman, for instance, has the right to garden upon the land of her group of origin, and she, like her children, is always welcome to "return." Similarly, men may claim the right to garden or plant trees on the land of their wives' descent groups, even if they are not resident with them, and they do so as the *tamazira* (here, "affinal kin") of those groups.

A man who has married *tamazira* (without payment of the brideprice and then taken up residence with his wife's group of premartial origin) is in a better position to avail himself of such rights. The rights that such men acquire vary considerably, and it is the promise of the acquisition of important rights and interests that may encourage a man to marry in this fashion; for *tamazira* marriages are often regarded as something to be avoided, contracted only by those too poor to pay a brideprice (before some of the missions forbade brideprice transactions)! The extent of the rights of a *tamazira* depends largely upon the status of the man in his wife's descent group with whom he is most closely associated by his marriage to her. Until recent years managers most commonly acquired men who were dependent upon them as *tamazira*, for managers were the ones who had the most to offer. They often married their "sisters" or favorite "daughters" to men who promised to reside with them, and they had to forego the acquisition of *kesa* through the brideprice in the expectation that an additional "hand" would help them to acquire even more *kesa* at a later date. It is sometimes said that a man will not take a proffered brideprice for his "daughter" or "sister," so great is his personal attachment to her, but the acquisition of a faithful ally is always at least a secondary consideration. It was with this expectation in mind that managers were careful to acquire only "good" men as their *tamazira*, men who were young, active, industrious, and perhaps ambitious too. A young man with promise, one who was "on the way up," might acquire *tamazira* too, but those already established had the most to offer such a potential ally.

A manager could establish a branch of his group through a man married to one of his "sisters" or "daughters" by setting aside one or more groves as the estate of that couple, and his *tamazira* became the custodian of those groves. He held them in trust for his children who, so long as he remained married to the "daughter" or "sister" of the manager, would have been secondary members of that group. His own cognatic kinsmen acquired no legitimate interests in that branch except that they might at times become his guests. The grove did not become, in any absolute sense, the property of a *tamazira* except, again, that he was its temporary custodian in the interests of his wife's children. Those children too are said merely "to eat" there, as their father and mother did. The groves and land around them are not theirs in any absolute sense. Nevertheless, branches so formed could become and remain discrete units for some time and, in the rare instance, even became independent descent groups. Groves once in the temporary stewardship of a *tamazira* and his wife are called "groves of women," but the usage rights of the couple were not confined solely to those groves. It is said, "in-marrying men look after everything in the *sinangge*," but all this means is that they may garden freely within the group estate and are not confined to any segment that might have been specifically set aside for them. A further implication is

that they are thoroughly involved in descent-group affairs; but
despite what he may become largely because of the status of his
sponsor, a *tamazira*'s rights and interests remain theoretically contingent.

Those who came seeking refuge (*bori*) received, together with
permission to reside, also the permission to use resources. In some
cases, especially if it appeared that the refugees were likely to remain for some time or if there were many of them, groves could
again be set aside for their use. If given permission they could
make improvements upon the land, such as planting trees, but the
land was, of course, never theirs to do with as they pleased. Refuge
was usually sought among kinsmen, but this was not always the
case, and in either event those seeking refuge had to present some
kesa to the manager whose protection they sought. In a sense,
then, they were "paying" for their protection, and certainly non-
kin would not have tolerated their presence and, therefore, some
possibility of an attack upon them all unless such a payment were
made. This payment, called *kapaka*, thus served as an indemnity
against loss of any lives by the "sheltering" group. Furthermore,
if anyone of the "sheltering" group died as a result of the refugees
presence, as through an attack by the enemies of the refugees, the
sheltering group could demand and receive further compensation.

Cognatic and affinal kinsmen of group members may also take
up residence with the group, either temporarily or permanently.
Those with rights over group property and personnel by virtue
of membership in its cognatic descent category (the *sasanggi*) are
said to be free to do this at any time. Most often, however, such
rights are exercised only temporarily and to a limited extent, and
no attempt is made to press them any further. "Visiting" is frequent, and men may go on extended visits to kinsmen some distance away. It is often said that someone has gone "to see" some
kinsman in another place and to "live with and support" him. In
the past during peaceful periods and at any time now, men and
their families may go on such trips and spend extended periods
with more or less close kinsmen of either party; young men with
few responsibilities often make such trips. Visiting may also take
place with kinsmen in descent groups where one is not a member
of the cognatic descent category associated with that group. For
instance, A may belong to cognatic descent categories I and II
and B to II and III, but if A is living with descent group I, B may

visit him there as his guest. B's privileges in descent group I are clearly contingent upon A's status there. A may, again, assign to B certain groves to use, if such are at A's disposal, and B may with permission make improvements upon the land, but when B or his descendants finally leave, as it is expected they will, any interests assigned to them revert fully to A and to descent group I.

The *de jure* rights of persons not resident with descent groups associated with cognatic descent categories in which they are recognized members vary considerably. Women and men who have just "married out" are said to lose none of the rights and interests they had before the marriage. Their children, it is also said, take over those rights and interests intact. Those who "remain behind" regard those who have just married out, and their children, as merely "being taken care of" by the descent group into which the latter have married. Indicative of the continuing recognition of such persons as members of the *sinangge* is the fact that compensation could be claimed for them and their children if such persons "died helping" another group. For a recently married woman for whom a brideprice had been paid, only a small compensation could be demanded (only one "piece" of *kesa*). Those who are away "visiting" for extended periods do not lose any rights and interests they may have in their descent groups of origin, and, again, a person adopted into a descent group after having already established membership in another, perhaps by filiation, does not lose his rights in the latter. His status remains what it was, and he is at least nominally welcome back at any time.

Divorced and widowed parties are said to be welcome back at any time too. To divorce a woman is simply "to return her to her own side," to return her whence she came. However, divorce is rare today, which may be in part due to the fact the protectorate government and the missions are strongly against it. Still, men who have married "by custom" can divorce their wives "by custom" too, but there are only rarely instances of this. I heard of fewer than a dozen cases from any time period during my entire stay on the island, and there are no more than four cases in census materials mentioning several hundred marriages in several decades.[8] Adultery and laziness are the major justifications for re-

[8] Further indication that marital alliances are stable, if not harmonious, and that the stability is not "artificially" induced by mission and governmental pressures, may be seen in the fact that on Simbo Island to the south, where

turning a woman. Theoretically, if a brideprice has been paid and if as yet no children are to be considered, divorce is a relatively easy matter. The husband simply "returns" the wife, and her kin then return the *kesa* they took for her. Difficulties may arise, however, if the wife's group of origin regards the divorce as without foundation. If the couple has children, they should remain with their father's group, but sometimes they do not, and in this instance the brideprice should be returned. If only some children remain with the father's group, this may be sufficient to prevent demands for return of the brideprice.

Again theoretically, a widow is obliged to remain with the descent group of her deceased husband which may arrange for her remarriage and claim a brideprice for her, though it will be a small one since her reproductive capacities may be limited. A widow may on occasion return to her group of premarital origin, but it is not considered proper. If she does, her group must pay the deceased husband's group what the latter would have demanded as her brideprice, or so it is said.

Finally, there must be considered those persons who belong to the cognatic descent category associated with the descent group but are not residents of that group—not because they have recently married out but because their ancestors did so long ago, and they are thus remote *sasanggi* of that *sinangge*. Much has already been said about the status of the children of previously primary or secondary members. Nominally their rights are in no way diminished by nonresidence, but what of the rights of their children, and so on?

The ancestor who forms one's first connecting link with a *sinangge*, whether or not one is domiciled with its descent group, is referred to as one's *nggavenggave nako* in that *sinangge*. To ask someone, "Who is your connecting link with *sinangge* X?" is to ask, in effect, through whom one claims to have any rights in respect of that descent group or which of one's ancestors was last considered to be clearly established as a member of that *sinangge*'s descent group. To ask such a question of domiciled and resident members of a particular descent group may be relatively meaning-

mission and governmental pressures are presumably much the same, I heard of far more divorce cases in a few days' time. Simbo and Choiseul social structures are similar, but in some interesting ways quite dissimilar (see Scheffler 1962).

less, for example, of persons who are and whose ancestors have been domiciled and resident members of that descent group for as far back as anyone can remember. Their "linking ancestor" in that descent group is the founder himself, or if they are members of a branch *sinangge* the "linking ancestor" would be the founder of that branch who links them with the major *sinangge*. But it may be meaningful to ask it of others, such as those who have "returned" after an ancestor "went out" at one time.

For nonresidents their "linking ancestor" with a particular descent group is the *vavae za unu me*, the "grandfather" who originated in or came from that group (*nggonggoe* may be substituted for *vavae* if the linking ancestor was a female). Now, nominally, a person has some rights and interests in a descent group if he knows he has or is admitted to have had a "linking ancestor" within it. Some Choiseulese insist that these rights and interests, although usually only potential, are "just the same" as those they have in the descent group with which they are domiciled regardless of the genealogical distance separating them from the "linking ancestor." Others are not so dogmatic and argue that such rights vary considerably; even though one speaks of oneself as a member of those *sinangge*, it is "not the same" as when one speaks of one's own descent group or that of, say, one's mother. They do, however, argue that one should always be able to take up residence with those descent groups, certainly temporarily and perhaps even permanently, if one "maintains good relations" with them. Aid, hospitality, and, at least, refuge in time of need should always be available, and in groups with which one has "maintained good relations," it is said to be possible to "return" and claim membership permanently. To do so is to "return to the side of one's 'grandfather' or 'grandmother'," but, since the terms *vavae* and *nggonggoe* are indefinitely extendible to all ancestors in and beyond the second ascending generation, no line is thereby drawn beyond which such "returning" is no longer possible; no genealogical range is specified. No one argues, at least after a little thought, that he could resume membership in such a distantly related descent group on the same footing that he has in the descent group in which he is already established, unless of course his standing in the latter is exceptionally low. However, it is always argued that it is not necessary to ask permission before "returning." One need not "beg" (*pene*, to ask for some thing rather than some information); the parties concerned need only "hear one another" or "discuss" the movement before hand. It is clearly stated by everyone that "returning cannot be denied" because, "we are all one *sinangge*," but it is recognized that if the original cause of separation from a descent group was some "big trouble," such as adultery, then it may be difficult to "reënter the group." It is also possible that "many generations" will have "covered" the ancient trouble and that difficulty will be forgotten or glossed over.

The most common privilege exercised over a descent group in which one is not domiciled is that of land usage, mostly for gardening (and today for coconut-planting). This is almost always conceded for it brings only a temporary and fleeting imposition, and it is, of course, most commonly exercised over the land of groups whose estates are near one's own residence. Again, just as in the case of "those born of women" succeeding "those born of men" as primary interest holders in the descent group if all the latter die out, the estate of the group may pass into the hands of nonresidents if the descent group as a whole should die out. Then and only then are nonagnatic descendants of the apical ancestor who are also nonresidents of the descent group in a position to assume primary rights over its estate. Otherwise, their rights remain contingent, but it is denied that the contingency includes the possibility of denial of membership in the group unless, as noted above, some "big trouble" marked the original separation of one's ancestors from the group.

The discussion to this point has focused upon Choiseulese ideology about kin groups and the meaning of affiliation with them. It has been necessary to make some reference in passing to the fact that this "ideal" order—in the sense of being a structure of ideas—is not necessarily the form taken by the actions of persons and groups in the situations to which the ideology pertains. Indeed, it is one thesis of the next and following chapters that the ideal order, certainly at its most dogmatic, could not be put into practice.

Chapter 3

*Some Aspects
of Descent-Group Structure
and Operation*

The discussion so far has concentrated upon what might be called the "norms" of Choiseulese society, but only upon some of those "norms" concerning the constitution and operation of kin groups and categories; and I have instead preferred to speak of dogmas or ideologies, those publicly espoused criteria which many people believe, or at least assert, to lie behind the conduct of themselves and others. My reasons for not discussing these matters in terms of "norms" are implied throughout this chapter; they are taken up again, explicitly, in the final chapter. However, it is important to note here how the Choiseulese themselves talk about those dogmas, what I translate when I say that people assert these criteria "to lie behind their own conduct and that of others."

These criteria are described by the Choiseulese as their "way" or "fashion" (*vatovato*), and, like our own meanings when we speak of custom or tradition, their meanings are ambiguous too; the reference may be to normative or normal conduct, to the "proper" or to the "average." The normative is, however, distinguishable as the "straight" (*totolongo*), or proper, way. Thus, the "straight way" of affiliation is for children to be born into and reared as members of their fathers' descent groups, for daughters to marry out while sons remain in their proper places. We are misled, however, if we assume that the Choiseulese feel any compulsion from "internal" sources in regard to these matters; there seem to be no strong feelings that the "straight way" is the way things "should" be done. *Mara* is the only word I could discover that conveys compulsion: It is the "third person, progressive" form of the verb "to be," and it is often used in the sense of "must" or "necessary." However, I cannot recall it ever being used spontaneously in reference to what some anthropologists like to call "rules," and on occasion when I brought up the issue of its relevance, I was told that these are "just our ways" or "customs"—a term taken from Pidgin. Nevertheless, on some occasions of debate about particular problems some parties would argue strongly that these are the "straight" and "proper ways" as opposed to someone's conduct which was thought to be not in keeping with them. But, as I try to show in the remaining chapters, such argument is an aspect of politics, in a broad sense, and not of personal conscience.

Expectations about one's conduct and that of others take into account the fact that dogma and practice may differ. There are, for instance, "good" and "bad" kinsmen, those who can be relied upon for support and those who cannot. It is understood that the enjoiner to support kinsmen is applicable to and expectable of only "good" kin, but no one admits to being a "bad" kinsman, except when it may be politic, and so the sentiment is qualified not in word but in deed. This does not imply a division between "ideal" and "actual" behavior, that the Choiseulese "say one thing and do another," but it does indicate that a social system consists in the transactions which give meaning to ideals and expectations. Dogma and fact, theory and practice, are not isolable one from the other, for they are part and parcel of the social system; the espousal of the dogma is a form of social action only to be understood within a transactional context.

The Choiseulese, like any other comparable group of human beings, are not motivated solely by current dogmas and expectations held by themselves and others. There are at least two prominent themes in Choiseulese life, and they seemingly contradict one another. One is "public" and the other "private." The former is that kinsmen must support one another; the latter is the sometimes verbalized understanding, and the actions based upon it, that to help others is to "down" oneself. One gets ahead in the world only at the expense of others, and others get ahead only at one's own expense. Since kinsmen share similar interests in property, and thereby the means to wealth and prestige, it is not surprising that kinship and affinity oppose as often as they ally. In the past these two themes received some resolution in the fact that one could meet one's ends only through other men who were, most often, one's kinsmen. Kinsmen rarely share "common" interests, but they do often share "similar" interests. Thus they can coöperate, and it is important to insure the support of others by assuring them of one's own support; everyone participates in and maintains the fiction, and certainly sometimes the "fact," that as kinsmen the dogma has their allegiance.

When the "straight way" and actual arrangements did not agree and when the instances were more or less modern, usually I was told that such was not the way in the past; people no longer follow "custom" as they should. But as I found more knowledgeable informants and examined similar instances from what was clearly the ethnographic "past," I found that "exceptions" were a part of the past too. I noted my confusion and misgivings to a particularly intelligent and perceptive, if somewhat cynical, informant who had long ago made an appraisal of his fellow islanders and knew what to expect of them. I was told:

> The mouths of men lie. It [the dogma] is only talk, but it comes to us from the past, and the lies come to us from the past too. It is said that men did not leave their groups in the past but that women usually did, but this is only talk, for men as well as women often left their groups. People say "I am this *sinangge*, and this *sinangge* and this *sinangge* too", but this is all rubbish. They are kin, that is all, and meaningless kin at that. The same is true about brideprice marriages. The customs are not firm, for it is in fact the offspring themselves who choose what will be done. They look out only for themselves, and they look for that which will help them to live well. This was just as true in the past as it is today. Our customs have never been firm. We do not follow one side.

Other informants too sometimes remarked: "Our customs are not firm. We look only for that which will help us to live well, and the rest is just talk." Nevertheless, this is not a general public sentiment, and to call it "just talk" is not, however, to demean the significance of the dogma: it is rather to say that, to paraphrase Stanner (1959: 215), people must sometimes choose between opposed goods and "situationally incompatible rules of custom," and often it is the "rule of custom" which is accommodated to the situation rather than vice versa. Nor is this to repudiate the value of the "rule," but it is to indicate that, to paraphrase Stanner once more, if the Choiseulese are governed by anything, then it is by their interests—"living well," wealth, and prestige—rather than by their principles or dogmas.

My thesis here can be no better stated than it was in Stanner's (1959: 216) critique of Turner's (1956) study of the Ndembu:

> It can be argued sensibly that it is precisely . . . the manipulative, bargaining, transactional approach to life, which *is* the system of their life. In other words . . . "endemic conflict" [including "exceptions" to the "rules"] is not an upset or defect or an aberration or a friction of some idealized or perfect system, but is *itself* the system, together with the accompaniments and consequences which, logically, follow when most interests can be attained only through other people, i.e. on terms either of agreement or of force. The generic model is universally recognizable: it is that of any society in which principle and circumstances are at odds, worldly interests attract and vitality remains. It seems to me as much the model of the Australian aborigines in association with Europeans as of American political democracy with its "rule of concurrent majority based on interests rather than on principles."

The *de facto* distribution of interests and rights in groups can be understood not as a simple function of the dogmas espoused about them but must be understood as only the relatively stable resultant of situationally conditioned interpersonal and intergroup relations or, perhaps to overstate the point, as facts of politics and property (cf. Leach 1961b).

Since rights over property constitute a large part of the meaning of descent-group affiliation and also played such an important part in the acquisition of prestige, it is only to be expected that people will be jealous of property and that disputes will arise over it. This is especially true since the avowed kinship idioms confer upon so many persons at least nominal interests in the same property; but because there were no formal juridical institutions wrongs, real or imagined, could be redressed only by self-help, and rights, operative or potential, could be maintained or activated only "on terms either of agreement or force." But, again, much of the power of self-help derived from property, for only the possession of it and the ability to distribute it and acquire more in its stead could make self-help effective. In this society of self-seekers, only control over property or the friendship of those who did control property brought security, and not so much from want as from the depredations of one's fellow man, with whom one was in competition for the valued goods of life, perhaps most importantly the esteem of other men.

All of this made the securing of descent-group membership a matter of prime importance, for the major properties are at least nominally descent-group properties. Property interests are consolidated by securing and maintaining descent-group membership, but since the activities implied by group membership may be practiced in relation to more than one group, it is possible, under some circumstances, to speak of a person as a member of more than one group, just as one can speak of a person as a member of more than one cognatic descent category.

BECOMING A DESCENT-GROUP MEMBER

It is perhaps not wholly accurate to speak of a person as becoming a member of a descent group, initially at least, simply through filiation, for it is residence through childhood and into adult life with a particular descent group that tends to establish one's firmest membership for oneself and for those to whom one is related. Again, it is not just the fact of residence itself but what residence implies. Through the activities in which group members engage in coöperation with one another—whether as "private citizens," as in gardening for themselves, or as descent-group members in the past, as in gardening for the manager or participating in vengeance, and so on—there is a tendency for each one to establish intimate and binding relationships with others of the group. Furthermore, as he develops strong vested interests in the property of a descent group through interpersonal relationships, through mutual obligations imposed between him and other members as coöperating "close" kin, and perhaps through the assignment of some group property to his relatively exclusive use, each person increasingly comes to regard that group as his own and proper group, regardless of his formal genealogical status within it.

Identification with a particular group and its affairs is further reinforced by the fact that continued association with that group necessarily alters one's relationships with all other groups, even though it may do so in varying degrees. Residence and extensive coöperation with one group must imply some lack of residence and coöperation with all other groups and, therefore, some degree of loss of interests in them regardless of one's formal rights. While one is consolidating one set of rights, other persons are doing exactly the same thing elsewhere and in relation to groups in which one also has some interests. But a person's consolidation of rights in one sphere means that his rights elsewhere will have to be neglected and left to others to consolidate for themselves. Thus the latter interests are held in relation to property and persons which have already become the vested interests of other parties. All of this follows simply from the nature of the descent groups: They are corporate groups, and rights in such groups are rights against others (cf. Radcliffe-Brown 1950: 12–13), the others being, in the instance of a nonresident, those who have consolidated their rights by converting them to vested interests, which, because of the jealousy with which property is generally viewed and because of its scarcity, the others are not likely to view as readily divisible. Few people forget these facts, and they in large measure, prevent a change of descent-group affiliation.

Some activities implied by residence are divisible; hence, by cooperating with members of several groups one may manage to establish vested interests in all of them, though to varying degrees. This is, of course, most easily possible when one can establish and have recognized a "close" genealogical tie with groups within one's own region. It may be that one of those groups is, or several are, situated close enough that one can effectively maintain the binding quality of the tie by contributing to the interests of members of that group. Thereby defined as a "good kinsman" one is likely to find that group membership is in fact open. If the descent groups of one's father and mother have adjacent estates, which frequently happens, and one's parent has a particular but limited interest in a segment of that estate, one may maintain effective membership in two descent groups by establishing a domicile with one while using the resources of both, particularly those resources, such as a grove, over which one's parent has or had a specific allotted interest. In this event, it is meaningful to speak of someone as a member of more than one descent group. (This from the analyst's view: The idiom of cognatic descent already covers such situations from the Choiseulese point of view.) Managers often occupied special positions, and it was true in this context too, for they were able to contribute more easily than other persons to the welfare of a group with which they were not resident. Again, because of their *de facto* power and potential for good or evil they were less likely to find themselves defined as "distant" kinsmen. On the other hand, managers were the ones with the greatest investment in a particular descent group, and, as I will show later, those least likely to want to or to have to repudiate those interests by changing descent-group affiliation.

This discussion of how one's identity as a descent-group member is and was acquired leads naturally to two further points. The first concerns the distribution of rights and interests within a descent group, that is, among those who are already domiciled with it. The second concerns the recruitment of persons to the group through what I term a *coöptative process*. The second necessarily involves facts relevant to the first, so I will now discuss how rights and interests are distributed among persons domiciled with a descent group.

ORGANIZATION AND DISTRIBUTION OF RIGHTS AND INTERESTS WITHIN THE DESCENT GROUP

The next chapter is concerned partly with the recruitment of managers and their activities. However, it should be noted here that there was more than one kind of manager, and *batu* had more than one type of empirical referent. There were the managers of descent groups or, at least, their estates; these were "managers of the land," also more generally referred to as *batu sinangge*. Most of them managed more than just land; they managed the whole descent group, its personnel, and its affairs. This required considerable talent and ambition, and, as is to be expected, not all men who qualified as managers by the genealogical criterion had those characteristics. But many men aspired to managerial status, and it was obtainable for some able men even though they did not meet the genealogical qualification. These are known as *batu sokele* (see chap. 4). Theoretically, the sons of those men who had only *achieved* managerial status did not succeed their fathers since they too were without the formal qualification. More of this later; the important point here is that effective control of a group was, and to a lesser degree still is, a matter of achievement, and although this achievement could be validated even further by formal criteria it was the ability to organize men and to gather and distribute *kesa* that was primary, and any ascribed qualities were secondary in determining whether a man was a manager in the fullest sense of the term.

The process of becoming identified for oneself and for others as a member of a group and establishing vested interest in it, applies to everyone regardless of his descent status in the group. The fact that one's parent may have done so before is sometimes relevant, but the process is necessarily repeated with each generation, with new personnel who must work out their own mutual obligations, trusts, and binding relationships. Agnatic status does not allow one to escape this process, and a person of agnatic status who is nonresident is just as subject to the loss of his rights and interests as is anyone else. It is true that he has some advantage over others since his status is an arguing point in his favor, but it is for others —those who have already consolidated their rights—to accept or reject his argument.

Outsiders were not obliged to distinguish between primary and secondary members of a descent group; they were "all the same" and to the same extent culpable for any offense attributable to that group or any of its members. This forced on each group the realization that in a real sense each member had an equal stake, in some sense "strong," in its affairs. The operation of the group in daily affairs as well forced this realization, for in every-day affairs agnatic affiliants are not distinguished from other kinsmen as a class, and the mutual obligations of kinship are just as strong regardless of its genealogical basis. Thus for any particular individual the basic fact is, from his point of view and to the extent to which this point of view was forced upon his group mates by the situation itself, that he is "strong" on the "side" with which he is most intimately associated.

It is conceded that secondary members (by genealogical criteria) may by some actions entitle themselves to a "strong voice in group affairs." However, it does require some notable service to the group before effective primary status may be attributed to or claimed by presumed secondary members. The most notable services were assistance in time of warfare, or securing vengeance, or promoting the success of a gift exchange. The contribution could be made in many ways, such as by lending one's physical presence and labor on numerous occasions, and, particularly, offering *kesa*. I have already said that *kesa* was descent-group property, but payments of *kesa* could be made to individuals as well as groups; and there were a number of ways of securing *kesa* as an individual who was not necessarily a descent-group representative (see chap. 4). Much *kesa* was in the hands of "private" individuals who used it to consolidate their own positions within a group. (Whether they did this intentionally is beside the point here, for the effect was the same.) Simply residing with the group for an extended period is not sufficient in itself, nor if one's parents and grandparents did so is that sufficient in itself, to convert secondary into primary rights, at least so recognized by others. Nonetheless, for any particular individual such interests are *his* primary interests whether others consider him entitled to a "strong voice," or not.

By filiation and subsequent domicile with a particular group and all that is thereby entailed, anybody may find himself affiliated with his father's descent group, and perhaps agnatically. His rights and interests in respect of that group—its property, personnel, and affairs—will be in fact "strong." On the other hand, when the same process has conferred affiliation with one's mother's descent group of origin he may find that, in apparent contradiction to the dogmas, his interests and *de facto* rights are "strong" and not "weak." They are strong because others are willing to recognize them as such.

Successive matrifiliations for several generations are rare indeed, and, of course, it seems hardly possible to have a series of matrifiliations, each building upon the gains made in previous generations, so that eventually one might find some persons tracing connection to the apical ancestor solely through females. This might happen if the process of descent-group affiliation were completely random; however, the whole system is (or was, at least in the days when descent-group affiliation was highly significant) biased in favor of patrifiliation if for no other reason than the presence of the dogma itself and because of the weight given to it as a sanction. There are other reasons: the establishment of a series of matrifiliations would require a quite improbable series of events, for instance, a series of *tamazira* marriages by the daughters of women who had themselves brought a husband into the group. This is unlikely because it would require an unusual succession of managers to arrange it and men to marry into it. The latter is least likely since everyone would know the political disadvantages. Some other combination of "returns" to "mother's side" and *tamazira* marriages could result in the same situation, but the disadvantages would remain the same. I found no instances of descent-group members tracing their connection with the apical ancestor or the remote sibling-set solely through women.

There are some instances in which two or three successive affiliations with "mother's side" have taken place, but in several of
those the men at the present time are having difficulty consolidating their positions. The difficulty arises precisely because
these men realize their situation and, becoming anxious about it,
have tended to overstate, to the annoyance of everyone concerned,
whatever case they may have for a "strong voice" in group affairs.

This raises once again the issue of how a matrifiliant, or anyone
without agnatic status, goes about establishing a strong position
in a group. For the unambitious there is no problem, for they do
not require a strong voice and are, in any event, largely unobtru-
sive. For the ambitious, however, it poses a double problem and
places them in a difficult situation. They must consolidate any
rights they may have and turn them into primary rights which
they may freely use, all of which requires some obtrusion into
descent-group affairs, but they must also develop their positions
carefully so as not to offend others who do already exercise a
strong voice. They are required to "keep their peace" when it is to
their disadvantage. Obviously, those in the best position to do
this are secondary members (presumed) whose rights are secondary only within the larger politically independent entity but who
have a segment of its estate set aside for their more particular use.

As noted in Chapter 2, while branches exercise in theory only
limited and relatively exclusive rights over their property, the
actual position occupied by a branch depended largely upon the
status of its manager. It was possible for someone who was only a
secondary member of a group to achieve the status of manager in
a wider sense than merely manager of a limited set of rights over
the estate of a branch and to convert that branch into an autonomous descent group. This was, of course, one way in which new
descent groups could arise. Although it was not possible for every
man so situated to carry the process of developing his status quite
so far, each one did have effective control over the limited and
relatively exclusive rights associated with a descent-group segment; this in turn gave him some power within the larger group,
for the limited uses to which he could put his property were often
sufficient to help him to acquire *kesa* and then render services to
the larger unit. Having done this much, or perhaps less, for, after
all, his interests were affected by the decisions the descent group

might reach, and especially those involving his property and life, he could assume and have recognized by others at least as much voice in group affairs as most others had.

Actually, the assumption of an active voice in descent-group affairs by long-time secondary members is no problem. They are generally accorded that much simply as members. The dogma that they must "keep their peace" is in fact applicable largely to those in the process of establishing themselves as group members or attempting to extend limited interests at the expense of others or, again, to some trouble maker whose secondary status may be held against him as a further stigma. One man expressed this point well when he noted, in effect, that so long as people "maintain good relations" with one another, dogmas mean little, but when the actions of a purported secondary member precipitate a dispute the dogmas are dragged out and deemed binding in their own right. The dogmas are then a "grammar of motives" utilizable as sanctions in a "rhetoric of motives" (see Burke 1955a; 1955b), but they were binding only when the protesting primary member had the means to back up his position with self-help (or, now, the courts).

The vocabularies of the Choiseulese languages are not deficient in words for trickery, deception, selfishness, and acquisitiveness, and these are used most often in discussions of property. It is commonly said, "everyone wants to be a manager," and there is enough truth in the statement to make it meaningful. It is certainly considered that all men should behave in ways appropriate to a man who is ambitious; they should not assume managerial airs—that would be looking for trouble—but they should at least be industrious, jealous of their property, and always ready to acquire more. It is expected of everyone other than a completely "lazy man," or "rubbish man" that this is just what every man is doing. One is, then, nearly always suspicious of the actions of others in relation to property. Any lapse in propriety concerning it is interpreted as a form of aggression, and it may well be. Kinsmen, of course, should always trust one another, but it is precisely kinsmen of whom one must be most cautious since they already share one's property interests and may be attempting to consolidate or expand their share at one's expense.

Several common varieties of "deception" are these: All managers of land, regardless of whatever else they were, were entitled to first-fruits from gardens on the land around their groves. These were important, not for their economic value or, we know, for their presumed "religious value" (making the crops grow well), but because they were indicative of the giver's recognition of the manager's custodial rights. (Today, knowledge of who took first-fruits for the use of certain lands is often important evidence in land-tenure disputes.) These prestations were thus jealously regarded, and the manager who did not receive them took the lapse as an affront to his own prestige, a contemptuous attempt to repudiate his rights. Not to present first-fruits was tantamount to saying that one had primary rights over the land in question. The offender "downed" the manager and at the same time elevated himself. One sanction against nonpresentation was that already alluded to: It was believed that unless they were presented the gardens would not flourish because of the anger of the ancestors. This, one supposes, would encourage gardeners, anxious for the success of their efforts, to make the presentations. I also heard it said that if first-fruits were not presented, and no complaint was made, then one could "keep" the land, but there were also vehement denials of this presumed right in particular cases when claims were made on the basis of it. That such claims were sometimes made, perhaps acted as a stimulus to managers to demand first-fruits, and they certainly support the contention that nonpresentation was equivalent to land-grabbing.

Another source of strife was the ability of managers to delegate or allot interests in land or groves in perpetuity. The allotments sometimes fell into disuse, and at a much later date someone would try to reactivate claims to them. This could be done, but a dispute might arise as to whether a particular person had the right in a specific instance. Someone else could argue that the claimant was attempting to take over interests that he or his ancestors let fall into abeyance too long. The situation worked both ways; false claims were made and so were false counter claims, and, of course, there was no court to determine "truth" or "falseness" of facts or even to test the "true" meaning of any dogmas or "rules." It was and still is common practice to wait until everyone with any first-hand knowledge of the original allotment or other transaction is deceased, so that there is no one who can speak with authority about it. Everyone concerned has only hearsay knowledge, and the situation can become thoroughly confused with lie and counterlie, or truth and countertruth if one wishes a more charitable interpretation. In the end, some agreement may be reached, and the intercession of a manager (see chap. 6) may play an important role in it. In the past, the winner was he who was able most effectively to mobilize self-help or present an effective threat of it. Those who make false claims upon the property of others are said to *ririki*, to claim what they know is not theirs to claim. The adjectival form is *rikiriki poreke*, the allusion being to the crocodile (*poreke*) who snaps and grabs at everything in his path.

Managers who were closely related, say, as members of the same major *sinangge* or of descent groups of one region, were supposed to trust one another, but if they shared interests in *kesa* they might have had good reason not to. *Kesa* was always hidden, usually in some special place deep in the jungle, buried and marked in some way so as not to be lost. The hiding place was shown to sons and especially trusted members of the descent group so if the manager died suddenly it could be recovered and, perhaps, used to avenge his death. It was sometimes shown to trusted managers from neighboring groups in one's own region for similar reasons, and it was deemed an honor to be shown the *kesa* of another man (or group). Not to show one's *kesa* to someone who considered himself to have a strong interest in it was to indicate distrust, and this was, of course, an offense upon which the offended party might act (see chap. 6). It was more common, however, to have trouble as a result of misplaced trust, for a confidant sometimes took it upon himself to misappropriate the *kesa*, removing it from the original hiding place to another known only to himself. This was done either by fellow members of one's descent group or by members of related or associated groups, and it was sometimes the cause of violent and protracted conflicts within and between descent groups. To steal *kesa* successfully was among the most clever of deceptions, highly despised publicly and not begrudgingly admired privately. It could occasionally be done with impunity, for fear of the sanctions took consideration of the likelihood of the offended party's ability to retaliate. If one had stolen all his *kesa*, and he had few "friends," it would have been difficult indeed for him to retalitate. For these reasons most managers, at least shrewd ones—and most of them were shrewd or they would not have been managers—attempted to keep the extent of their *kesa* holdings a secret, and hid it not in a single place. Fearing trouble, they also moved it from place to place, but fear of losing it either to themselves or their descendants encouraged them to trust in some persons, and unfortunately perhaps the wrong ones.

Most acts described required some temerity, and while avarice sometimes led to recklessness, it more usually took a cautious form—cautious in that it was less obtrusive and there was perhaps less chance of being recognized as grasping at the property of others. But the consequences could be equally deadly. I refer here to the practice of sorcery (*sukita*). Sorcery is regarded as most heinous, practiced only by those who are thoroughly evil. Sorcery accusations were, however, quite often only pretexts, rationalizations for the implementation of self-help when the true cause of anger was an offense not publicly deemed sufficient to warrant the death of the offender. There is probably much less sorcery practiced than there are accusations made, and today open accusations are rare too (see chap. 4).

Sorcery is commonly reputed to be a "woman's doing," but it is recognized that men practice it too. Whoever does it, it is thought to be most commonly prompted by disputes or jealousy over property, though certainly any grudge may suffice. In any event, sorcery is used to dispose of an irritating party by removing him or her from the world of the living. Interesting as they may be, the details of the practice are irrelevant here. The practice itself may be described as "sympathetic magic," but we are here concerned with the patterns of expectation and accusation. It is commonly expected that women of the same descent group will practice sorcery in the interests of their offspring, eliminating potential rival claimants to property. Thus if two women, A and B, belong to the same descent group, A may be suspect of practicing sorcery against the children of B to eliminate them as rival claimants to the property of the group. Informants often gave illustrations, not actual cases, although I do know of one in recent times, in which the accused party was a woman who had married into the descent group, but there was otherwise no indication, and certainly not stated as such, that in-marrying women are especially suspect. On the other hand, I recorded a case in which a man was actually caught (probably in the 1930's) in a sorcerous act against a fellow descent-group member, and many men are suspect of similar acts.

To return to a point made above: The Choiseulese are well aware that sometimes the accused was innocent, but the death of a relative was taken as a pretext to make a sorcery accusation against him so that the accuser could expand his own interests. Thus the accusation of sorcery as well as sorcery itself was an agency for the aggressive. It is sometimes argued that one need fear sorcery only from those with whom one shares property interests, but even so it is more widely feared.

Since sorcery is so nefarious, managers did not use it regularly as a form of sanction. In fact, managers were supposed to have only the welfare of their groups at heart, and so sorcery was completely outside their sphere—or so it should have been. Yet some people suspect managers of having practiced sorcery to eliminate rivals or potential rivals even within their own descent groups. Managers, with their *kesa*, had other means, also despicable to their followers, to assure conformity to their wishes (see chap. 4), and did not have to stoop to sorcery. Even if they were suspect, few people would have been foolish enough to tempt fate—an almost certain fate—by earning their ire through an accusation.

One could go on detailing situations of conflict arising from property interests, but I refrain at this point and take up the issue again later in relation to some particular cases.

The described examples are some of the situations that prompted the application of the dogma that secondary members must "keep their peace," and these examples are sufficient to indicate that the dogma in itself is hardly effective either as a preventative or a remedy. It plays a role as a sanction, not only against secondary members, to further legitimate actions taken by those who feel their vested interests are threatened. Of course, it may be that the interests of secondary members as well as those of primary members are threatened, and it may be primary members too who offer the threat. Where primary members are in conflict the appeal is not to relative rights but rather to group solidarity, to the idea that "we are one *sinangge*, and it is not good to fight," an idea that had a solid basis since those who were disunited internally were easy prey to those on the "outside." There was nothing mystical about this, for the appeal had force only when and only so long as there was a real threat from the "outside." There are few such threats today, and descent groups have little solidarity.

Although the Choiseulese are reluctant to admit it, intragroup quarrels were often the cause of residential separation and a subsequent tendency for increased coöperation with "outsiders" within the same region. People generally preferred to live dispersed upon their own limited holdings, so long as peaceful conditions permitted, because life in compact villages bred quarrels and because residence on one's holding was the surest way to maintain a clear title to it. Disputes were important, too, in the rise of a new descent group which might assume a significance equal to the group from which it sprang. In an example given above (chap. 2), it was said that one of the managers of a descent group divided its estate among his sons specifically to prevent them from fighting with one another, thereby assuring *sinangge* solidarity. Most of the divisions in time became independent descent groups, or so it is said. It may be that the whole story is a myth, and the major genealogy of Kesi may have developed as a fusion of many smaller genealogies composed as a charter for the relationships that grew up between previously wholly independent descent groups. The Choiseulese, I am sure, would argue that this speculation is nonsensical, and I cannot refute them. Indeed, my evidence regarding intergroup relations would indicate that amalgamation on such a scale was unlikely (see chap. 4). But myth or otherwise, Kesi was famed for its internal peace, and some informants attributed this to the clear-cut divisions of interest within it.

My earlier remarks about consolidating one's position apply equally to all secondary members, regardless of how they became such, as matrifiliants, adoptees, captives, "returning" parties, or even as patrifiliants with a female link somewhere in their ancestry. "Matrifiliant" implies that filiation has taken place through one's mother, so it cannot be taken as a translation of *popodo nggole* ("born of women"). The latter includes not only those whose mothers form their female ties to the descent group but also those whose grandmothers or great-grandmothers form those ties. Those "born of women" constitute a mixed category, not in terms of what the dogma says, for they are all simply secondary members, but *de facto*. Those whose grandmothers form their female link may be patrifiliants, that is, their fathers may have been descent-group members and they themselves have become such partly as a result of their fathers' affiliations. A man who is a patrifiliant but not of agnatic status still refers to his descent group as his "father's side," ignoring the non-agnatic nature of his status. Indeed, it *is* his "father's side," and this may be given some consideration by others despite the lack of continuous paternal filial bonds with the group. Thus patrifiliation may be of some importance, but this is not necessarily true. Opinions vary; those who are merely patrifiliants are likely to regard one patrifiliation as just as valid as a whole series, which is after all how agnatic status is usually acquired, by "cumulative patrifiliation" (cf. Barnes 1962: 6). But persons of agnatic status, on the other hand, see some inherent virtue in the series of successive patrifiliations.

There are still other patrifiliants with female links some three to four generations from the present, but they are few. In principle, their rights and those of men whose female links are even further removed are no different from those of matrifiliants, but in fact they do have some advantages over recent matrifiliants. Their ancestors may have performed notable services for the descent group, and this they may be able to use to their credit. On the other hand, one of their ancestors may have been troublesome, and this may be revived to their disadvantage. More often, however, when requesting the support of the group (for instance, in brideprice and rights of land usage) or countering denial of support, a nonagnatic descent-group member can point to perhaps several generations of continuous affiliation and allegiance by his ancestors, and he can usually cite significant activities on their part in support of the group. These are points in his favor, and it is said that such considerations may "kill" the "rule" which could be construed in his disfavor.

Ideally, support cannot be denied to descent-group members regardless of their status, but if a man is a trouble maker his nonagnatic status, regardless of its basis, may be stressed; and what he takes to be his rights may be denied on that basis. Property rights and strife over them are not the only basis for disputes within descent groups. Adultery, family squabbles, disputes over children and their petty troubles, may all contribute to one's reputation as a trouble maker, and if the grudge against a person of nonagnatic status is of sufficient strength and generality it is unlikely that appeals to extenuating circumstances will be allowed to "kill" the dogmas that may be unfavorable to him. The dogma is then taken as sufficient reason to deny support.

There is no reason why each descent group should present a united front on all issues, and there is much evidence that it does not. There may be those who support the claims of nonagnatic affiliants against those who would deny them. They may have their own personal reasons for so doing, and some of those reasons may be honorable. The self-interest model that I have chosen to help elucidate the organization of Choiseulese society does not preclude consideration of nobler motives (nobler from the Choiseulese point of view), and people are not unappreciative of favors done them. Thus if a person of nonagnatic status is hard-working, helpful to his kinsmen, and does not alienate the bulk of the descent group through lack of coöperation or by attempting to extend his interests in its estate at the expense of others, the fact that he is a secondary member would not, in the first place, be likely to arise, and if it did he would probably find supporters who would minimize it by helping him find mitigating circumstances.

Besides, even presumed secondary members have their own sanctions with which to assure support. Since most disputes of the sort envisioned here (those in which the dogma of secondary membership could be applied) do not concern questions of membership but only the relative privileges and advantages of it, the parties remain interdependent long after the particular issue has been settled, or, more often, after settlement has been postponed. Thus a claimant may exercise subtle coercion not by threatening to withdraw his services, which some members of the group may desire more than others, but merely by indicating cautiously that this could be done. Furthermore, there were instances of spurned parties who took revenge by arranging attacks upon their own groups! (See chap. 4 for a similar case.)

Again, these latter remarks apply to persons of any membership status, primary and secondary, and of course they had greater force at the time when intergroup conflict was rife and kinsmen were more dependent upon one another than they are now. They followed from the nature of descent-group operations and intergroup relations and were, therefore, equally binding upon all group members. Since no formal juridical institutions existed to arbitrate claims and counterclaims, every man was in the same boat, and every man's rights and interests were contingent upon those of others and upon what he could coerce others to do for him or aggravate them, perhaps without much effort on his own part, to do against him. For descent-group operations to be effective some solidarity was necessary which depended upon the willingness of individual members to coöperate in the interests of the larger whole. The interests of presumed secondary members had to be given fairly equal recognition in fact; otherwise their depressed status would have led to a division of allegiances that would have been fatal for some group members or, at the very least, impaired the efficiency of group operations. Furthermore, if secondary membership did in fact confer an inferior position, who indeed would have put himself in such a position? (Cf. Fortes 1959: 211–212.) Persons did sometimes place themselves as secondary members, or even as contingent members, in groups where there was little hope of consolidating their positions, but they did this only for compelling personal reasons (for instance, to escape some dispute that might have resulted in death and would not be shortly resolved) or because there were situations in which it was better to be a secondary member of one descent group rather than a primary member of another. Those circumstances are better discussed in detail in the context of intergroup relations (chap. 4).

To summarize the situation of those who are presumed secondary members: There are no simple criteria to determine exactly and under what circumstances their interests and rights shift from secondary to *de facto* primary status, for indeed the change is assumed gradually and is never completely beyond debate. If a grudge against a purported secondary member is sufficiently strong and general in the group, appeals to extenuating circumstances are not likely to have much effect on opinions. But primary and secondary members alike consolidate their rights by establishing vested interests, and both are given more or less equal recognition in the ordinary course of events. Crises precipitate the application of the dogmas about secondary members. The exact rhetoric used varies with the type of secondary member and the circumstances, but the principle is always the same: secondary members have no rights or interests other than those recognized by primary members. However, the dogma does not take account of the extent to which such recognition may go. Similar crises arise between primary members, and then the appeal, which is only one sanction among many applicable to both primary and secondary members, is to another dogma. The dogma about the status of secondary members, indeed, even the conception of such a category, is conditional, but the conditions which result in variable interpretation and application are given by the relevant situations and not within the dogma itself. In most situations, and in intergroup relations, a descent-group member is simply a descent-group member; the appeal for his allegiance is upon that basis, not upon the basis of second-class citizenship, for, indeed, how could it be otherwise? Americans do not appeal to Negros *as Negros* to enlist in time of war.

Contingent members are in a somewhat more equivocal position, of course, because they have no descent-based claims. They have, in principle, only those rights delegated or allocated to them by specific persons, and their descendants do not inherit or succeed to them; some persons do assume some conditional rights or interests held by their parents, but only with the tacit understanding that the consent of the original allocating party still holds good. It is rare, but not unknown, for contingent members to remain with a descent group for several successive generations. To the later generations in such a series that group is "home," and they may know no other. What they exercise as privileges they come to regard as rights, the only ones they have, and there is some understandable reluctance to surrender them. But, dependent as they are upon the good will of only a segment of the descent group rather than the whole, they must tread carefully and keep their peace to an extent not wholly expected of secondary members.

Men who have come into a descent group through *tamazira* marriage are in the best position to escape the limitations imposed upon contingent members in general, largely because of the status of their sponsors, usually managers. Managers at one time acquired *tamazira* specifically for the assistance they might render and then delegated considerable powers to them for that purpose. *Tamazira* may hold segments of the group estate in trust for the children of their wives and they thereby acquire some power within the group. Managers also sometimes gave them *kesa* with which to get a start at acquiring more. Seldom, however, was this an outright gift. More often it was acquired by acting as the appointed representative of the manager at a gift exchange in which he was to be presented some *kesa* (see chap. 4). With the sanction of managerial authority such men spoke out in discussions, voicing an opinion as to the wisest course of action, but they avoided making it apparent that the opinion voiced gave undue consideration to their own interests.

The actual role played by a *tamazira* depended not only upon his sponsor but also himself. Again I refer to differences in ambition. Some men who were neither obnoxious nor ambitious preferred to or had to marry *tamazira* because, being unambitious, they had no *kesa* of their own, nor were they able to get it from others since there was little prospect of recouping the loss through the actions of the unambitious man. On the other hand, disinclination to industry made such a man undesirable as a *tamazira* too. (See pp. 171–172 for further discussion of the role of *tamazira* marriage today.)

As the parent of secondary members—and the children of a "daughter" or "sister" of a manager are no ordinary secondary members—an in-marrying male has a *de facto* interest in the group, which may be recognized by its members. He may speak or act in behalf of his children, but his actions, words, and the limited powers recognized are his. Thus a *tamazira* may suffer little from the stigma of contingent membership, but he can go too far. It was not unheard of for a *tamazira* to become the *de facto* manager of the group into which he had married. Some proved so markedly superior to primary and secondary members that they assumed managerial powers, but they could not assume them without the consent of the managed, for a man achieved managerial status only when others, recognizing his abilities and the potentiality of benefiting from them, began to address him as *batu* and to defer to him in a fitting manner. The point here is that some *tamazira* began to assume managerial airs before others were ready to recognize them. In that instance he was likely to be reminded of his contingent status, provided that the risk of standing up to him was not already too great.

Although in principle only the temporary manager of a segment of the descent group estate, a *tamazira* could establish himself a separate residence upon that estate and begin to attract kinsmen or affines who would be his allies in the acquisition of more *kesa* and prestige. Thus he could effectively found a descent group, and this did occur and is recognized in genealogies. However, he was always acting, at least nominally, in the interests of his children and perhaps the original descent group as a whole. So long as he maintained good relations with the larger unit there was no objection to this procedure, for he and his following were valuable allies, and the members of the original unit had no reason to feel a threat from him militarily or in loss of land. A *tamazira* may be "like a son" to the manager and is sometimes referred to as such. So long as it is not felt that he is alienating something from the group, he may do largely as he pleases if he has the open or tacit consent of his sponsor.

This process of segmentation or descent-group formation by a *tamazira*, or for that matter anyone who was not indisputably the true son of a manager, was frought with potential difficulty, especially for later generations. At a much later date, after all of those with first-hand knowledge are dead, certain persons purporting to trace cognatic connection with the *tamazira* may make claims upon property that once was "his." The claim need not be to exclusive interests, and its basis is therefore variable. For instance, it may be argued that the property was held not temporarily or contingently by a *tamazira* but rather by the same man construed as a primary or secondary member of the descent group of the claimants. Thus the claimants need not be his direct descendants and may claim interests as members of his descent group. This may happen between two adjacent descent groups, since it was common practice to take *tamazira* from adjacent groups and allot them groves that bordered upon the estates of their original descent groups. In this way a *tamazira* was able, if he wished to reside upon the land of his grove, conveniently to maintain relations with both groups. If his descendants were to "return" to his original descent group they could lose their interests in that grove, but they did not necessarily do so as long as they continued to use it and permitted others of the originating descent group to do the same. Thus the land of, say, descent group I could in effect fall into the hands of members of descent group II (see Fig. 9), but the Choiseulese deny that it happened by arguing that not the land was involved but rather only the groves or rights to use the land. It may be argued too that a branch of

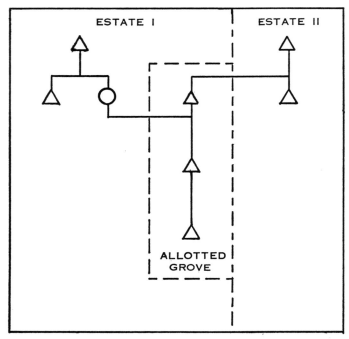

Fig. 9. The Allotment of Groves

descent group I was merely coresident with descent group II, which is one way of looking at it, but it requires one to ignore that the branch probably interacted more with descent group II and was therefore actually more a part of descent group II than it was of descent group I. This is an instance of variable definitions of situations, for those people residing with group II probably considered themselves to be members of it, and they probably considered the land to be that of group II.

Knowledge that such situations did occur may lead some persons in group II, through malice or otherwise, to claim at a later date that the grove in the estate of group I is their own, that of group II. The claim may be made that since some members of group II used that grove it must, therefore, be a grove of group II. If it is pointed out that they did so as the descendants of a *tamazira*, this may be countered with the claim that the rights of a *tamazira* and his descendants cease with nonresidence and the grove reverts again to the allotting group. Therefore, those who it is claimed used the land in the past must have used it as their own. Of course, this argument contradicts the dogma of descent-group openness and availability of resources to those who have "gone out" and their descendants. Such situations are not easily resolved, and in the past if the powers of the contending parties were fairly equal the disputed property would "go un-used," as it sometimes does today when court action proves ineffective. Obviously, there is no clear-cut rule, and the "rules," such as they are, could only be tested by the relative strengths of contending parties. Agreements are difficult to reach because neither party wishes to back down from its position and thereby be "downed," and neither do they want to lose the property. In the past, one party might have been able to institute self-help, or threaten to do so, and quite effectively squelch the other's claims. Since self-help settled the issue, there was no guarantee that the party with "truth" on its side, if indeed there was one, would win out.

Other contingent members delegated similar interests and rights may precipitate similar situations. Long-term guests were sometimes allotted groves, and their descendants could continue to use them so long as they were guests. Guests presented an indemnity for their presence, and they could, upon departure, present a small feast and some *kesa* to the manager of the host group as a token of appreciation. This marked the return of the grove to the host group. Any of these acts may serve as the basis of a dispute. For instance, it may be said that the token of appre-ciation was never presented and is still owed by the descendants of the guests who have "gone home," and this could be used as an excuse to refuse hospitality to them again. Descent-group segments could also arise, perhaps only temporarily, when guests resided separately in a discrete hamlet and began to take wives or husbands from the host group. If the segment persisted, some question about the extent of its estate or its rights to alienate the land might arise, but the issue could be resolved only by agree-ment or force, which prevailed depending again upon the ability of either party to mobilize self-help.

However, trouble was not often precipitated by the presence of guests for two reasons. First, guests usually went home, and the groves allotted to them reverted to the host group. People became guests principally to escape trouble at home and returned, only too happily, when they felt it was safe. People also took on guests, especially when they were numerous, largely for what was to be gained (*kesa*) and were often only too anxious to have them leave, a fact which—cautiously—was not allowed to escape the notice of the guests. The other reason is that they or their descendants did not long remain in the status of guests, for they began to marry members of the host group. Guests then became spouses, and their descendants became either primary or secondary members by filiation.

A pertinent question here, and one that is difficult to answer with certainty, is whether groups of guests or single guests were ever assimilated into the genealogy of the host group, thus becoming secondary or primary members. So far as the original guests themselves are concerned, this seems quite unlikely. The Choiseulese emphatically deny that such a thing could happen; to admit it, even were it true, would be an admission of damage to the dogma that guests must "keep their peace." It was the assumption of strong interests on the part of guests that one had to be on guard against. Furthermore, genealogies are taken as representing biological and only certain social facts, such as adoption; the Choiseulese would deny that a valid genealogy would treat a guest as a *sinangge* member. This is not to deny that anyone ever falsifies a genealogy; they sometimes do, but the falsification is branded as just that by those who feel they know better. However, there is some evidence that incorporation may have occurred.

There are, for instance, some major *sinangge* genealogies which are not unitary wholes, that is, in which there are several segments whose genealogies are said to be parts of the major *sinangge* but admittedly cannot be united except by vague imputation. The "origin" of such segments is "unknown." There are, I think, at least two possible interpretations of such situations. Informants were quick to attribute them to their own ignorance or to the presumed general loss of genealogical and other forms of "customary" knowledge in modern times, but this is now a convenient rationalization or excuse and does not necessarily preclude the existence of comparable situations in the past. It may be, then, that this genealogical condition represents not so much a loss of knowledge as a stage in the uniting of previously discrete genealogies. The evidence for the latter possibility, admittedly not particularly compelling, is this: Whether the segment presumed to be related to the larger genealogy is large or small, interested parties seemed to me at times to be experimenting with explanations which would satisfy others. They seized on little bits of isolated information and attempted to build a coherent picture from them. Some admitted they were guessing and others claimed they "knew." Someone would say, for instance, that he knew the earliest person in the presumably related segment called the then-manager *bubue* ("mother's brother"), or *kakae* ("older brother"), or whatever, but he would admit that he did not know that it was a "true" (that is, biological relationship. On the other hand, he would say that he cannot prove it was not, so "maybe yes and maybe no." It is common practice that when a person professes some knowledge that he is not certain others will be willing to accept, he tells it as hearsay, adding "maybe yes and maybe no." Usually this can be understood to mean that the speaker gives some credence to what he has said but is waiting for a response from others before he affirms it. This is so in public; but in private among trusted friends he may tell his tale as a truth that has been handed down through the generations. Men with dubious genealogical backgrounds (dubious to others, that is) teach their versions of those genealogies to their sons without dubiety. Their sons espouse them as the only truths they know. In time, and as interpersonal relations change and perhaps mellow, more and more people may come to accept as undeniable knowledge what were once hesitantly given assertions and mere "personal truths." I know of no single case which could illustrate this process *in toto*, but many cases illustrate probable aspects of it.

Furthermore, we know from comparative ethnographic evidence that kin-group genealogies seldom represent true and simple genetic facts, but are in fact "social documents." Choiseulese genealogies are too much like those of comparable peoples [1] to be

---

[1] For instance, from New Guinea where often "the genealogical structure of the group is stated to be a single descending line of males with no remembered siblings leading to a large band of brothers about three generations above living adults" (Barnes 1962: 6).

anything more or less than the result of processes similar to those reported for the latter. Since any processes that may be shaping genealogies today are probably not strictly comparable to those of the past, I cannot "demonstrate" this assertion, but it does seem probable that there are no impediments to such a process as the following: Elderly men who preserve the genealogies of descent groups could link up fairly easily all long-term residents with the local core of the descent group by assimilating their own less remote ancestors to a sibling model, or something approaching it, to form a unitary genealogical structure of no great depth. A genealogy so constructed could link descent-group members and at the same time include some descendants of the reputed sibling set who had earlier "married out," and fictive or distant kin ties could be converted to "real" bonds of kinship. In any event, such "forging" of genealogies may be unnecessary since descent groups are agamous and those with dubious genealogical backgrounds may make them irrelevant, certainly for their offspring, simply by marrying another and better-established descent-group member.

One final but important point: The discussion above, taken by itself, presents a somewhat distorted picture of even those few aspects of descent-group operation that I have discussed so far. For instance, many allotments of groves to group members were made, used, and finally fell into disuse through the extinction of the segment to which they were given or through some other process by which that segment eventually ceased to be a part of the group. Usually, nothing much ever came of it. The groves were eventually allotted by other managers to yet other parties, and the process began once more. The point is that disputes over such issues were and are probably not as frequent as the number of opportunities for them. When they arise the dogmas then become an issue, given situational significance only when circumstances combine the possibility of such an issue with the presence of a person or persons with "an axe to grind." Even so, they did not arise as often as they might because the parties concerned might have been unevenly matched in ability to mobilize self-help. Often an aggrieved party goes about muttering his discontents, but only when he feels that he has a chance of winning in the end—strictly a matter of force in the past if he had no persuasive arguments with which to coerce an agreement—will he take any action to implement those claims. (The next chapter discusses how self-help was used in such situations; one of the reasons for the many land-tenure disputes today is precisely that self-help or the threat of it is no longer operative.)

In the preceding discussion I have been concerned only with some of the operational criteria by which various dogmas about descent-group structure become qualified in certain circumstances. I have not been able to detail all varieties of situations and permutations of conditions which are relevant to my basic theme. They are more numerous than can be covered here, and, besides, this is not a treatise on Choiseulese "law." What has been said should be sufficient to demonstrate how some aspects of descent-group structure, particularly the dogmas, are used in action, and I have, I trust, shown that *all* rights and interests are in fact contingent, even if in varying degrees.

RECRUITMENT OF "OUTSIDERS"; THE COÖPTATIVE PROCESS

Active recruitment of potential members to descent groups is confined either to immediate offspring of persons who have just married out or to particular "crisis" situations. (Today there is little active recruitment going on, but the processes by which it did occur, and still does on occasion, are frequently discussed in relation to cases of continuing interest to particular groups.) If one is not resident with one's mother's descent group (of premarital origin) the representatives of that group may not be content merely to profess concern and openness of group membership to their "sister's child"; they may actually encourage him to desert his father's group and come to live with them in disregard of the brideprice payments. A similar situation exists with regard to a child who has become affiliated with his mother's descent group through the *tamazira* marriage of his father. His father's group may appeal to the dogmas and argue that since the "father's side" is "strong," it would be only proper for him to affiliate with them. Such appeals must disregard the "rules" associated with brideprice payments.

Parents, too, sometimes choose to disregard the fact that the brideprice has or has not been paid, and they may change their group affiliation. Their children go with them. If a brideprice has been paid, the father's group will probably protest that not only have they "thrown away" their *kesa* but they are losing the children as well. The mother's group, benefiting both ways, does not protest, but an attempt is usually made to maintain good relations and to placate the father's group. A compromise of interests may be reached whereby at least one child of an age sufficient to permit separation from its mother (no longer nursing) may remain with the father's group and be adopted by one of its members. When children need not yet be considered or when the children are still too young to be separated from their mother, it may be promised that when they come of age some will be returned to their father's descent group. If the marriage has been *tamazira*, the same still holds. The mother's descent group may protest that it is not only losing a woman but is getting no *kesa* to show for it, and the group may be promised one or more of the offspring as compensation. The problem here is that children may not be "returned," for the group with which they live may continually postpone returning them, and when they reach adolescence they may not want to "return." People become "settled" or "tame" within the group in which they have grown to maturity and are understandably reluctant to move elsewhere for other than compelling personal reasons. If this is so, no one will force them, and, in any event, if one is returned, he may return again to his mother's or father's group at a later date. If the group with which he wishes to affiliate is willing, as it should be, then there is little anyone in the "losing" group can do about it other than to threaten withdrawal of services or recognition as a member, but such a threat is unlikely unless some "big trouble" is involved.

Sometimes a *de facto* change of local group affiliation may come about as a result of visiting, either deliberately or otherwise. For instance, a couple may go to visit the wife's (or husband's) group and be persuaded to remain permanently, or they may go with intent to stay but conceal their intentions. If asked when they plan to return to their "proper" place, they may claim that they are visiting only temporarily and will return in due time. This may never happen, but meanwhile visiting serves as a convenient pretext to avoid any quarrels over the disposition of children, and allows the parents to suspend a decision which might anger one "side" or the other.

In order to induce a change of affiliation on the part of an offspring of a one-time member, a group may offer him a grove or groves as his own, or it may offer, through one of its representatives, to pay his brideprice or any other form of aid which might be attractive. It may be pointed out that an ancestor of the potential member had a particular interest in a segment of the group estate, and the resumption of that interest may be offered to the potential member. Such offers were most often made when a group was suffering depletion of its membership or when a particular individual in that group wished to increase his own following. A man who has no sons of his own may appeal to a "sister's son" to return and live with him as a son, taking over his proprietary interests in time. Such an offer was most attractive to the person concerned and to his parents when it held considerable promise, as when the offer came from a manager who could urge a "sister's son" to return to him to become manager after he died or to act in his stead while he was still alive.

Offers could also be made to persons further removed than the offspring of one who had just left the group. However, groups other than those of one's mother or father are not expected to take such a lively interest in one as a potential member, nor do they usually do so. Neither could they claim compensation. They do not, however, even today, profess any disinterest in him. He is, after all, one of their *babazuna*, "grandchildren," and they do constitute a large part of his kinship circle. Referring to him as one of their *sinangge* is usually no more than a way of expressing their recognition of kinship and its more general attendant obligations and rights. An active attempt to recruit a person to a descent group was more likely to occur if that person or his parent had made some meaningful contribution to group interests or more or less actively maintained whatever interests he may have had. In other words, one cannot expect to be offered descent-group membership if one has allowed one's interests and rights to become completely dormant or if one's parents have done so. Nor can one cease meaningful interaction with the members of that group and expect even rights of usage to be recognized unless both parties have something to be gained from re-activation.

This is not to imply that being, as it were, two steps removed from a group entails complete loss of interest in it. No "side" is ever "lost," or so the Choiseulese would say, but they would not deny that the interests and obligations become attenuated and the parties become more likely to define the relationship as "distant" and of no particularly binding quality. However, there is little chance of an individual's relationship with a particular group being defined as "distant" by himself or others if his mother or father was clearly established as a member before or after marriage. Nor even if the connection is somewhat more remote is there much chance of having it defined as of no significance, if those groups are all of the same region.

On the other hand, if one's father (or mother) took his (or her) spouse from a distant group, from another region for instance, interaction with members of that group is likely to be considerably less than with members of closer groups who may not be so closely related genealogically. A certain amount of disinterest and disinclination to involve oneself or one's group is likely to develop between individuals and distant groups to which they may be closely related. The reason is simply that, as becomes apparent later, one has more to lose than to gain by involving oneself in the affairs of those with whom one does not share immediate and vested interests. Depending upon the spatial distance and the intergroup relationships that separate such persons and groups, the attenuation of obligation and interest may be mitigated by visiting, perhaps of an extended variety amounting to temporary residence, and in the past by assistance with feasts, gift exchanges, gardening activities, and so on. The same may be done, and with greater ease and frequency, with nearby groups with which one is perhaps not so closely connected by genealogical ties.

Case I

The situation of one man I knew well may serve as an example of one similar to that envisioned above. Tanavalu's father, Madoko, married a woman named Ngulava from the Senggaluboro descent group in one of the Varisi-speaking regions on the opposite side of the island from his own descent-group estate, Gabili. They met and married on an occasion when their groups were living temporarily, because of a war, in a large village on the land of *sinangge* Kesi, the truncal segment of Madoko's mother's natal major *sinangge*. She was the daughter of Sodabangara (see Case IV, chap. 6) who was the manager of the Votuae branch of major *sinangge* Kesi. When peaceful conditions prevailed, Madoko and his followers returned to their own estate, taking Ngulava with them. Throughout his life Tanavalu has seen little of his mother's kinsmen. His genealogical knowledge of them is limited; he knows only the names of his mother's parents and siblings. As the manager of his own descent group he knows its genealogy and history well, but he also knows much about major *sinangge* Kesi and especially its Votuae segment. Kesi is a large major *sinangge*, both in numbers and in size of estate, and its estate borders on that of Gabili. Furthermore, the amalgamation of residential units in recent times has brought most of the people of the Votuae segment into Tanavalu's village as permanent residents. It was partly because of the kinship connection and for economic and political reasons (see Case IV, chap. 6) that they chose to reside with Tanavalu. But he would probably be just as well informed about them genealogically even if they had not taken up residence on his land. Aside from his own descent group, which is fairly small, they represent the bulk of his kinship circle. His knowledge of his father's mother's *sinangge* links him with an even larger number of people (other segments of the major *sinangge*) about whom he knows little genealogically. Tanavalu interacts daily with people to whom he is related through his father's mother, but he sees his mother's people only rarely, such as when either he or they are traveling, and little mention is ever made of them. When I asked him to which *sinangge* he belongs, he told me Gabili (of which he is now the manager) and Kesi, the major *sinangge* of his father's mother. (People sometimes define their *sinangge* membership in terms of major *sinangge* rather than minor *sinangge*. When asked why they do this, they say that the major *sinangge* is the "most important," perhaps to emphasize their connections with a wider range of kinsmen than identifying with the minor *sinangge* would permit. This is also consistent with the dogmatic emphasis upon major *sinangge* land rights being undivided.) Tanavalu often speaks of himself as a member of Kesi, and he is in a real sense, for living together as they now permanently do, his own descent group and that of his father's mother are "coresident" (*vari kapakapa*). Tanavalu too has married a woman from the opposite side of the island—he met her when he was a mission teacher—and his children see or know little of their mother's kin. Tanavalu says that the *sinangge* in which they have the greatest interests are again Gabili and Kesi. Clearly, he has little interest in the *sinangge* of his mother, or they in him. His resources are more than adequate, and he has no designs upon the property of his mother's group, nor if he had would they be likely to come to much, for his inability and disinterest in maintaining intensive contact with them has deprived the kinship connection of most of its significance to all concerned. Furthermore, other persons who have remained resident with his mother's group have doubtlessly developed strong interests in any land or other property in whch he might have derived an interest through his mother. Allowing Tanavalu to activate claims upon such property would, of course, mean giving up some of their own interests. Naturally enough a fiction of mutual concern and availability of resources is maintained because as long as there is no need for an open breach in the relationship it will be avoided. In this case, as in many others, the fiction costs nothing and may be worth a great deal. Both parties know that Tanavalu is not interested in changing his group affiliation, and both know that if he should suddenly decide to it might prove difficult, but neither is he likely to try. The fact that he is the manager of his descent group makes a change unlikely, and also makes it of possible profit to keep on friendly terms with him. Were Tanavalu to decide to change affiliation, it is far more likely anyway that he would attempt to affiliate with a group in his own region.

This case is typical, except that it is not common practice to marry persons from distant descent groups. Another case representing a somewhat different situation will illustrate the important point already made, that the dogma of descent-group openness is not to be taken literally.

Case II

Four generations ago Kaegabatu of the Sirosengga descent group (an autonomous branch of Kesi, residing now in the Varisi region) married a woman from the nearby descent group named Tapika. He paid a substantial brideprice for her. They resided patrivirilocally with the Sirosengga people, but after a number of years Kaegabatu died and his wife returned to Tapika, taking her two daughters with her. Widows were not supposed to return to their groups of origin, and, further, neither were children of a brideprice marriage supposed to return to their mother's "side." Nevertheless, both sometimes happened, and in this case, as in many others, it was possible because the woman had been industrious and could argue that she had "killed" her brideprice by helping her husband's people in their group activities, such as by assisting with gardens and pig-tending activities in preparation for feasts. Even so, she was not supposed to take her children, or at least not all of them. Yet Kaegabatu's wife got away with both of her daughters so that their children and grandchildren are now affiliated with the Tapika descent group. The managers of Sirosengga and Tapika have discussed the situation often over the years, and they both agree that "properly" (the "straight way") these descendants, or at least some of them, should return to Sirosengga and resume their rights over Kaegabatu's property (some groves) there and "help" the Sirosengga people in everyday activities and also, more importantly, group activities, of which today there are few. But the Tapika manager points out that they have lived with Tapika all their lives and so had their immediate ancestors; they are "settled" there, and there would be no point in uprooting them even if it could be done. The manager of Sirosengga reluctantly agrees, but he says he feels that Sirosengga has been cheated because Tapika got both the *kesa* and the children. However, he says, any time they want to return to Sirosengga they should feel free to do so. They probably won't, because all good coconut land there has long been occupied, and they are, as their manager says, settled into Tapika, they and their ancestors having lived there for three generations now. They have their own interests in the Tapika estate, and Kaegabatu's old groves hold no attraction for them. Perhaps if they tried to change their affiliation now and move into the Sirosengga settlement its manager might argue differently, but meanwhile he proclaims the "openness" of Sirosengga to them, despite the fact that he knows that they are not particularly interested. One might ask why he continues to remind them of the history of their affiliation with Sirosengga and why he continues to bring up the issue with their manager. Why not let the whole issue drop into oblivion? The answer is that it is a simple matter of politics. Tapika and Sirosengga are both in the same region and have a long history of close coöperation despite some unpleasant incidents. They conceive of themselves as closely related and friendly groups, and it is to the advantage of the manager of Sirosengga to have something to hold over the manager of Tapika, a little something extra with which to remind the Tapika manager that he owes the other an occasional favor or small service. Discussion of it now and then also gives the Sirosengga manager opportunity to remind the Tapika manager that the former is a good fellow and holds no grudges, that the two groups must be good friends or they would not allow such a situation to continue. The latter can afford to admit that the former is right in asserting how things "should be," for there is no danger of Kaegabatu's descendants returing to Sirosengga. The situation is effectively out of their hands, but discussion of it now and then can serve other ends. It may be kept alive although several generations have elapsed because there is no formal "rule" concerning the number of generations that are too few to "cover over" a tie that once existed and because it does involve the infraction of a "rule." But the concern was and is not so much that a "rule" had been broken (when Kaegabatu's wife returned with her children despite the brideprice payments) but rather that the Sirosengga people have lost out all around. The Sirosengga manager notes that if the Sirosengga people had "bad hearts" they could argue that Kaegabatu's descendants had been away too long or that there is insufficient room for them at Sirosengga. But Sirosengga is "a good *sinangge*" and would not do such a thing.

There were times when a descent group lost much of its membership through warfare, and at such times active recruitment was probably neither infrequent nor confined to the offspring of those who had recently gone out. The same was probably true when a would-be manager was building a following (chap. 4). He was not so much concerned with the kin ties which might contribute to his following but rather with the quality of allegiance rendered by those kin and others. Would-be followers were also little concerned with kin ties; what they wanted was the protection of managerial prowess and prestige.

However, if we can for the moment assume a situation with neither intergroup conflict nor managerial competition, then, little permanent movement would have occurred. Most moves would not have constituted permanent changes of affiliation but rather only visiting designed to maintain relationships or to solicit the aid of kinsmen in some project. Residence elsewhere than with the descent group in which one considered oneself a member does not necessarily constitute a change of affiliation unless there is a declared intention of doing so. An intended change of affiliation may not be declared but allowed to develop gradually out of a "visit." Again there are political reasons for this. To declare that one is going to change affiliation may amount to renouncing the descent group with which one is presently affiliated, and renunciation may not be necessary unless there is some compelling personal reason for it, for instance, when the person changing affiliation has made himself so obnoxious that he is not wanted in the group. Most people would, however, prefer to leave their status in doubt for as long as possible, closing no avenues unless absolutely necessary.

These remarks apply equally to the right to establish a residence with a descent group and to rights of usage or services—both forms of membership, but nonetheless analytically separable. The Choiseulese do not separate them terminologically, but in practice they are differently treated. Recognizing someone's membership in the latter sense is different from going so far as to recruit him as a descent-group mate, even though similar services may be involved. The extent of mutual involvement remains less in the latter instance. Using land or receiving aid from descent-group members on the basis of belonging to its associated cognatic descent category may require only fleeting interaction and little commitment of personnel and resources, but, on the other hand, meeting such requests does allow the claimant a foot in the door, so to speak. Taking someone as a descent-group mate implies more, for it entails the recognition of kinship obligations in their most meaningful form. It involves almost daily interaction and the fullest acceptance of the presumed obligations of kinship. It is not surprising then that, for this reason and others, claims made against descent groups in which an individual is not domiciled are often claims against rights of usage or services and not right of membership in its fullest sense. Persons can get most of what they want from another descent group without actually assuming residence with it. Through visiting one could obtain "shelter" from a conflict in which one's own group was affected, and one may make temporary use of resources upon request.

The rights to residence and to the use of descent-group resources are nominally conferred by cognatic descent, yet it is clear that the validity of these rights, and indeed the recognition that they do exist in a particular instance, depends upon the quality of the interpersonal relationships obtaining between claimants and already established descent-group members. Through services rendered to the group or to various of its members, a claimant may establish the validity of his rights, but the recognition of his rights does not depend solely upon any services he may have rendered or which may have been rendered by his parents or ancestors. Potential services are also an important consideration, and the extent to which they may be needed or desired may qualify other considerations relevant to claims being made.

When one's genealogical tie with a particular group is distant and when "many generations have covered" the separation of one's linking ancestor from that group, and especially when one's own group and that other descent group are not of the same region, it may prove difficult indeed to become fully a member of that group. I say "may" and not "will" because there may be mitigating circumstances which make it possible to activate membership in such an instance. But in any event, "closeness" or "distance" of genealogical connection is neither formally nor factually *the* deciding criterion in resumption of descent-group membership. There are many criteria which may or may not be brought into any particular case, but always fundamental and determinative of those criteria which finally prove important are the *de facto* rights and interests of those who constitute the present personnel of the descent group.

An individual wishing to assume descent-group membership may put his case to the manager and elders of that group, and they will usually hear him out; they are obliged to do so as his kinsmen, and they must keep up the pretense—although it may not be a pretense—that they have his interests at heart as good kinsmen. But they are the powers that be within the group; they are the primary interest holders, *de facto* or by the "rules." One does not simply move in on any group with which one would affiliate; one must be sure of one's welcome beforehand. This is necessary since, as a member of a group, one is dependent upon one's fellow members, and they become obligated to one in a variety of ways which may transcend the limits of their responsibility before one's assumption of actual membership. People may be understandably reluctant to extend their responsibilities and for that reason alone be reluctant to have someone as a fellow descent-group member.

To give one example here, the person wishing to assume membership generally has a good reason for wanting to leave wherever he is already, and perhaps the best reason is that he is no longer welcome there. Sorcery, presumptuousness about rights, adultery, and so on may all serve as sufficient reason not to want him as an associate, and for the same reasons he may be unwelcome elsewhere too. For all these offenses in the past could lead to the implementation of self-help and in the end the whole group could become involved (see chap. 4). (Today kinsmen are not so necessarily involved in one another's affairs, yet no one likes a trouble maker around, and some people are simply not welcome.) In order to close group membership to an undesirable person it is not necessary to repudiate the dogma of openness in general; it is only necessary to find extenuating circumstances which make closure reasonable in the particular instance. People may, for various reasons, be reluctant to charge the would-be member with offenses which are generally attributed to him, and then it is only necessary to argue, for instance, that "our group is already too full"—there are already too many people for the land available. It is not important that the would-be member may know this to be false, for he too has the responsibility, in this instance quite strong, to avoid an open breach in the relationship. Were he to charge the representatives of the group with lying, his relations would quickly degenerate, an open breach would occur, and he would find himself completely *persona non grata*. Many considerations and incidents could then be found to justify denial of the validity of his claims. One such basis for denial is that "too many generations have covered" the original separation of the claimant's ancestors from the group. How many generations are "too many" is not defined as a matter of dogma, so persons are free to interpret this condition in any way convenient for them. Or some ancient trouble between the group and the claimant's ancestors might be resuscitated and given significance whereas before the breach it was deemed meaningless.

The nature of descent-group membership makes it necessary that one be at least tolerable as a member in order to become or continue as one. The services of one's fellow members were indispensable in daily and especially political life, and fellow members were both assets and liabilities to one another. This is less true today, but one can still become a descent-group member only by the continuing consent, or lack of dissent, of that group. Where a claim was contested, as it perhaps seldom was when the claimant had something to offer and no pronounced liabilities (but claims are often contested today), the onus of the proof of the worthiness of it was (and still is) upon the claimant. Estab-

lishing the worthiness of his claim is not limited to establishing
its genealogical accuracy, although that too may become an
issue, for the validity of the claim may hinge upon almost any
incident in the past and present relations between the claimant
and his ancestors and the established members of the descent
group. Any event may be deemed relevant or irrelevant to one's
claims; relevance is not absolute but depends largely upon the
individual's desirability as a group member or perhaps other
considerations such as the relative availability of primary resources. (Population density, however, is quite low and was
probably not significantly higher in the past so that pressure on
land was probably not a significant factor in the refusal of membership rights. Today, however, considerable pressure exists,
though it is difficult to measure, upon land suitable for coconuts,
the only cash crop. Not all descent groups possess estates including such land, and the members of those groups poor in this
respect would like to affiliate with the relatively well-off. But
the option is not generally open to them, and they are well aware
of it.)

Thus an individual may maintain interests and rights in the
estate and persons of another descent group with which he is
not resident, where he does not maintain a household and coöperate regularly in daily activities. But the essential sociological
point—probably so obvious to the Choiseulese that there is no
need to express it in dogmas—is that one's rights and interests
in any group other than that with which one is resident or in any
property one is not immediately using, and in relation to which
one shares rights and interests with other persons, are contingent
upon the rights and interests of other persons who have already
assumed their rights and consolidated their interests. It is true
that one may "choose" membership in another descent group,
granted that certain kinship qualifications are met, but those
are not the only qualifications, and, furthermore, choice can be
exercised only with and through the consent of others. It is
equally true to say that a descent group chooses its members as
it is to say that the individual chooses his descent group. It
seems a closer approximation to the complexity of the facts to
speak of a coöptative process rather than individual option.

Just as there is not ordinarily much encouragement of nonmembers to desert present affiliations, there is also little conflict

over the right to establish membership in its fullest sense. There are good reasons for this. First, attempts to change descent-group affiliation are and probably were less frequent than one might expect under the dogma that they are possible and that there is so much residential mobility. Much of the mobility is, and was, only temporary and occurred under special circumstances, as in time of intergroup conflicts; and also it is not necessary to be residentially or even categorically affiliated with a descent group to receive benefits or services from it. Secondly, the dogma of descent group openness is not taken literally by anyone with "good sense." The cognatic descent idiom relates not only to right of access to an estate but equally to the mutual obligations of kinsmen. To declare one's descent group open to another is to declare oneself a good kinsman, ready and willing to offer aid. On the other hand, to take this too literally and to attempt to exercise the right of resumption of membership when one has not maintained binding relationships with descent-group personnel is to impose upon the dogma and to overburden the morality of kinship. But even those who have maintained their interests must be cautious not to burden the rights that have been recognized; they must "keep their peace" too. They must refrain from attempting to extend what rights and interests they have, or face the possibility of encumbering even those. Their situation is quite similar to that of secondary members of the descent group, but it is even more delicate for they do not have the asset of active membership working in their favor.

Those who already exercise rights of usage usually refrain from extending them at the expense of active group members, and those whose rights exist in theory refrain from attempting to convert them to realized interests, for people know that, though the right of assumption of descent-group membership exists in theory it may not be exercised freely in fact. They refrain from attempting to exercise or to extend the right because they know that to do so would be to provoke reaction from those who already exercise a *de facto* control over the group and its resources. Of course, the extent of the reaction that may be provoked depends upon the extent of the claims and upon the extent to which those claims have already been recognized and the claimant given a foothold. Therefore, a situation may appear to a would-be claimant favorable to the extention of claims; the possibility of severe reaction may be judged to be low. He may then attempt to extend his claims. Needless to say, mistakes in judgement do occur.

The dogma of openness can persist precisely because openness can be refuted in particular instances and because, perhaps most importantly, by refraining from exercising it people do not place too much of a burden upon it. The dogma can persist as an idiom of kinship allowing persons access to descent-group estates in a limited manner and expressing the mutual responsibility of kinsmen, and their property, to one another because there is a tacit understanding, more appreciated by some than by others, that it is not to be taken literally. The understanding must remain tacit, not a part of the "public" dogma, for to question the idiom would be to question the morality of kinship itself.

But the restraints upon changes of affiliation or attempts to extend interests are not to be found solely in the knowledge of the difficulties that may be encountered from those with vested interests in other groups. Restraint derives too from the nature of descent-group membership. What is meant here is perhaps best understood by asking why one might want to change his affiliation and why one might not want to do so even though some advantage could be gained.

Since descent-group membership implies interaction, mundane or otherwise, and mutual responsibility, it is necessary to maintain good relations with descent-group mates in order to reap the benefits of group membership. Perhaps as a consequence of the recognition of this, the dogma that members of one *sinangge* (in all senses of the term) must not quarrel is emphasized. Nonetheless, as already noted, there is and was considerable intragroup conflict, especially over property. People do, of course, quarrel for other reasons: because their children get into squabbles, because they feel that another has not rendered sufficient return for a favor done him, because sometimes garden produce is stolen, because pigs get into gardens, and so on. Often the immediate quarrels themselves do not amount to much but a grudge continues to be harbored. People may, for various reasons, restrain themselves from overt conflict, but this is not to say that they necessarily love one another. They do so out of necessity, out of continued need of the services they can and must render to one another. (Again, all of this was much more true in the past than it is today.) In any event, there is always sorcery, and one need not quarrel openly, for revenge can be had with less difficulty.

Any person is likely to maintain the descent-group affiliation conferred upon him by the residential choice of his parents. The difficulties of changing affiliation, (especially if one has not maintained, through circumstance or choice, the type of tie that may be converted to active membership) are only part of the reason. Most people have vested interests in the groups with which they are affiliated, and changing means establishing vested interests elsewhere—a long and sometimes difficult process—and it means more or less giving up those one has already established. Those vested interests include not only property interests, which some persons may have more extensively and firmly than others, but also personal bonds between individuals which extensive interaction and the intensive exchange of services have rendered binding or obligatory. Unless he has managed to establish effective relationships with influential members of other groups, a man is solely dependent upon such relationships as he has with his own group mates—dependent upon them, especially in the past, for all forms of assistance from gardening to aid and protection in times of interpersonal or intergroup conflicts. Again, depending upon the conditions under which one renounces one's descent-group membership, one also to some degree renounces those interests that one has developed. Separation may occur amicably and one's former fellows may continue to regard one as a group member, leaving open the possibility of return. Even so, one's exit from the immediate scene may open up possibilities for others to expand their interests both in property and the allegiance of other group members. Since property interests are so important and must be consolidated and maintained primarily by securing and maintaining descent-group membership, it is easy enough to understand why persons do not change descent-group membership by mere whim and why such conduct would not be allowed. The surest way to maintain one's rights is to keep them active and the surest way to do that is to maintain one's descent-group membership. No man wishes to be dependent upon others, as everyone is to some degree; but no one wants to be put in the position of "being fed" by others, that is, living on their land and having only what they will allow. Each man wants his measure of independence in the form of his own groves and *kesa* if possible,

and ambitious men want even more. Changing affiliation has its
drawbacks, and changing it often would make it impossible to
secure a good position in any group. It was especially important
for men of ambition who wished to acquire prestige and power
over other men through the handling of land and *kesa* to acquire
and maintain their descent-group affiliations. On the other hand,
there were means of gaining wealth that were not necessarily
tied to descent-group membership. For instance, one could hire
oneself out as an assassin, be paid in *kesa*, and then use that *kesa*
to obligate a descent group to oneself by paying its debts (see
Case V, chap. 6, and also chap. 4). However, this was a dangerous
business, and few could do it without making sufficient enemies
to meet an early death.

Various circumstances may mitigate the disadvantages of
changing descent-group affiliation. An amicable separation is
one such circumstance, as, for instance sometimes happened,
when a person was called to another descent group to be adopted
by its manager. His former fellows then had something to gain by
maintaining good relations with the departing person. On the
other hand, a person's position in his group may, for various
reasons, seem disadvantageous and he may feel that he has more
to gain than to lose by changing affiliation if it can be done. The
desire to change affiliation often arises from the feeling that a person's interests, as he sees them, would be better served elsewhere,
for as we have seen, a basic consideration in descent-group affiliation is "looking for that which will help one to live well." Thus
a person may be motivated to move because of consistently poor
gardens, personal or family health, persistent quarreling, or, most
importantly, sorcery accusations or fear of sorcery, both of which
arise primarily from conflict over women and property. Persistent
quarreling may be the result of the same cause, and the excuses of
poor gardens or personal or family health may be no more than
pretexts, the real reason being that the individual feels that his
property interests are not being given sufficient recognition or
that others are attempting to better their positions at his expense.
We have already seen too that the avarice of some people makes
them less than desirable as fellow members, and others may
begin to apply various subtle or not so subtle sanctions against
them, making their lives with that group miserable.

The disadvantages as seen by the individual may be real or

imaginary. People do attempt to better their own positions at the expense of others, sometimes going so far as to practice sorcery against others to remove them from the scene. Jealousy of another's success may lead to the practice of detrimental magic against his gardens and pigs. Such practices are real enough, but they are probably not as frequent as suspicion of them. There is probably just enough truth in suspicions of such practices, for people have been caught at them, to enable someone whose fortune has been running consistently poor to believe that he and his family might do better elsewhere.

Stated simply: Where a person "lives well" he is not likely to wish to change his descent-group affiliation, but he must also "live well," that is, maintain good relations, with those with whom he would opt to affiliate or they are not likely to allow him to do so. In fact, the right to affiliate with other groups is a privilege. A person who has acquired a poor reputation for himself, for instance, as an adulterer or a sorcerer, is not desired as a member of any group. In order to be able to change one's affiliation it is also expedient not to have to change it. Nonetheless, those who are not wanted in one group may find it possible to acquire membership in another. Since sorcery accusations, for instance, are commonly known to be sometimes fallacious, only a pretext covering other motives, the accused may find kinsmen willing to take him in, especially if he is industrious and offers some promise of assistance in group activities. Or, as sometimes happens, he may find a willingness to accept him as a visitor or a contingent member with no particular rights. This too may be a source of difficulty; we have seen that such persons may begin to attempt to consolidate their positions and to imagine or to argue that their rights are more extensive than they once claimed (again see the case history in chap. 6 for an example of a similar situation).

Fear of violent conflict between groups also led persons to make temporary or permanent changes of residence. The validity of this fear as an excuse for opting out of a group and remaining free to return to it later varied with one's personal position and the position of one's group in the conflict. For instance, if one's group went to war against another group in which one had kinsmen, especially close kinsmen, one was not obliged to participate. Descent groups generally did not get involved in conflicts as aggressors unless there was fairly unanimous consent among their members, but it did happen that a manager occasionally got out of hand and involved the group in a dispute with which the members were not wholly sympathetic. A manager who did this was in danger of losing his following, or at least part of it, for some persons would opt out and assume temporary residence elsewhere waiting until the manager got his due and it was safe to return. Thus opting out under certain circumstances did not constitute a renunciation of descent-group membership. However, if a group were attacked, it generally dispersed, if anything were left of it, bade its time, and built support for the occasion upon which it could take the offensive. Some of those who dispersed might not return to participate in further hostilities, and it was not necessarily to be held against them. On the other hand, if one's group were the aggressor and the general consensus was that aggression was necessary to protect the prestige and property of the group, and thus right and proper, one could not opt out of the situation without impairing future descent-group membership for oneself and one's descendants. For nonmembers, participation in vengeance activities against the descent group could constitute sufficient cause to terminate all rights of future membership, but again not necessarily so. These events could be thought of as things of the past and of no significance, or they could be given considerable weight. If group representatives choose to stress hostile actions against the group in the past (usually by one's ancestors) they may even today argue that those actions effectively "cut" the genealogical connection and deprived it of its validity as a basis for any claims. The validity of hostile actions against the descent group as an operational criterion for group closure depends, then, like perhaps all other operational criteria, upon the immediate situation—upon what is to be gained or lost to the group or its representatives by recognition of the rights of the claimant.

A further cause of change of affiliation was fear of vengeance against oneself. Refuge could be sought with kinsmen in a distant descent group, and this was easiest where one's mother or father came from that place. Even so, the maneuver was not always effective since aggrieved parties would go some distance to get revenge. Change of affiliation was not always necessary if one had some *kesa* with which to secure protection among non-kin (see the discussion of *bori* in chap. 2), but in any event the movement could constitute only a temporary change of residence, and not necessarily of affiliation. However, this change, like others discussed earlier, could become permanent.

The sanctions available to those who are refused what they take to be their rights are few, but they are nonetheless sometimes quite effective (though, again, this is much less true today). Threat of the withdrawal of one's coöperation or services as a kinsman may be effective if those services have been or show promise of becoming important and useful. But since mutual dependence between members and a nonmember is not as great as that between members, such a threat can hardly have the force it might if made by a secondary member. Self-help could hardly be threatened because it would defeat one's presumed intent to become a group member, but fear that a person who was denied his claims might have recourse to self-help for revenge if he felt his pride injured, could restrain group members from exercising their fiat arbitrarily. The fear of possible revenge did not exist when the claimant was a man of no account, but it increased with an awareness of the abilities of the claimant. One could also resort to self-help in the form of sorcery, and fear of it would also act as a restraint upon arbitrary repudiation of claims. But all these sanctions had to be exercised with great caution—the group had to be made aware of their possibility. An open threat would again defeat the goal by destroying the façade of amicability which was usually carefully preserved and might even result in the group itself initiating self-help to eliminate the claimant. The persuasiveness of such threats and fears depended upon the relative powers of the individuals and groups.

An issue to be considered here is the range over which the rights conferred by the cognatic-descent idiom may be exercised. We have already seen that the dogma itself holds that one may become a member of any descent group in which one had an ancestor who was a member, but that it is generally recognized that claims to full membership are not usual. Claims are instead to services of kinship and perhaps only relatively limited rights of usage of the group's estate. While *sinangge* genealogies are said to contain all descendants of the apical or founding ancestor, it is apparent that they do not. Some informants were clear about the fact that what the genealogies do is to link most persons resident with the descent group as members of its "core." Outside of that unit any genealogical retention is more or less incidental, and the maintenance of oneself in it, if one is not resident with the descent group, must be the result of keeping the group mindful of one's status and of validating the recognition of that status by contributing to the interests and welfare of group members.

The attempt is usually made to accede to minor claims or at least to present oneself or one's group as generally willing, even though circumstances may make it difficult. In any event, wholesale repudiation of such limited claims is not the general practice. Limitations of time, space, and other resources, including human energy, make it difficult to maintain an active interest in groups other than those in one's own region. It is within the region that a person exercises or generally attempts to exercise whatever rights he may have in other descent groups. It is, then, not so much the type of kin-tie he may have with other groups that is important but rather their availability and the possibility of making extensive use of them that leads him to attempt to activate his rights or to maintain those of his parents. The closeness or distance of the kin-tie is not nearly as important as are considerations of group welfare as seen by the group. Thus persons from neighboring or nearby groups may be granted the privilege to plant gardens or to reside temporarily with the group even in the absence of a binding kinship obligation so long as the descent group feels it is in its own interests.

The Choiseulese stress only the fact that it is *as kinsmen* that they coöperate and grant one another rights of usage and services. They do, however, sometimes say that certain kinsmen are particularly friendly because their fathers had the "same" father, but the same sentiment may be expressed about any set of kin ties, and the fact that certain ones are agnatic is not crucial. Thus, one might construe as of no particular importance the pattern of distribution that the actual usage of rights may have at any one time, especially within the region and between neighboring descent groups. That is, other things being equal, one would expect, in the absence of a dogma stressing a particular type of relationship as the basis of coöperation, that all types would be used with equal frequency. (There are, of course, such dogmas concerning relative rights, but the idiom of cognatic descent confers at least limited rights of use and entitlement to descent-

group affiliation to all members of the cognatic descent category.)
I suspect that this was so, especially with regard to usage of the
more common forms of service between kinsmen, such as coöperation in gardening and even the granting of rights of usage of
land. However, I cannot demonstrate this; sufficient information
regarding the recent past is not available. At the present time,
however, taking rights to use coconuts or to plant gardens as an
indication, it is clear that persons make claims, or ask permission
where they have no formal claims, on lands near their residence or
from any kinsman who has such resources and who they think may
be willing to share them. The type of kin tie was never pointed
out as important other than for the fact that it existed as a kin tie.

When it comes to the crucial issue of actual changes of descent-group affiliation, data concerning the recent past and the
present are somewhat more complete and useful in both instances.
The cases I studied represent affiliational histories for several generations. However, those for which I have extensive information
are not numerous—perhaps half a dozen—and cannot be construed as a representative sample. A sociological census of two regions gave somewhat less intensive information about sufficient
cases to constitute a representative sample of patterns of descent-group affiliation at the present time and also to indicate
something of the situation in the past.

My sociological census covered all 103 adult male family heads
within the two regions extensively investigated. I recorded information about present and past affiliations and limited information
about the affiliations of their parents and grandparents if available. I also recorded general outlines of life histories including
information about marriages. From these data I have been able to
abstract Tables 5–8. From the histories of affiliation, and especially from those few about which I have extensive information,
and, finally, from numerous general statements by informants, I
have abstracted the information concerning general processes
presented in the foregoing discussion.

Choiseulese dogmas about relative rights in descent groups
conferred by genealogical status, lead to the expectation of a
sizeable number of serial patrifiliations, a low frequency of matrifiliations, and a still lower frequency of serial matrifiliations, a
low frequency of *tamazira* marriages, and a low frequency of
changes of descent-group affiliation. Numerical data might reveal

how rare or how frequent changes of affiliation are, and whether there is any tendency for persons to activate certain possibilities of affiliation more so than others. (Numerical data can hardly answer the question why this should be, but without them the question might not be posed at all.) At least for the first set of expectations, however, I have already indicated that they were and are so many circumstances mitigating the application of the dogmas that they must be seen and understood not in their literal phrasing but as idioms of interpersonal and intergroup relations. Thus although numerical data do confirm these expectations, the conformity is not necessarily due to any compulsion that the Choiseulese feel to act on the dogmas but, as seems more likely, to efforts of persons to maintain or to establish modes of affiliation in which the dogmas enhance the statuses of themselves and their offspring. It turns out that changes of affiliation are rare and that the range over which such choices are exercised is narrow. These points are discussed below.

Since the information does usually run back into the past for several generations it is also to some extent directly relevant to that time. The most important series of changes affecting descent-group affiliation were those that came about in settlement patterns. However, in some regions, such as Varisi, because of the particular distribution of *sinangge* estates, less reorganization was needed to meet the requirements of the modern situation. Only one of the four villages in that region is composed of more than one descent group and comparatively fewer people have had to leave their own estates and take up residence elsewhere. More of the aboriginal descent groups have remained intact. Thus the situation in the Varisi region today is perhaps closer to that of the past in general, but clearly none of these data are exactly representative of the particular distribution of modes of affiliation at any time in the past. The frequencies of various modes varied at different times and places in the past just as they do today. The various figures recorded here were changing even as I recorded them, and it was necessary to "freeze" the scene at one point in order to be able to present a general picture. I chose the month of my arrival on the island (November 1958).

But despite all the change, there has been a form of continuity. The processes of descent-group affiliation remain what they were —filiation and the coöptative process—and the basic motivation to change of affiliation remains too. What has changed are the particular things men desire to enable them to "live well." Even when the settlement pattern was changing new affiliations were being made on the basis of conceptions of what kinsmen could and should do for one another. It is true that some "customs" are useful today only as "history," as criteria upon which to base judgments about the veracity of claims based upon presumed historical events, but other "customs," certainly those concerning the criteria for descent-group affiliation, are still applied, and so many of the same criteria remain operative. If someone seeks to change his affiliation today he may come up against difficulties he would not have encountered in the past, such as the availability of coconut land, yet such difficulties are perhaps no more than old-fashioned ones in new dress.

Table 5 expresses the composition of the fifteen descent groups in the two regions of the census. These are not the same units as those presented in Table 3 above (chap. 2), for the latter are cognatic descent *categories*, not descent *groups*. The categories (in Table 5) "Adult Males" and "Adult Females" include everyone who claims membership in the descent group through membership in its cognatic descent category. These, along with their "Children" (including adopted ones) form the "core" of the descent group. Adults who were at one time adopted into the descent group are included in category "P" (resident with patrikin); this is reasonable since it is men who do most of the adopting in a formal way.

In order to avoid confusion it is important to note here that the total population of the two regions is approximately 601. Table 5 includes only 551, leaving fifty persons unaccounted for. Of those, twenty-eight are in Tepazaka and twenty-two in Varisi. For one reason or another they were difficult to classify in Table 5. They are for the most part persons whose status is ambiguous or who are not members of those descent groups. They might be classified as guests and their children: most of them are persons related through another cognatic descent category to a group member who is their sponsor in that place, and they live in close association with him.

Table 6 indicates the genealogical status of those male family heads who are patrifiliants with their descent groups. The non-agnatic patrifiliants are categorized by reference to the ascending

TABLE 5

Descent-Group Composition

Descent Group	Adult males A	P	M	Adult females A	P	M	Ch	M nm	F nm	Total
						Tepazaka				
Gabili	1	0	4	0	3	2	22	2	4	38
Votuae	0	1	1	1	1	1	19	2	1	27
Eromo	5	0	0	1	0	0	14	1	3	24
Baukolo	0	2	1	0	1	0	13	1	3	21
Singgotu	1	3	4	3	2	3	43	3	2	64
Korasokana	0	4	6	0	2	2	34	2	8	58
Kubobangara	0	4	1	0	0	0	17	0	5	27
Kubongava	1	1	0	0	1	0	14	1	2	20
TOTAL	8	15	17	5	10	8	176	12	28	279
						Varisi				
Sisikua	1	3	4	1	3	1	31	0	4	48
Korasa	3	5	4	0	3	3	38	1	6	63
Zevekana	0	4	0	0	0	0	13	0	4	21
Rogabatu	10	0	1	4	0	2	46	2	12	77
Barisengga	2	4	0	1	1	0	23	2	7	40
Kalekubo	1	0	0	0	0	0	4	0	1	6
Sirobangara	3	0	0	1	0	0	9	1	3	17
TOTAL	20	16	9	7	7	6	164	6	37	272

Key: A = agnatically affiliated
P = affiliated with patrikin (excluding A)
M = affiliated with matrikin
Ch = children (including those of deceased members) and adoptees
M nm = male nonmembers, married to female members
F nm = female nonmembers, married to male members, or widows of deceased male members

generation in which the female linking ancestor occurs in the group's genealogy (second, third, fourth, or other). In few cases are there more than one female in the linking descent line.

Table 7 summarizes the distribution of modes of descent-group affiliation for all adult male family heads (including agnatic affiliants in the general category of patrifiliants, cf. Table 5). It also indicates whether this affiliation was acquired by natal filiation or by other means. Included in the "other" category here are some men who acquired that affiliation by a parental change of affiliation (e.g., when their mothers "returned" and took them along).

Table 8, summarizing the data on both maintenance and change

TABLE 6

GENEALOGICAL STATUS OF MALE FAMILY HEADS
WHO ARE PATRIFILIANTS

Generation of female link	Tepazaka		Varisi	
	N	%	N	%
Agnatic	8	15	20	39
Second	4	8	6	12
Third	4	8	8	16
Fourth	3	6	0	0
Other[a]	4	8	2	4
TOTAL	23	45	36	71

[a] A residual category, including adopted persons and those whose female link is more than four generations back.

of affiliation for the same men, shows that coöptative change of affiliation is uncommon; few men exercise the right nominally conferred by cognatic descent. Only seven men had changed affiliation by this means and then persisted in that change. The remainder, with a few exceptions, have either maintained the descent-group affiliation conferred by their parents' residential choices or they have married and affiliated elsewhere as *tamazira*. The men so affiliated are categorized in Table 8 according to their previous affiliation with patrikin or matrikin; these figures show that matrifiliation does not seem to be a factor predisposing to *tamazira* marriage. This is not surprising since many patrifiliants are just as much "secondary" members of their descent groups as are matrifiliants. However, established agnatic affiliants seldom marry as *tamazira*. All 18 *tamazira* appearing in Tables 7 and 8 are affiliated with the descent groups of their wives' fathers, and this

TABLE 7

DESCENT-GROUP AFFILIATIONS
OF ALL MALE FAMILY HEADS

Region	Residing with patrikin				Residing with matrikin				Residing with affines	
	Natal		Other		Natal		Other			
	N	%	N	%	N	%	N	%	N	%
Tepazaka	14	27	9	17	10	19	7	13	12	32
Varisi	32	63	4	8	6	12	3	6	6	12

is consistent with the generally lower political and economic status of men who marry in this way (that is, they are generally unable to acquire *tamazira* themselves).

There is more mobility now, and there was more mobility in the past, than these figures reveal. During the two-year period of my field work, for instance, there were several additional changes. Some of these were brought about by men who had married as *tamazira* returning to their original descent groups. Furthermore, a few men who are here listed as now affiliated with descent groups in which they are members by filiation (natal or otherwise) had changed their affiliations at one time, usually by *tamazira* marriage again, but later returned. And, again there is also much

TABLE 8

MAINTENANCE AND CHANGE OF
DESCENT-GROUP AFFILIATION

Region	Maintenance of last parental residence			Changed affiliation		
	With patrikin		With matrikin	Tamazira marriage		Coöptative change
	Agnatic	Other		previous patrikin	previous matrikin	
	N %	N %	N %	N %	N %	N %
Tepazaka	7 13	13 25	16 31	7 13	5 10	4 8
Varisi	19 37	15 29	8 16	3 6	3 6	3 6

"visiting" that may or may not turn gradually into changes of affiliation.

The general picture in the Varisi region, where less dislocation of descent groups occurred, may be, for that reason, somewhat closer to the situation in general in the past. Affiliation in the Varisi region changed little within recent years, yet most changes occurring between 1959 and 1961 were in that region. Part of the reason for this is that one descent group (Rogabatu) is now beginning to lose many of its members because it is situated in the "bush" some distance from the coast, and the people have no place to plant coconuts and thereby earn cash. Several of its members have managed to persuade kinsmen living within the region, but on the coast, to take them in, and others are trying to do the same. In any event, in 1958, of the fifty-one adult married males in that region forty (78 per cent) had maintained the residence and descent-group affiliation conferred upon them by parental residence and two others had changed affiliation at one time (through *tamazira* marriage) but later returned to their natal descent groups, making a total of forty-two men who have in effect maintained the residence and affiliation conferred upon them by parental decisions. Six (12 per cent) had chosen to reside patriuxorilocally through *tamazira* marriage, and only three (6 per cent) had opted to change affiliation for other reasons and then maintained that change. Furthermore, none of the three "chose" to reside where neither parent had not done so before or had not maintained vested interests in that descent group, usually in the form of property rights such as groves; and in each case the person changing affiliation had maintained those interests before assuming full membership in the group. In some cases those changing affiliation had resided during childhood with the descent group to which they "returned." In no case that came to my attention did a person "return" to a descent group other than one of those with which one of his grandparents had been most closely identified at one time. Changes of affiliation on the basis of cognatic descent are almost always within the same region.

Only two of the seven coöptative (or non-*tamazira*) changes of affiliation recorded in Table 8 could possibly be considered as exceptional to the foregoing remarks. In one case a young man who was born and reared with his mother's descent group returned to the one from which his father had originated in another region. He took his wife and children with him. A man who is a classificatory "brother" to his now deceased father paid his brideprice a few years ago and finally managed to persuade him that he should return to his father's original place. He was enticed with promises of further economic aid and privileges, and these seemed alluring because his sponsor was a relatively wealthy man. But the young man's wife was not happy away from her own kin, or so it was said, and after two years of vacillation they finally returned to the young man's mother's descent group in 1961.

In the other case a young man, K, married *tamazira* to the sister's daughter of the manager of a descent group close to the descent group from which his own father's mother had come upon marriage. K's father had been resident with that group for a short time, but avowedly only temporarily, and he planted some coconuts there. After his marriage, K was approached by his father's mother's sister's son, P, also a member of his father's mother's descent group. P reminded K of his property interests in P's descent-group estate and encouraged K to come live with him. P also had considerable interests, through the demise of his father's *sinangge*, in other land, and he was able to offer K extensive privileges in relation to that land as well. K moved in with P, and both of them say (privately) that he resumed membership in his father's mother's descent group. However, his status is somewhat ambiguous for he does not publicly claim membership in his father's mother's descent group, and he does not garden on its land. K and P say that K is now a member of his father's mother's group as a way of expressing their relationship, but K gardens only upon the land which P gained control of through his father. It is clear that K has taken advantage of his link with P to further his own economic position, and P has encouraged K to do so and thereby contribute to the beginnings of a following for P.

While thirty-six (71 per cent) of the Varisi region men are resident with patrikin, only twenty of these (39 per cent) are agnatically affiliated. Comparable figures for Tepazaka are much lower, but the contrast between the two regions is not due to any differences in the values placed upon types of kin or descent ties. It is due rather to the historical circumstances discussed above. The exact incidence of affiliation with the descent group of one's father varies considerably from group to group, as does the incidence of agnatic affiliation. In only a few cases are all adult married males within the descent group agnatically affiliated, and in other cases none are. It is obvious from Table 7 that the rate of agnatic affiliation in the Varisi region is much higher than in the Tepazaka region, and frequency of affiliation with matrikin is much higher in Tepazaka. Again, the differences result largely from the rearrangement of the settlement pattern in the early 1900's. The higher rate of *tamazira* marriage in Tepazaka is related also to the higher rate of affiliation with matrikin and the lower rate of agnatic affiliation. There is only one rather dubious instance in which a man who was agnatically affiliated to his descent group made a *tamazira* marriage. A young man from the Varisi region, recently married, lived with his three brothers as guests on the land of another group in which they could, but did not, claim membership. They consider their primary interests to lie in the estate of the *sinangge* in which they have agnatic status but of which they are now the only representatives. He married a girl from the same village and as a consequence has not become separated from his brothers by more than a few houses. Men frequently marry *tamazira* in an attempt to better their economic positions, but agnatic affiliants are less likely to have to do this. As for the young man, the girl had considerable attraction as the sole claimant to a large parcel of land, and there is reason to doubt that the *tamazira* marriage means much in this case.

These data demonstrate one thing conclusively: affiliation with descent groups is most usually a product of filiation, most usually by patrifiliation. "Filial kin rights" are by far more important as forms of entitlement to membership in descent groups than the more general rights by cognatic descent. For, even though it is not an absolute condition, only rights established by one's parents by conversion to vested interests and subsequently maintained or elaborated by oneself are in fact secure of recognition. To my knowledge, the Choiseulese have no single term or phrase which conventionally describes the pragmatic recognition of filial kin right. Perhaps, if there is indeed this lack of a term, it is because it is not one's parentage that matters so much as it is what one's parents have made of their rights and what one has continued to make of them. It is not so much the nature of the kin-tie that makes filial kin rights seem so important as it is the situational conditions which frequently make it difficult for a person to maintain effectively his ties with groups other than those of his father and mother. Where he can do this (that is, maintain the interests established by a linking ancestor rather than a parent) the situation is covered by the cognatic-descent idiom. But my usage of filial kin right describes a general practice and does not translate a Choiseulese concept. They may have no need to conceptualize this practice and do, I believe, derive some advantage from not doing so. They do not formally distinguish parents from ancestors, as anthropological analysts sometimes find convenient. To the Choiseulese then, filial kin rights are covered by or contained in the cognatic-descent idiom and may be given only a *de facto* recognition, thereby allowing the cognatic-descent idiom to remain useful in other ways because of its possible implications. The social significance or meaning of the cognatic-descent dogma must be sought elsewhere than in its literal presentation. I have suggested that much of its significance is to be found in its wider reference to the more general obligations and interests shared by kinsmen.

MARRIAGE

The *sinangge*, in any sense of the term, was and is an agamous unit—there is no cultural "rule" of endogamy or exogamy. The only explicit marriage regulation forbids marriage to a kinsman within first-cousin range, but, as I have already mentioned, there is not perfect agreement on this either. A few instances of first-cousin marriage, past and present, were recorded, and sanctions against such marriages seem minimal. A kinsman beyond first- (or second-) cousin range is, however, the preferred spouse, both ideologically and statistically. This is not simply because he, or she, is a kinsman but for other reasons as well.

The Choiseulese sometimes marry for "love" or personal attraction, and the sentiment is appreciated and given expression in songs and folklore. But more often a spouse is chosen with more practical interests in mind. A man wants a woman who will be a good worker in the house and gardens, will give birth to many children, and will not indulge in malicious gossip. A woman wants an industrious and courageous man who will treat her well and not fail to provide for her and the children. Parents prefer to find a suitable spouse for their child, but the more or less casual sexual relationships between young people often grow into marriage. Premarital sexual relationships are not openly encouraged but neither are they strongly forbidden, and sooner or later one relationship may begin to stabilize. When parents feel that love interests and other considerations coincide, there is no problem, but otherwise they may attempt to terminate the relationship. The lovers may be forbidden to see one another, sometimes by an "oath," and if they are "good" children they abide by parental decision. Since not all children are "good" children, elopements occur, and if it becomes public knowledge, as it usually does, the parents may do little about it because the shame precipitated by any further fuss is considered best avoided.

Ideally the brideprice is paid (the Choiseulese use the same term as for any purchase, *volivoli*, which is distinct from the term for an exchange, *vari sokasoka*) before the assumption of common domicile. In elopement, however, the brideprice must be arranged afterward, and the transaction is then often prolonged and difficult, for once the marriage is an accomplished fact the husband and his kinsmen try to get by with as small a payment as possible. An elopement may also occur if the parents bicker too long over the brideprice or other issues after they are more or less in agreement about the advisability of the marriage.

The amount of brideprice is said to depend upon what the girl's parents want, but it depends too upon what they can get. In the past, an "ordinary" girl was seldom worth more than three to five *kesa* unless she had an exceptionally good reputation as a worker. The daughter of a big-man was sometimes worth considerably more because of the potential value of the affinal bond to the parents of the groom. Initially the parents of the bride set a price, and parents of the groom always offer less, usually claiming that they are unable to pay so much. After some discussion, in which the girl's brothers may participate, the amount is usually set or the marriage called off. The brideprice is usually paid by the father of the groom directly to the father of the bride, each paying or receiving in his own name even though the *kesa* may be "borrowed" from others. If the parents are dead the *kesa* may come from any kinsman who can be persuaded to help, but it usually comes from a fellow member of the groom's descent group. One of the services a manager used to perform for his people was to help them with brideprice payments. They were not obliged to repay him in kind, but the service increased the obligatory nature of their allegiance to him.

The payment or receipt of brideprice is not conceived of as a descent-group affair, and it is not divided, much less in any particular way, among the kinsmen or descent group of the bride's father. He may use it to repay other debts, but he is not obliged to distribute it as brideprice among his kinsmen. The Choiseulese sometimes speak of *sinangge* paying and receiving brideprice, but what they have in mind is that such transactions are affairs between kinsmen of the bride and groom. An exchange of pigs and other foods accompanies payment of the *kesa* but does not occur at the same time. The bride's parents present baked pig and taro to the groom's parents, and this is known as "the pig that covers the footsteps" of the bride. This gift is a token of receipt of the brideprice and is not regarded as a direct exchange for it; yet it is also said to "kill" the brideprice, that is, it eliminates any further claims against the bride's kinsmen and any claims on their part upon the children of the marriage. At the same time the groom's kinsmen present to the bride's kinsmen "the pig that turns back the brush" along the path over which the girl was brought to them, a symbolic reference to the closure of any further claims against them. The mother of the bride is given one *ziku* (a shell bracelet) or *kesa*, in payment for the nourishment of the girl as a baby. In return the mother must pray to her recently deceased ancestors to help the girl's gardens prosper or to make her marriage generally successful by helping her to tend pigs and rear children. In a *tamazira* marriage none of these transactions take place.

Another form of marriage, fairly frequent today, is *busi volomo*, a "meaningless" marriage that is neither *tamazira* nor *nanggisi*. No brideprice is paid, and residence is usually patri-virilocal. There is some question whether *busi volomo* occurred in the past. Some informants insist that "before" no one would let a woman go without getting *kesa*, but *busi volomo* did happen occasionally, and I know of several instances in which the brideprice was never paid, although there was some discussion about it that ended in no agreement. It seems obvious that "ideally" no one would let a woman go without getting something in return. But conditions sometimes made the "ideal" (most desirable) impossible of attainment, as in some instances of elopement. The high frequency of *busi volomo* today is largely the result of the banning of brideprice payments. But the ban has not been entirely effective, and many people still believe strongly that it is foolish to let a woman go without getting *kesa* for her unless the marriage is "politically" or economically expedient. There is some evidence that *busi volomo* was common practice only in intragroup unions. Today men sometimes say that they let their daughters or sisters go "for nothing" so as to have an enduring claim upon any offspring—they express themselves in terms of enabling the offspring to "return" if they wish. Many men realize that *kesa* is nearly useless today and would prefer not to have a brideprice in the way as an argument against their claims on future occasions. In the past, however, *kesa* was highly meaningful, and giving women in marriage was one of the ways of obtaining it (see chap. 4). Thus even in intragroup unions the brideprice was often demanded, but it is recognized that it could have been forfeited in the name of group solidarity. Nevertheless, the wife-takers probably preferred to pay if they could as a matter of prestige.

Because of disagreements over whether brideprice should be paid and over the amounts, difficulties in arranging marriages are not uncommon. After the Choiseul Council was established it decreed that "one *kesa*" should be considered as equivalent to three Australian pounds and that the standard brideprice should be "three *kesa*" or nine pounds. The Council can hardly act against mission wishes and has refrained from ruling on whether the brideprice should be paid. However, there seems to have been general agreement that wife-takers should accede to the wishes of wife-givers and meet the demand when it is made. When a brideprice is paid today, the other transactions take place on a much reduced scale, if at all.

It is generally felt that it is best to marry a kinsman. The Choiseulese recognize, the various advantages and disadvantages of marrying kinsmen, but the most noted reason is that it is not good to give up a woman, or a man, who will go among non-kin or distant kin and "help other people." Indeed, the brideprice is sometimes spoken of as compensation for the loss of help and children caused by the surrender of a woman. Giving a woman or a man to another group is seen as being doubly disadvantageous. Not only is help lost but it is also given to others, and I have already noted the ambivalence of the Choiseulese to this. Giving a woman (or man) to distant kin or non-kin is especially to be avoided when it entails the removal of that person from the region, since this means effective removal from the interactional sphere.

Marriage within the descent group itself is not particularly stressed. Although there are advantages to intragroup marriage they may be outweighed by the disadvantages. Intragroup marriage does not expand the number of kinsmen who may exercise claims over the group's estate, but it limits the number of groups or kinsmen who may be called upon for assistance. However, marriage within the region strengthens the bonds between the groups of that region and at the same time keeps the marriage partners within useful range of the kinsmen of both. The effect of all of this, again clearly recognized by at least some Choiseulese, is to create a fairly complex network of kinship ties within the region or between already closely related descent groups, which enhances group and regional solidarity but also minimizes the number of kin-ties, and consequently coöperative relationships, between groups and especially those of different regions.

By encouraging marriage within the region or between cognate groups, a balance is struck between the expansion of the number of claimants to personal and group resources, on the one hand, and the extension of the kinship circle and cognatic descent categories, providing an increased range of aid, on the other. These various types of intra- and intergroup marriage had important consequences for intergroup and interregional relations (see chap. 4), and as a consequence of the various social changes that have occurred marriage still has great personal and familial significance but much less significance for intergroup relations.

The Choiseulese have many terms to express the various forms of marriage to kinsmen and the effects that such marriages have. Only a few are directly relevant here. Marriage to a kinsman is called *busi napu*, "to marry again"; *busi ule*, "to marry" and "return," is to marry within one's own descent group; *busi va ule*, "to cause to return by marriage," is when one marries a person from another group who is already potentially a member of one's descent group through cognatic descent. The marriage then "returns" a potential member to that descent group.

Firth (1957) and others have noted that the nonexogamous nature of "ambilateral" kin groups has correlates similar to those noted earlier for Choiseulese groups. Total endogamy would result in extreme conservation of goods and services, but it is not feasible because, the groups being small, the number of spouses available within a single group would be limited. It is also undesirable because it would result in severe restriction of the sphere from which aid must come. One does need kinsmen, and many of them, but because of the cognatic descent idiom it is not advisable to make too many marital unions between groups not already allied. Nonexogamy permits groups to make affinal alliances with other groups when it is to their advantage, but it also allows them a measure of control over the extension of claims to resources. Thus marital alliances could be used differentially to enlarge or maintain social ties, and marital alliances within the region made the best choice because they allowed the maintenance and intensification of kinship bonds that already existed, but they did not expand the sphere of obligation or at least did so only minimally. Although marital alliances were sometimes arranged with such considerations in mind, it should be noted too that intraregional marriages were the most probable form since the political and demographic situation minimized inter-regional contacts anyway.

Managers frequently married polygynously, usually in order to increase their spheres of influence and possible assistance. Increased obligation was the price they and their followers and descendants had to pay for the benefits he and they derived from having many wives and thereby many *ivana*, "brothers-in-law." Other men could have more than one wife, but the expense was often prohibitive, and unless a man was generally considered a manager polygynous marriage was presumptuous. Managers took women for wives by means other than "purchase" (see chap. 4) depending upon their powers of self-help—in other words, by their ability to frighten a woman's kinsmen into submission to their wills. Such marriages were not *busi volomo* because they usually resulted from some debt, fancied or real, and the women were taken in lieu of payment of the debts.

Available data on the exact frequency of various forms of marriage pertain to modern times. Modern conditions have considerably affected marital arrangements between groups, families, and individuals. Brideprice is forbidden to Methodists and Seventh Day Adventists, even though some Methodists still persist in the practice. Catholics, on the other hand, are free to pay and take brideprice, and as a consequence most marriages in the Varisi region, where three of the four villages are Catholic, require brideprice payments. Peaceful conditions possibly allow a greater frequency of marriage between regions, but even in the past there were normally some marriages, at least on the borders of regions and because of the movements from one region to another in time of intergroup conflict. One factor promoting inter-regional marriages today is mission affiliation. Some villages are surrounded by others with different mission affiliations, and the missions urge the people to marry persons of the same religious affiliation. Mission affiliation also may promote marriages between proximate villages if, as in the Varisi region, they are the only ones in a larger area which have the same mission affiliation.

Another difficulty concerns the incidence of *tamazira* marriages. Most informants insisted that there is more of it today than there was "before," for then only managers could get men to marry their "daughters" or "sisters" that way. But today, since every man is trying to be a manager at least in some sense, if one has a marriageable daughter or sister he may try to get a man to live with him rather than take *kesa* for her or let her go for nothing. In this way he can think of himself as an important man building a following. Some men who are relatively well off in coconuts can attract *tamazira* today, but others still refuse to let their daughters or sisters marry unless the men come to live with them. For this reason some girls marry relatively late, but others settle the question themselves by eloping, and some men marry *tamazira* with no intention of residing permanently with their wives' kinsmen. The higher rate of *tamazira* marriage today in Tepazaka reflects the generally more prosperous economic conditions in that region as compared with the Varisi region. In Tepazaka men are building followings by using their wealth in coconuts or good land as an attraction, but in Varisi, where coconut land is limited, this cannot be done.

Tables 9–11 express some of the information recorded about marital arrangements in the two regions today, again for the 103 adult male family heads in the two regions. No attempt has been made to extract similar information from genealogies, because they are neither sufficiently detailed nor complete. Partly this is my own fault for not being aware of the relevance of certain information until much of the census and genealogical data had been gathered and for not persisting when informants claimed ignorance of such things as the descent-group affiliations of grandparents or the type of marriage they contracted, and so on. But probably it would be impossible to get such information for most persons, and what could be obtained would be of dubious accuracy. Like genealogies, it would be slanted to favor the informant; furthermore, there is a tendency to proclaim any marriage of unknown type a brideprice marriage simply "because that was the usual way"—certainly the most prestigeous way.

Table 9 demonstrates a pronounced tendency to marry kinsmen. The exact nature of the relationship is known in about one-half of the marriages to a kinsman, and in many of the remainder it could be "discovered" if some effort were put into it. The difference between the two regions is partly attributable, again, to recent changes in settlement patterns. Many persons affiliated

TABLE 9

MARRIAGE TO KIN

	Tepazaka		Varisi	
	N	%	N	%
To Kin	42	81	35	69
To Non-kin	10	19	16	31

with descent groups in Tepazaka are descendants of members of groups that dispersed and no longer exist as discrete units, and many of their kinsmen through those *sinangge* are now living in other regions. Thus even when they marry a person from another region it is more likely that they marry a kinsman.

Table 11 assesses the frequency of intragroup marriage and requires explanation. It shows clearly that only one-fourth of all marriages are to persons outside of one's own region. This does not mean that all other marriages are between persons belonging only to *sinangge* domiciled within the region. For instance, the rows labeled "Same Village (only)" and "Same Region (only)" include marriages contracted between persons living in the same village or region, but only sometimes are they marriages between parties both of whom "belong" to neighboring descent groups. In other cases they are secondary marriages of, say, women brought into the village or region and subsequently widowed only to remarry within the same village or region, and several marriages are to a temporary resident or guest of a member of a local *sinangge*. These figures, then, represent the frequency of choice of a spouse from the persons locally available.

It is not easy to separate the factors of kinship and proximity as they exert an influence upon the choice of a spouse. Since

TABLE 10

TYPE OF MARRIAGE

Type	Tepazaka		Varisi	
	N	%	N	%
Nanggisi	7	14	39	76
Tamazira	11	23	6	12
Busi volomo	33	63	6	12

spouses are usually chosen because of personal characteristics, not group membership, persons tend to choose their spouses or to have them chosen for them from people they know well through frequent interaction. But the tendency to marry kinsmen is not solely caused by the fact that spouses are chosen from persons locally available who just happen to be kinsmen; it is caused at least partly by a stated preference for marriage to a kinsman, a preference founded on the recognition of the advantages discussed earlier.

About 30–40 per cent of all marriages are between kinsmen related within second- to fourth-cousin range, and some marriages between reputed kin might also fall within that range. Again, this is only to be expected as a result of preference for

TABLE 11

INTRAGROUP MARRIAGE

	Tepazaka		Varisi	
	N	%	N	%
Same descent group (major or minor)	14	27	10	20
Same village (only)	16	31	9	17
Same region (only)	9	17	22	43
Different region	13	25	10	20

marriage to a kinsman and choice of a spouse from persons locally available. As far as I could determine there is no conscious preference for marriage to persons related within second- to fourth-cousin range, and the incidence is probable related to the correlation between closeness of kinship and closeness of residence.

Finally, some comment on the row "Same Descent Group (major or minor)" in Table 11. In Tepazaka most of those marriages are between persons from adjacent villages and, therefore, between branches of one major *sinangge*, but in Varisi they are almost entirely between members of the same descent group living also in the same village. This is so largely because in the

Varisi region all branches of one major *sinangge* are now resident in the same village, whereas in Tepazaka major *sinangge* are often dispersed with branches or descent groups in different villages. This situation is the result of fairly recent changes in settlement patterns. These figures alone do not give an adequate idea of the extent to which intramarriage restricts the number of claimants to personal and group resources since marriage between persons of the same cognatic descent category would have that effect too. Thus any marriage between kinsmen has the effect of limiting further expansion of the cognatic descent categories and kinship circles, but the extent to which it does depends upon the closeness of the relationship between the marriage partners. The more closely related one's parents are to one another the more confined is one's kinship circle and one's property interests, and the constricting effect of marriage to kin is greatest when marriage partners come from the same descent group. This is so because, as I have shown, it is filial kin right which is most usually the operative criterion in determining one's *de facto* rights and interests. It can be only a rough estimate, but probably forty per cent or more of all marriages are between persons having at least one parent each from the same cognatic descent category. This means that the offspring of those marriages have their potentials for exercising claims against cognatic descent categories or groups reduced by at least one-fourth or perhaps much more, depending upon the degree of intramarriage in their parental backgrounds. Theoretically it should be possible to determine for each individual the number of descent groups against which he has the nominal right to make claims of various sorts simply by extracting from him the relevant genealogical information. But this would be an extremely dubious procedure productive of ambiguous and unreliable information. As I pointed out earlier, such knowledge is not always active, and therefore it would not come immediately to mind. Furthermore, people are often poorly informed about the descent group and cognatic-descent-category affiliations of their ancestors, even for some of their grandparents. More important is the fact that the number known is not really important because other considerations are the crucial factors in determining potential for affiliation and because the claims of kinship are primarily exercised within the region, often regardless of *sinangge* ties, and depend far more upon the es-

tablishment of personal obligations than upon genealogical specifications.

Intragroup marriage does frequently reduce the number of
groups against which an individual may make claims. But it is
only one of the many factors having that effect. Although the
Choiseulese sometimes think of marital arrangements in such
terms, it seems to me that they more often view marriage as a
means of creating or maintaining alliances between social units at
various levels. Much is often made of the fact that marriages
between descent groups bring those groups "close together," and
in at least one case careful count has been kept of the number of
marriages between two descent groups. It is viewed as an index
of their friendliness towards one another. In keeping with their
dogmas relating to "following the father's side" it is often argued
that "it is women marrying about who bring groups together" by
creating overlap between their cognatic descent categories. It is
true that marriage may make and keep "friends," but it is also
true that it may precipitate quarrels and lead to conflicts between
groups, as over the payment or repayment of brideprice. Then too,
sexual relations with another man's wife is a very grave offense
against that man, and he had the right to kill the culprit or one
of his kinsmen to avenge injured prestige. Such revenge could
lead to war (see chap. 4), but in these affairs the wife's descent
group did not take part. However, a man did have the right to
kill an adulterous wife, particularly if she was an habitual offender. Her descent group could avenge her death if it were powerful
enough and if it were felt that the killing was not justified.
Quarrels arose more often over the disposition of children or
sorcery accusations. I have already noted that in-marrying women
often are suspect of sorcery against personnel of the descent
group "core," but it may be that they are innocent and the accusation is a convenient means of displacing hostility that might
more accurately be directed against a descent-group mate.

It was noted that divorce is rare, and this seems to have been
true in the past too. Today divorce is difficult to secure because,
though most marriages begin by "custom," they are almost
always confirmed by a formal church rite too. Protectorate law
allows for the dissolution of "custom marriages" by "customary"
means (definition of this is left to the discretion of the native
courts), but those solemnized by the church can be dissolved

only by court action at the highest Protectorate level. Pragmatically, this is virtually impossible for any islander to manage. However, the government officers are lax in enforcing marital arrangements, and in two cases that came to my attention men simply deserted unwanted wives and took others, leaving the original wives to fall back on their kinsmen for support. Both original wives had become physically disabled. The actions were regarded as scandalous contempt of good Christian behavior, but little more than talk ensued. Local headmen reported the incidents to touring government officers who, on several occasions, reprimanded the men and threatened punishment if they did not return to their wives. To my knowledge, nothing more has come of either case. In another instance, one prominent manager became enamored of a widow living in a nearby village and announced he was going to leave his wife. The wife fled immediately to the house of another influential man in the village and asked his assistance in getting her and the children back to her natal village on the other side of the island. This would have been problematic since she had had practically nothing to do with those people for a great many years. He intervened and persuaded the husband to postpone his actions, for, he argued, the scandal would hurt the village and surely threaten the husband's status as an influential man. Some other people took it upon themselves to inform the local European missionary who refused to tolerate the suggestion of divorce and punished the husband by restricting his church activities for a year.

The sociological census uncovered only one other case of divorce—sometime in the 1920's—which was by "custom" and occurred because, it is said, the wife was lazy and inclined to malicious gossip.

Women disputing with their husbands may be supported by the husband's kinsmen, but for the sake of harmonious relations between husband's and wife's kin groups women are strongly discouraged by both parties from calling upon their own kinsmen for support, and it is not considered their privilege to intervene. I was told of incidents in which women fled their husbands because of maltreatment by them or their kinsmen, but these women were forcibly returned by their own kin. The managers of the parties concerned arbitrated and encouraged the disputants to be more restrained in their actions lest there be trouble between the groups. Informants did stress that once the brideprice transactions had been completed people were reluctant to dissolve a marriage, partly because there would be ill feelings over the need to demand the return of the *kesa*, and the wife's kin could find many excuses for refusing to return it. But I have no data on how the amount of *kesa* exchanged might have influenced such actions.

There is some ambivalence here: Strictly speaking, marriages were not formally contracted by descent groups, yet they did implicate groups in one another's affairs. Managers therefore took it upon themselves to discourage marriages they thought inadvisable and continued to take an interest in harmonious relations afterwards.

Considering some arguments put forth to explain marital stability or instability, especially in Africa, the low divorce rate on Choiseul appears problematic. A woman's kin continue to take an active interest in her and her children; as noted, it is sometimes said that the husband's group is only "looking after her." Marriage does not formally curtail any of her interests in her natal group, and although the type of marital contract nominally affects the formal status of her offspring, pragmatically their actions with regard to descent-group membership may be little influenced by such considerations. What a man seems to acquire most unambiguously in marrying a woman is an exclusive sexual interest in her. Nominally, offspring are his too if he has paid the brideprice, yet this right is easily compromised.

Statements to the effect that it is the circulation of women that unites the people of different groups and that the husband's group only "looks after" the woman for her own group would seem to indicate that marriage in this society is (or was) partly a form of alliance between two bodies of kin, and the strong emphasis on solidary and harmonious relations between brothers-in-law confirms this. The presence of offspring further united the bodies of kin and their constituent groups by giving them a kinsman in common (through the cognatic descent idiom).

Chapter 4

The Larger Society:
Intergroup Relations

The basic residential, proprietary, and political segments of Choiseulese society have been described so far in terms of a "descent group model," and this is indeed how the Choiseulese present them to the ethnographer and talk of them among themselves. Today the descent ideology is ascendant, but in the past it was only one element in their operation, for these groups were more strongly proprietary and political units than they are now after much of their operational significance has been lost. Thus the social significance of the descent ideology has to be understood in the political and economic context which the ideology was professed to define and regulate. This chapter stresses the political, and especially the intergroup, aspects of *sinangge* operation. In particular, attention is focused upon the interdependence of the big-man complex and the descent-group aspects of the *sinangge*.

MANAGERS

Each descent group is said to have a *batu*, big-man or manager, who is its principal leader. According to the dogmas, managerial status "crosses" from father to elder son. However, a group may contain several men who are spoken of as *batu* and still others, adult, able-bodied men, with families, who are called *kazigarata*. All these men, regardless of their descent statuses have a right to a voice in group affairs, yet some are entitled to a "stronger" voice than others—stronger in that their opinions deserve and demand greater consideration. The man who meets the genealogical qualifications of primogeniture and agnatic status is known as the "true *batu*" or the *batu* "who originates in the land" (*batu ununa pua*). Other *batu* are *batu sokele*, with the implication that they are "almost but not quite" true *batu*. Thus *batu* implies not only formal qualifications but also behavioral attributes. These latter qualities are those required to be a good "manager" (a term which I have borrowed from Burridge 1961 [1]). A *batu* in the fullest sense, then, is one who meets both the genealogical and practical qualifications.

The Choiseulese recognize that in some situations the dogma cannot readily be applied and provide for such contingencies. A manager with no sons is succeeded by his brother's son or, failing him, a sister's son or even an adoptee, and more or less in that order of preference. However, as noted before, the Choiseulese are not addicted to rules, and, in fact, anyone who is a descent-group member is eligible to be the *batu* of the group, and the possibilities are numerous. The essential attributes of a manager are not the formal qualifications but rather managerial abilities. In the past these abilities were particularly demonstrable in the realm of economic and political relations with other men, both within and between groups. The common Melanesian pattern of the acquisition of prestige through competition and public gift exchange prevailed here too, and no man could be a manager in the fullest sense unless he were markedly successful in competition with other men, even those within his own descent group. Even the formally most qualified men had to earn renown in the political sphere with which to back up the presumed powers acquired by formal succession.

The single most fundamental fact about Choiseulese society seems to have been that it was without formal juridical institutions: Each man could attain and maintain his interests only through other men and only on terms either of force or agreement. He had to become a big-man himself or acquire the protection of another man who was one by allying with him and rendering as-

---

[1] Among the Tangu, managers operate "without the aid of an office" (Burridge 1961: 74); therefore my use of Burridge's term is not meant to suggest an exact parallel between the big-men of Tangu and those of Choiseul. Certainly, some interesting parallels exist; for an enlightening general discussion of big-men in Melanesia see Sahlins 1963.

sistance in the realization of his ambitions. The resources through which big-man status was realized were sufficiently scarce that only a relatively few men could succeed, but this did not keep many from trying. Managers, through their control of property (especially *kesa*) and their ability to distribute it and then acquire more in its stead in the course of allying with or opposing other managers and their followings, protected themselves and their followers or allies from the depredations of others. Prestige and proprietary rights were thus closely intertwined and both were sources of conflict. Even agnatic affiliants were divided among themselves by their shared but not necessarily "common" interests in the same property and by the political ambitions of one another, which could be realized only by control of their common property.

The emphasis or value placed upon prestige motivated men to compete with one another in various ways. Indeed, the Choiseulese seem to view interpersonal relations as typically competitive, or at least they often so interpret the motives of others (including the Europeans with whom they must now interact). A characteristic retort is, "Do not try to 'down' me!" Men competed, and often violently, for both prestige and the property through which it was realized, not simply for prestige and property but ultimately for the power and security they conferred. Others helped them for similar reasons. It follows that allegiance was not given on the basis of some abstract "principle" but of self-interest as seen in terms of certain values. Kinship and kin-group affiliation opposed as well as allied persons, and a group was seldom a monolithic structuring of the undivided and common allegiances of those who comprised its membership at any one time. Yet in the absence of formal juridical institutions, the necessity of attaining one's interests through others forced some coöperation and temperance of self-interest, and groups managed to persist even in the face of the divided allegiances of their members.

With this much of a preliminary outline, this situation is now discussed in greater detail with particular attention to the interplay of these two aspects of *sinangge* organization: the competition for managerial status and followings, worked out largely in the realm of politics and intergroup relations, and the conceptualization of them as descent groups.

First, however, some explanation of the use of "prestige" is in order. As Nadel (1951: 171) noted, "prestige is no doubt one of the vaguest terms used in sociological description." However, I do not wish to be ambiguous. Following Nadel, prestige here describes a quality attributed to individuals or groups which differs from rank or status in being less formalized, namely an "acquired pre-eminence of individuals over one another" or "some acquired command over one another's actions." Prestige, unlike rank, is voluntary, without specified sanctions to enforce recognition, and diffusely accorded to individuals and groups.

To rephrase Nadel (1951: 172), prestige, so understood, is visible in the deference shown to an individual (or group) in the readiness of others to support him in varying ways, to take his advice, imitate his example, or merely express their admiration or approval. The influence of prestige is diffuse, visible generally rather than confined to "specified contexts of activity." The Choiseulese express the possession of prestige or the desire for it by saying of a man or group, "he stands out" or "he wants to stand out." *Vitovitongo*, the reduplicative form of "name," or "fame," may express the same idea.

Prestige was accorded to men and groups who were successful in the most important intergroup activities, such as vengeance warfare and gift exchange. Success in these activities required such qualities as "cleverness," "ability," "power," and "wealth." Each manager had to demonstrate his own worth before and while "in office." If he did not he would find himself gradually superseded by another who had earned the favor of descent-group members. The Choiseulese say that in effect the "people" sometimes chose their manager by "discussion" (*vatovato*), a term which is also applied to the more or less formal discussion of particular issues among descent-group members. To make someone a *batu* was to *va batua*, but there were no formal ceremonies of installation. Therefore, recognition as a manager, and even as *the* manager, came about gradually and informally; it was the product of a gradually developed understanding within the descent group. It is said that the people would discuss the matter informally, come to a consensus, and then eventually appoint one of their number to communicate to the chosen party their wish for him to be their manager, but consensus sometimes probably came after the assumption of political predominance within the group.

Becoming a manager was essentially a process of acquiring wealth *and* a reliable following. One acquired wealth, primarily *kesa*, in a variety of ways, detailed below, and one acquired a following by maintaining one's wealth while at the same time using it to the benefit of others, most usually members of one's own descent group. A man who did this without meeting the formal genealogical qualifications was known as a *batu sokele*, but so long as there was no serious contender with better formal qualifications as well as the pragmatic ones, a *batu sokele* could operate as though he were *the* manager in the fullest sense. There are cases even today in which a man who is a nonagnate is generally recognized as the manager even though there are men more fully qualified in the formal sense. I was told that in the past both men would have been given deferential treatment but the formally qualified individual would have been only the titular leader while the people would have depended on the *batu sokele* for true leadership. Ideally, both men should have coöperated in the interests of the group as a whole. Informants differed about the consequences of such a situation for future succession: Some maintained that the son of the "true" manager would be the next one, others felt that the son of the *batu sokele*, or some other man, would succeed him. It will become apparent that either could happen, but formal and *de facto* status as manager would hardly have remained separate for long in the indigenous situation.

The deferential symbols of prestige were due to a man with the formal qualifications whether he exhibited managerial abilities or not. Yet, lacking the abilities, he also would have lacked the means to sanction nonconformity with the "rules." Furthermore, since residential groupings in the indigenous context were relatively unstable, a capable man could found his own group and establish a formally qualified line within it. Such possibilities are discussed below.

A manager's prestige was demonstrated in interpersonal interaction by various signs of deference. He was addressed as *batu*, and in a deferential manner, but at times he had to appear to be deferential in order not to seem too concerned with his own interests as opposed to those of his followers. Other people could not stand or sit higher than his head and might have to crouch before him in order to avoid this. His person and possessions were, more so than those of other men, particularly *tabo* to women, and to touch or walk over either constituted a grave offense and injury to his pride which he had to avenge. His house had a special door through which he alone might pass.

In the competition for wealth, power, and prestige, the sons of incumbent managers had the initial advantage. Managers often groomed their successors by taking promising young men, and especially their own sons, and encouraging them to develop the necessary qualities, instilling in them the attitudes necessary to a manager, teaching them practical knowledge, and, perhaps most importantly, showing them their *kesa* and assisting them in acquiring *kesa* of their own. The manager then made it generally known that it was his intention for that man to succeed him. Sons inherited their father's wealth or knew the whereabouts of descent-group wealth in their father's care. Fathers usually favored their sons, though I recorded a couple of cases in which a younger son was "chosen" rather than the eldest son. Even as youngsters, the sons of managers were deferred to by their father's followers. Sons of managers were known as *batu voru*, "new" or "young managers," and they were treated respectfully. The wife of a *batu* was given the same considerations, and an offense to a manager's wife or child was equivalent to an offense to him. A son who came of age while his father was still active was often delegated limited responsibilities and acted in his father's name on important occasions. I heard no accounts nor saw any indications of strife between father and son over managerial position, but I cannot positively say that there were none. The early delegation of responsibility to sons may have obviated such disputes.

It is hardly surprising that among my informants those who maintained most strongly and consistently that sons always succeed their fathers as managers were themselves managers with sons to succeed them. In contrast, other informants went so far as to say that "any wealthy man is a *batu*," basing their view on the fact that anyone with wealth had some power to mobilize self-help. But not all men with wealth used it liberally to support their descent groups and other kinsmen. Some men "kept things to themselves alone" or "thought only of themselves," and therefore were accorded less prestige; people were less willing to render allegiance to them. If they used their wealth in behalf of their kinsmen they gained prestige, which was conferred interpersonally by addressing them as *batu* and rendering them respectful behavior. The terms and symbols of deference could be rendered without the substance.

Thus the agnatic genealogical qualification derived its significance primarily from managerial status. A lineal descendant of the descent-group founder had a prior moral claim to the allegiance of group members, but he was effectively followed only in the presence of demonstrated ability. An ambitious man was better situated if he was agnatically affiliated, for the dogmas then worked for him even though it was possible to succeed in one's ambitions in spite of the dogmas. When the dogmas ran against him it was not so much that he was working against a "principle" as it was that he was working against other men who might have been in a position to use the dogmas in their favor. When the competition was for the allegiances of other men within, or more or less associated with, a particular group or for control of the property of a particular group, then the dogmas could have become useful to one of the competitors, indicating his presumed inherent worthiness for the position. But it was up to the individual to give his claim substance through his actions for the group. Thus when the conflict or competition was between groups, genealogical considerations were of even less importance. The ability to assume responsibility and to direct men and their affairs was what made a manager. Of course, managerial status was derived from the realm of intergroup relations, but it did not remain confined to such "specified contexts of action." Prestige so derived carried over into other realms of action or social life.

A manager's primary duty is to "care for" his descent group and also his other kinsmen. In the past, he felt compelled to do this because only in their continued allegiance did the title have any meaning. By fulfilling his duties and by doing so in competition with other managers, a man built his own reputation as someone to be reckoned with. This in turn provided his group with security as others came to know his powers.

As the word "manager" indicates, the duties of a *batu* may be described as managerial. He is in no sense a "chief," exercising great authority with formal sanctions; he is *primus inter pares* among the "important men" of the descent group. Acting as the custodian of corporate property—land, groves, and *kesa*—as the principal preserver of a genealogical charter, estate boundaries, and significant knowledge relating to events of special importance to the group, such as the contraction of debts, its own and those of other groups towards it, the manager is the principal representative of the group in intergroup affairs. In affairs of concern solely to the group itself he is the one who organizes discussion and who should have the most significant voice in what may be decided. In many activities he is the leader, signaling when they shall begin and ordering their progress, but never ordering people about.

The manager holds meetings to discuss group affairs, such as the entrance of would-be members; the relative rights of members; whether to involve the group in the affairs of another group when assistance was requested; whether to acquire a wife for some member and how much to pay for her; whether to extend aid to nonmembers; the arrangements entailed in feasting and *kesa* exchanges; in the past, whether to take revenge or go to war. On the occasion of such discussions and on other occasions the manager must be a "strong talker"; he must not order or bully, but he must manage to effect favorably the actions of others by manipulating their sentiments and obligations toward him. He must, in short, play upon his prestige. The extent to which he can do so depends upon his oratorical and political skills and on the strength of his prestige in his own group and in other groups. In relation to other groups a manager exercises only influence and no formal authority. His authority is confined to his own group, but his reputation and a respect for his abilities, or (again, in the past) a fear of them, spreads to others and then exercises a sort of feed-back upon members of his own group who give him greater deference as his more general reputation grows. The amount of influence a manager exercised within his own descent group was, therefore, directly dependent upon his influence in intergroup affairs.

A manager must be industrious, never tiring of physical or mental labors. He is not exempt from subsistence activities; in fact, when this role was more important than now, it greatly expanded the subsistence activities in which he and his family were engaged. Feasting required large surpluses of foodstuffs, especially taro, pig, and nuts. Therefore, a manager had to maintain extensive gardens, but he had plenty of help in maintaining them. Part of the help came from his several wives (some managers in the distant and perhaps mythological past are reputed to have had as many as ten or fifteen) and the *tamazira* he acquired by foregoing brideprice for his "sisters" and "daughters." But the bulk of assistance consisted in the efforts of descent-group members working in his gardens. A manager had to maintain gardens much larger than those of other men because he was often called upon to provide hospitality to visitors, but when he prepared for a feast he maintained especially large gardens and periodically organized his followers to work in them.

Managers also exercised religious functions in relation to their groups. They often "kept" a *bangara* or "god" who assisted in the maintenance of group welfare both directly and indirectly by protecting the group in general and by assisting the manager to do the same job. The *bangara* and *manuru* (ancestral ghosts) assisted and protected group members principally by giving them good fortune and occasionally by inflicting direct damage upon enemies. For instance, some *bangara* are said to have exercised an influence over sharks and crocodiles, and one could pray and offer sacrifices to them to send such agents against one's enemies. More commonly, however, *bangara* and *manuru* assisted directly by giving *mana*, which the Choiseulese describe as "something that makes a person's body live," that is, makes it active and strong. *Mana* is a personal power, bestowed by the gods or ancestral spirits (now the Christian God), which maintains a man's success and becomes apparent in that success. Following the proper observances towards the spirits and gods—"feeding" them, giving sacrifices—assured the bestowal of *mana*, but *mana* was maintained and grew through enterprise and doing good for one's descent group.

A manager's interest in his descent group continued even after his death. Most descent groups cremate their dead, and the ceremonies attendant to cremation were especially elaborate for deceased managers. Ashes and partly burned bones were preserved and placed in simple pottery vessels, but a special effort was made to preserve intact the skulls of managers. These were placed in special shrines and given extra attention as the physical embodiments of particularly potent ancestral spirits. The spirits of deceased managers were thought to "sit in assistance" when the "important men" of the group held a discussion. They also went to war with the group, giving them good luck by causing the spears of the enemy to miss their marks. They also attended gift exchanges and helped living managers play their roles successfully.

Thus a kind of mystical relationship existed between the manager and his descent group, but the Choiseulese now at least seem far more aware of the practical relationship that obtained between the two, and they are also aware that a manager's obligations to himself were closely bound up with his obligations to his descent group. He had to be careful, in his own interests and those of his group, to maintain his status. Managers were proud and careful of their prerogatives and the deference that should have been shown them. They were quick to take offense lest they be "downed," that is, allow others to insult them freely and thereby show sign of weakness, an open invitation to attack or general misuse. Managers had to maintain their prestige in order to protect themselves and their groups from the depredations of other managers and their groups who were, it was thought, ever ready to take revenge or elevate their own status by "downing" another.

One of a manager's principal concerns and obligations was, then, to strive for wealth and prestige. Ideally, it was not only for himself or even primarily for himself that he did this but rather for what success enabled him to do for his descent group. Generosity was a prime managerial virtue, partly because the wealth with which a manager was generous was not "his" in any absolute sense to begin with, but also because wise handling, and not holding, of wealth was an essential managerial task. No selfish man was a "true" manager, even though through intimidation he could earn the deference of some. However, mere possession of the symbols does allow some men to make the pretense of managerial status and to exercise a limited control over the actions of others. This is especially true today now that the economic situation allows some men to accumulate more wealth than others, and largely without the help of others. The termination of violent intergroup conflict has lessened the essential dependence of men upon one another, and it has also made impossible the validation of managerial status. This will become apparent in the discussion of intergroup conflict and competition.

Upon extreme provocation, managers could arrange to have a person killed, or so it is said. Normally, homicide of members of the same descent group was considered thoroughly reprehensible, and if it was considered necessary the manager might have had to give *kesa* to an outsider to do the killing. I collected no actual instances of such events, and I suspect that matters seldom went so far within the group. The unwanted party probably would have recognized the deteriorating situation and would have left. Furthermore, a "good" manager protected his people rather than terrorized them and could not legitimately take such matters into his own hands. The "important men" of the group would confer and agree to have a troublesome group member killed if, for instance, he had himself killed a fellow member; an "outsider" could have been hired to do the job or an "insider" could have been delegated the responsibility. In the latter instance, informants say, a close kinsman would have done the killing in order to avoid any further vengeance. Sometimes, however, the killing of a group mate was justifiable, as in the case of adultery, and counter-vengeance was not publicly justifiable.

This brings up the matter of internal politics again. A manager's influence within his own group was related in a complex fashion to the relative powers of other big-men or ambitious men within it. Men of ambition were somewhat limited in their actions by the presence of a "true" *batu*. They could not too actively court the allegiances of his followers without arousing his jealousy, but if careful they could use his friendship to enhance their own statuses. A *batu* needed powerful allies, but it was in his own interest to see that they did not get power at his expense. He could permit their ambitions some expression by minor deference to them or by delegating them limited tasks in his own name. Thus an ambitious man could "talk strong" about group affairs, but he had to be careful to express himself in terms of group interests. But more of this later in relation to the segmentation process.

As the Choiseulese put it, the manager "covered his people like an umbrella," and they in turn were "only his hands." Groups took their prestige from their managers, contributing to managerial prestige by supporting and benefiting from that prestige in return. Consequently managers were (and still are, though to a lesser degree) sensitive to the needs and desires of "their people," but their own needs, as perceived by themselves, sometimes were at odds with the needs of their people, as their people perceived them. Thus skill at "impression management" (Goffman 1958) was a prime requisite to managerial status. For instance, a manager could acquire renown and, perhaps more important, *kesa* by affording protection to persons who were not members of his descent group. Yet his followers sometimes feared the consequences of getting entangled in the affairs of others, particularly a war. The manager should have deferred to the wishes or fears of his followers to avoid angering them and thereby lowering his own prestige, and theoretically "he could not do anything the people do not want." But, on the other hand, he knew that "his people" were dependent upon him and his renown, and this dependence could facilitate his ignoring of their wishes despite the possible consequences. This is not to say that managers could openly flout the wishes of their followers; there was no surer road to disaster, for followers wielded the ultimate sanction of changing their allegiances. A manager's freedom of action depended upon his power and the extent to which he had managed to isolate it from dependence upon particular individuals. But, in any event, it was always best if he could foster the impression of acting only in the interest of his descent group. More than mere tact was required to manipulate situations to meet one's needs, to balance "public" and "private" understandings, to accommodate conflicting interests and principles while seeming to give allegiance to the higher principle of group welfare.

Informants described the maneuvers of several eminent managers in the past in this way. One of them was Madoko, manager of the Gabili descent group, who died around 1917. Madoko was widely respected and drew to his group many people other than descendants of its founder. Many came to him for protection and contributed to his wealth in the process. He also attempted to establish a reputation as a peacemaker during the early missionization period. Several instances were cited in which he was offered *kesa* to execute someone who had fled to him for protection. Some of his followers reportedly wanted him to do so, but he refused and instead accepted *kesa* from the fleeing party and protected him from the depredations of his enemies. The dissenters argued they would all be killed, but this did not happen; for Madoko's reputation and his past alliances and continuing friendship with other more powerful groups were such that others refrained from carrying out their threats.

The granting of prestige to a man afforded him a degree of freedom of action; at least it assured him of the ready support of some men. But the continuance of this support demanded that he meet certain obligations and responsibilities towards those who granted the prestige. Thus the Choiseulese exerted some control over the actions of others, and especially their managers, by granting prestige. Despite what "good" managers should have done, some abused their powers. Like some other Melanesians with similar political systems (see, e.g., Sahlins 1963), the Choiseulese maintain that a manager who abused his powers could be disposed of by violence. This seems plausible, yet I recorded no actual instances of it, unless the case of Zale (see below, pp. 227 ff.) can be so considered. Rampant abuse of power was probably checked by the growth of factions within the descent group. If there were others who posed a serious threat to the manager's powers he had to be extremely careful in the exercise of the more extreme sanctions available to him.

THE SEGMENTATION PROCESS

Chapter 2 discussed how the Choiseulese conceive of the segmentation of descent groups in genealogical terms. But segmentation did not follow systematically from genealogical considerations, nor were the other factors giving rise to factionalism and consequently segmentation or fission [2] such that one could predict the genealogical lines along which they would occur. Barnes (1962) has contrasted this situation with that occurring in many African societies where division takes place regularly between certain classes of kinsmen, for example, brothers having the same father but different mothers, or between mother's brothers and sister's sons. In those societies, the formal distribution of the interests involved in segmentation contains the seeds of future discontent. This predictability of the lines of cleavage leads Barnes to speak of this variety of segmentation as "chronic" as opposed to "catastrophic," a word which he would apply to the form of segmentation processes in many New Guinea Highland societies. There, factionalism and segmentation persistently occur and are in this

---

[2] "Segmentation" here refers to both the condition of internal division and the process of division. "Fission," on the other hand, refers to the extreme form of segmentation in which a social group becomes divided into two or more distinct groups, no longer united by kinship (cf. Barnes 1955: 20).

sense "chronic" too; but that segmentation will occur is predictable only in the most general terms, and when, where, and exactly how or between whom is not nearly as predictable as in many African societies.

This, I think, was true of Choiseulese society too and seems to have been a corollary of the ambiguous relationship between the not too clearly defined formal distribution of interests in property and the political processes. This relationship has to be understood in terms of the general ecological and political circumstances prevailing in the past (as Barnes attempts to do for the Highlands). Again, I can deal here with only the political factors. These, however, were not altogether different from those obtaining in many African societies where wealthy or capable men gather followings.

If there were ambitious men within his descent group, it is said that a manager was pleased, since they represented additions to his power. They could help him to take *kesa*. But he sometimes saw them as a threat, for as one man "went up," others "went down." Usually he tried to avoid open breaches with them for obvious reasons. Factions could form within the group when various members formed more or less close alliances with different managers or would-be managers either along kinship lines or merely to seek advantage. A faction could become formalized as a branch of the original descent group, and as such it could continue to reside with the larger whole and not seek to establish a separate identity. It was given a "share" in the larger estate and could choose to establish a separate hamlet upon it, but so long as the faction remained formally with the larger unit it was obligated to participate in group activities and could be identified by outsiders with the larger unit. Branch status, then, might mean little except an addition to the prestige of the head of that faction who could then consider himself a manager with his own land ("grove"). Leaders of such factions could be called managers, but each was still the "hand" of the "big manager" and only "helped him to speak." He, the "lesser" manager, could acquire his own *kesa* and use it to gain further wealth, but he could not legitimately operate on his own in relation to other groups. His actions could be considered by outsiders to represent the actions of the larger unit.

Branches could also break away from the larger whole and

"stand on their own," that is, become effectively autonomous units. Autonomy was formalized with a *kelo* (a feast) and *kesa*, both given to the manager of the truncal segment. This *kelo* was called *kelo kaesi*, but if a *kelo* were difficult, if the resources were not available, then the presentation of a baked pig is said to have been sufficient to mark the formal separation. It is said also that formal separation was not necessarily the result of a quarrel— the manager of the segment could have wished merely to have his independence of action—but separation did often result from jealousy between "brothers." As noted previously, Bose, the erstwhile manager of Kesi and a man of great repute, is said to have divided his estate among his "sons" specifically to reduce jealousy among them. But his eldest "son," who took his place as the manager of the whole of Kesi, was reputedly jealous of the growing status of his "younger brothers" and, it is said, gave them cause for offense by ordering them to move their hamlets from one place to another "for no good reason." Some of them resented his actions, presented him with *kelo kaesi*, and established their formal autonomy so that he could not order them to move about. They did not make a full breach with him—"there was no anger"—but they did force him to concede their status.[3]

Formal separation was not to be undertaken lightly. The would-be manager of the new branch had to have sufficient following to make separation meaningful and sufficient *kesa* to make the *kelo kaesi* and then support his followers too. In short, he should have been able to take care of his own affairs, to "stand alone." But despite formal separation, the branches (then actually separate descent groups) usually remained closely allied with truncal units, and continued to depend upon one another. Autonomy was only "more or less," not absolute or, in formal terms, there was only segmentation, not fission. In ordinary domestic affairs the distinctiveness of the branch descent group was rela-

---

[3] These orders to "move about" are said to have stemmed from jealousy of "higher places"; the sites upon which the "younger brothers" lived were higher and more strategically placed than the site of the "elder brother," and he was therefore jealous of them. There is also some indication that a higher location represented greater prestige for those living there. It may well be that the whole tale of Bose's actions, and those of his reputed "sons," is simple mythology, a "just so" explanation of the way things are today or were not so long ago. If so, I cannot say what did in fact happen.

tively complete, as much as the overlap of membership between cognate groups allowed. As an independent unit it was in a stronger position to deny usage rights to members of other segments which were, or were not, independent too. Technically, however, it would remain at the aid of other segments and share resources freely, but its *de facto* status and power allowed it to interpret its obligations as seen fit by itself.

Members of cognate descent groups sometimes refer to one another as of the same *sinangge*, indicating the major *sinangge*, and it was noted earlier (chap. 3) how, on some occasions, persons may identify themselves with the major *sinangge* and say that *it* is what "matters" in contrast to its component units. Nevertheless, it is recognized that the aspiration of each branch was to "stand alone" and not to need the aid of cognate units. Minor descent groups entered into and completed transactions with other descent groups, even cognate groups, segments of the same major *sinangge*. Their goal was the same goal shared by all descent groups—to gain in status and repute by competing with one another largely in transactions involving exchanges of *kesa*. But in a crisis it was not always possible to retain independence, and a branch might have had to call for aid from or render aid to cognate groups on the nominal basis of common membership in a more inclusive unit. For instance, cognate groups were most likely to be called upon to *bona* for one another; that is, if a descent group could not meet its debts to another group and that group was about to apply sanctions to obtain payment, the former could call upon one of its cognate groups to meet the debt. The latter, though it was under no firm obligation to meet the request, was at least more likely to respond affirmatively than any other group. "Outside" descent groups could render such assistance but there were likely to be considerable pressures exerted to meet the debts thereby incurred to them. Debts to cognate groups should have been repaid too, but sometimes the cognate groups preferred to allow the debt to remain as an assurance of reciprocal services in the future.

In a crisis, an alliance between two groups was rendered more likely by formal membership in a larger unit based upon the same genealogical principles and on the same more remote ancestors, probably because their individual interests were more likely to be similar as a consequence of previous involvements. But there were no formal sanctions for the alliance, and it might have been between only some of the several cognate groups. Ultimately, such an alliance was based on the same considerations that operated in the formation of alliances with "outsiders"—promise of gain or the opportunity to meet previously incurred obligations. Cognate descent groups usually acted as autonomous units and rendered one another the same services as could be rendered by other groups. In vengeance, too, minor descent groups acted separately, at least so long as it was confined to a small scale. Cognate groups were not obliged to avenge offenses against one or the other of their number, but, as the scale of vengeance grew, the identity of the major *sinangge* as a solidary unit could become apparent in concerted action against the enemy who then became the common enemy. Because kinsmen in other cognate groups could become implicated, a minor descent group should not have initiated war without the consent of the others, but that consent could be garnered with promise of *kesa* or as an obligation for services previously rendered. Then, too, cognate groups readily became implicated in one another's affairs since the enemy was not obliged to confine his retaliation only to the offender or his descent group. If A and B belonged to different minor descent groups of one major *sinangge* and A offended someone, the offended party could retaliate against B as well as, or instead of, A if, for instance, A were difficult to get to, for to him they were "one *sinangge*." Then both branches were involved, like it or not, and it was a major *sinangge* affair, though again there was no necessary or "automatic" involvement of the whole major *sinangge*.[4]

The manager of the truncal segment of a major *sinangge* was in no sense a "paramount chief" over the cognate units. He is said to have "cared for" the whole major *sinangge* just as he "looked after" the truncal segment, but actually any interference by him in the internal affairs of the branches, unless solicited, would have been resented. He acted largely as a "keeper of the peace" between them and not as their "boss." He had no au-

---

[4] Admittedly, it does seem implausible that an offended party would risk countervengeance by an even larger group. Yet I recorded instances in which it is said to have happened, and it could indeed happen frequently since the agents of vengeance might be ignorant of the appearance of the offender or his kin. Also they had to kill someone or they did not get their *kesa*. See below for further details.

thority to impose a settlement of differences between cognate units; his power derived from the same source as that of the managers of the autonomous minor descent groups, from his participation in competitive political activities. The truncal unit itself differed little in its operations from its cognate but independent so-called branches. Its manager retained custody of the unclaimed "groves" of the major *sinangge,* and the truncal segment was generally, but not always, known by the name of the larger unit. Its actions were its own and did not necessarily implicate independent branches. Thus the major *sinangge* did not exist as a unit with permanent and continuous functions vis-à-vis "outsiders" or even in the relations between cognate branches.

Managers may be seen as focal in the formation of descent groups. In forming a new descent group a man was not limited to his sons and to *tamazira* and their families in recruiting a following. A good manager was one who "fills the group" and thereby makes it more powerful, more capable of competition. One way to "fill" the group was to encourage persons born into it to remain with it throughout their lifetimes; such persons are said to "stay and make firm" their rights and interests in the group and its resources. Another means was to attract potential members to "return," and yet another way was to attract distant kin who eventually might become assimilated into the *sinangge* genealogy. Some reference has been made already to this latter possibility (chap. 3): The Choiseulese do not give it conceptual recognition; as far as they are concerned, publicly at least, the genealogies of descent groups represent the facts as given therein, but, again, some individuals are not above "forging" genealogies and others are not above agreeing to "forgeries" if it suits their interests.

Those residing with a manager and pledging to give him their permanent allegiance formed a single unit for domestic and political activities alike regardless of their genealogical status in relation to him. They worked together as his "hands" and effectively shared vested interests in the same property even though their interests in that property were differentiated. From the "outside," too, they formed a single unit for purposes of vengeance. Some were only "sunshine soldiers and summer patriots" and would desert their manager for another who offered greater protection for fewer risks, but if a person switched his allegiance too often he was considered as having no "roots," and he found neither satisfaction nor friendship anywhere.

But this mode of analysis can be carried too far, for groups could persist even after the deaths of their managers and choose other managers from among themselves. The estates provided some continuity, focal points for organization through resources to be exploited—but only through group action—and, furthermore, they provided significant statuses to be filled.

The political activities of descent groups influenced their personnel in other ways. Success attracted members and bred more success, but failure repelled members or potential members; a descent group that had been dispersed in warfare might never reunite to become a meaningful social unit again. Descent groups did "die out," but their deaths were not so much genetic as political; death was not the result of a failure to breed but of a failure to sustain the lives or allegiances of those born into the group. The estate of a descent group segment reverted to the descent group to be reincorporated into the larger estate and perhaps to lose its identity. It could be reallotted and perhaps serve to resume the process of segment- or descent-group formation. If, on the other hand, it were a completely independent descent group, then its estate passed to members of its cognatic descent category who were members of other descent groups. Did the estate become incorporated into that of the descent group of the inheritor? I found no such instances, but they do not sound impossible. There are many unused estates on Choiseul today, but almost all are deep inland and therefore unsuitable for coconut plantations. Their number is accounted for partly by the changes of allegiance and descent-group dispersals under "contact" pressures in recent times; but even though they are not in use, there are still claimants who keep their interests alive at least in talk. Some are estates of groups that have completely or almost died out, leaving perhaps only one or two claimants. These have not been incorporated into the estates of the descent groups of their holders—indeed, I would not know about them if they had been—and some are periodically used for gardens by other persons with the permission of the holders. In time they may become incorporated into the estates of the holders' descent groups, and this seems most likely where they adjoin the estates of those groups. But separation even at some distance may not be a barrier, for although most descent-group estates are in one piece, I discovered a few that were not. Informants were unable in each instance to offer any explanation for this. It was conceded to be unusual and admitted that one of the sections must have been acquired somehow, but no one knew how.

How far the segmentation process could go is a further question. Could a branch, for instance, rise to obscure the truncal segment and assume that status itself? Or could it become so thoroughly autonomous as to sever all genealogical ties with the truncal group? There are major *sinangge* consisting of branches only reputedly related to one another and others consisting of branches whose connections with one another are "known," and in some cases both possibilities occur in one genealogy. Whether these various types of linkage represent stages in the loss of genealogical knowledge or stages in assimilation of previously discrete genealogies to one another, or perhaps either or both of these processes at different times and places, I cannot say. On many matters, the Choiseulese are not good oral historians, perhaps because it may be advantageous to "forget" some things.

There is some evidence that it was possible for a branch to rise to obscure the truncal segment. The manager of a branch could assume *de facto* control of the whole *sinangge*, major or minor, if the power of the original truncal segment waned and it died out or amalgamated residentially with a branch. Former members of the truncal segment began to identify themselves with the branch and were so identified by "outsiders." The branch name then superseded that of the truncal segment and "covered" the whole as the manager of the branch then "stood out" more than any other man. A descent group may be identified by its manager's name just as he may be identified by reference to the name of his estate; descent group members may define or have their affiliations defined for them in terms of allegiance to a manager or interests in an estate by reference to the name of one or the other. The use of one name as opposed to the other is not entirely a matter of context; if the manager of a branch came to "stand out" more than any other then his name or that of his branch could become most current to refer to the whole group. I know of at least one instance, not among the groups in my census, in which this process is apparently going on today. The original truncal segment of one major *sinangge* is no longer an autonomous unit because some time ago it became allied residentially with one of its branches that had itself come to "stand alone." The truncal segment's portion of the total estate was "willed" to the manager of the branch, a man of wide repute, only a generation ago. But already the name of the original truncal segment has fallen into disuse, although it is still remembered, and the whole major *sinangge* is now known by the name of the branch estate because its manager "made it stand out." There is considerable confusion in the minds of some men over the issues involved, though often the confusion is only the result of simple ignorance. The present manager conveniently prefers to ignore the past status of his branch and even tries to rework the genealogy to make his branch the truncal segment in line with the *de facto* situation; at least, this was one interpretation offered to me.

The possibility of total separation or fission taking place is apparent. As I have already remarked, the present state of some genealogies may indicate stages in such a process (or they may, possibly, represent the loss of genealogical knowledge because of the diminishing significance of such things for many purposes). Surely in the course of population expansion, fission took place many times as new groups sprang up and as communication between them diminished; but the evidence for this is admittedly only circumstantial since all these processes came to an end some time ago.

Religious activities are only a poor measure of branch status. Chapter 5 presents what meager evidence I could obtain about the relations between religious and descent-group organization.

Taking *Kesa*

Managerial wealth consisted largely in land, its improvements, and *kesa*. Wealth in land derived from genealogical position within a descent group and was a matter of internal succession. Wealth in *kesa* could derive from inheritance, usually from one's father, or perhaps from some other kinsman by whom it had been "willed," and if one's father were a manager one could assume his position and control over the *kesa* of the descent group. Managerial status also gave a man a measure of control over the disposition of *kesa* held by group members who had earned that *kesa* for themselves. On crucial occasions when the total wealth of a group was important and managers "counted their *kesa*," they included in their count all the *kesa* held by all descent-group members. They could call upon them for it, and they could not be refused, or so it is said. Such occasions arose when, for instance, a group had to avenge itself after an attack or recruit aid when an attack was imminent. On other occasions—gift exchanges not arising from vengeance activities—which concerned only his own immediate interests or only indirectly those of his descent group, a manager was more or less on his own. It was not his privilege to demand the *kesa* of others, but he could solicit their aid or borrow *kesa* from them. In general, however, borrowing was to be avoided because no one liked being in debt to others.

Kesa could be acquired in yet other ways, some of which were open to all men, being noncompetitive or competitive in such a way that few men were effectively barred from participation. Some means required individual action and others group actions in which the manager acted as group representative and acquired or received *kesa* in the name of the group. Some means of acquiring *kesa* are described below.

Kesa consists of sets of thin-walled cylinders which appear to be made from the fossilized shell of the giant clam. But according to the Choiseulese, *kesa* was not made by men. Thus its significance in politics was magnified by an other-than and greater-than human origin. There was, they say, a time when there was no *kesa*, and men were poorer for the fact. It was made and given to men by *bangara* Laena, a water god residing in the sea somewhere near the offshore islet of Nuatabo on the north coast of Choiseul. He made it specifically to be the "mark" of big-men.[5]

Sets of *kesa* usually consist of nine cylinders, but the sets vary widely in size and quality and, therefore, value. There appears to have been no definite standard of value against which *kesa* was compared. Nothing else in Choiseulese existence, from their point of view and before the coming of the Europeans, approximated it in value. Today, the Choiseulese have worked out an equivalence in Australian pounds, whereby the smallest set commonly used in transactions is worth three pounds (or about $6.75). In the past, if one did not have *kesa*, ten men's *ziku* (arm rings) could be substituted for each basic set. (Ten *ziku*

---

[5] For a complete account of the reported origin of *kesa* and a more complete description of it, see Scheffler 1964a.

were worn on the upper arm as a "mark" of *batu* status.) However, then as now the equivalence is purely for purposes of substitution, and *kesa* was always the preferable and most prestigious medium of exchange wherever it was appropriate.

Kesa sets are divided into two classes—"working" *kesa* or "for exchanges," and "large *kesa.*" The latter was kept for prestige purposes and security, and was used in exchanges only as a last resort or to bind a particularly strategic transaction or alliance. Working *kesa* comes in five sizes, each now valued in Australian pounds at three times its ordinal size; that is, the "fifth" size is equivalent to fifteen Australian pounds or about $35. "Large *kesa*" seems not to have been so neatly standardized and depended for its value more on the context of its use and its own reputation from previous transactions in which it had been used. Some Choiseulese remember in great detail the "personal histories" of the "large *kesa*" they have in their possession.

Each set consists of nine separate cylinders, each one called a *mata*, or "eye." Three *mata* are bound together in ivory-nut palm leaf and called a *salaka;* three *salaka* are bound with cord and form "one *kesa.*" "One *kesa*" is a conveniently ambiguous term, for it may refer to a set with the value of "one" or to one set of any size, and so also with "five" or "ten" *kesa.* They can be more specific, however, since there are terms for the five sizes of working *kesa* and for a few of the more standardized larger ones. Whenever *kesa* is exchanged it must be displayed so that its size and quality may be estimated by both parties to the transaction.[6] This is done by causing it to "stand up," placing the cylinders one on top of the other. The midrib from an ivory-nut palm is inserted in the stack to keep it from falling and to measure its length. The length is measured against the arm. The smallest standard *kesa* should measure approximately from the finger tips of an outstretched hand to about three inches below the inner crook of the elbow. The fifth size should reach to the center of the biceps. The largest *kesa* anyone claimed to have seen was over a fathom in length, and each individual *mata* was said to measure from the tip of the thumb to the tip of the small finger over an outstretched hand (eight to nine inches). It is obvious that these measurements vary from person to person, even though within a

---

[6] As I have already indicated, there are a few exchanges of *kesa* even today, but these take place only in brideprice transactions.

limited range. Nevertheless, the variation gave room for debate about the relative worth of particular sets. Some men notched on their club handles the lengths of *kesa* they possessed or which were outstanding to them. The value of any particular set also varies in a vague and not readily calculable manner with its condition as well as its size, so again there was some room for debate about the equivalence of any pair of transactions.

One could acquire *kesa* by rearing and selling pigs which were always in demand since they were an essential part of the foods presented at all feasts. If not enough pigs were available from one's own stock or from other men as gifts, then more had to be bought. A big feast could require ten to twenty pigs, but only one or two were required for the more frequent and relatively minor exchanges of *kesa*. Within the descent group, pigs were given, not bought, with the understanding that return would be made in kind and more or less freely. *Kesa* should not have been demanded for them. When a kinsman in another group needed a pig for a feast it was given without immediate compensation, but again the understanding was that a return in kind or *kesa* would be made sooner or later. Pigs could be bought outright, but there was no set scale of value in *kesa*. The amount paid depended upon the size of the pig and the strength of the demand for that particular one. No one could "get rich" simply by selling pigs, but it was often the way in which one got a start, acquiring the initial *kesa* to invest in more profitable means of acquiring more.

Kesa could be acquired through brideprice transactions. Three to five *kesa* was the amount usually given, but this varied with the desirability of the woman, partly a matter of the status of the wife giver, and what the "market" would support, that is, what the wife givers wanted and what the wife takers could afford to pay. The amount of *kesa* that could be acquired in this way was, of course, limited for any one individual, and, as with selling pigs, this means was seen as essentially supplementary. But men who were already established as managers could lay claim to the brideprices to be paid for women who were relatively unattached, that is, orphans without influential kinsmen or those who had been acquired as "slaves" by the group. Of course, women were not "sold" simply to get *kesa;* brideprice payment did not make a woman the chattel of the husband. He acquired exclusive sexual rights over her and, nominally, primary claim to the possession of his children by her. He also acquired rights to her productive labor, but she retained social identities apart from her status as a wife.

Compensation in *kesa* could be claimed for someone who "died helping": a man whose son fell from a nut tree and died while helping another man could claim *kesa* from that man in compensation. The amount varied with the circumstances and the parties concerned. If they were already on poor terms demands were greater, but five *kesa* was the most that could be demanded according to "custom." Fear of self-help was the only sanction for payment of compensation. Only representatives of the immediate family of the deceased could claim it; other close kin could request a share from them but not from the original compensating party. Compensation was also paid for losses sustained by those who helped another group in warfare. Losses were not tallied and then compensated individually, one-by-one, but heavy losses enabled helpers to demand a higher payment when they were compensated for their assistance in general at a gift exchange after the termination of the conflict.

"Pulling persons" (*tonggo basoe*) was a way of expressing what amounts to acquiring *kesa* in exchange for them. There were a variety of conditions under which this could be done, and sometimes it was used as sanction against nonpayment of debts or the commission of an offense. Usually a child was involved in these transactions, but persons of any age (and of either sex) could be victims. Sometimes the victim was used in a sacrificial rite or adopted into the receiving descent group as the "child" of the purchaser. As noted earlier, this was not entirely reputable and, therefore, usually took place in secret.

Acting as executioner for another party could also earn one *kesa*. It was not necessary to take vengeance directly upon the offender nor was it required for the offended party or his closest kin to carry out the revenge themselves. They could hire the services of a third party. A certain amount of *kesa*, usually one to three, was promised upon completion of the task, and the *kesa* was presented to the killer at a feast some time later. It was not difficult to find someone to take on the job, for everyone wanted *kesa*, and if they were unrelated to the party or parties to be killed and fearless enough there were no formal obstacles to accepting the chore. Furthermore, many men were always ready to "show their strength" and gain reputations as "killers of men."

Nggave was a form of "visiting" used only on specific occasions when *kesa* was needed urgently for some particular reason. It was a means of coercing one's kinsmen to give *kesa* with minimal counter-obligations. For instance, a man could go to visit some kinsman living in a distant village and announce that he had come to *nggave*. His kinsman then prepared a small feast of pig and pudding and presented it to the guest. The guest announced that he could not eat the pig unless *kesa* were put with it, and the host was then obliged to add *kesa* to the food. If he did not, the guest would say, "do not down me with just pig," for it is not proper "to eat pig on no special occasion." To give pig without *kesa* was an insult. The guest took the food and *kesa* and returned home. Later, the host could become the guest and effectively demand equivalent return of the *kesa* he gave, but the transaction is not expressed in that way. In the case of *nggave* it was not essential for the exchange to be equal or for one party to come out ahead. Furthermore, *nggave* exchanges did not "pyramid" as many other types of exchange did (see pp. 304 ff.). Obviously, *nggave* was not undertaken lightly nor could it be done with just any kinsman. The parties had to be on good, perhaps intimate, terms, and it seems probable that *nggave* was in effect a rather stylized means of requesting a loan on relatively liberal terms and assuring an affirmative response.

Young men could also extract *kesa*, with no obligation to return it, from their "mother's brothers" or "father's brothers" by presenting them with a gift of baked pig and pudding. There was no formal limitation placed upon the number of times that this could be done nor was there any specified limit to the closeness or distance of relationships involved. It is perhaps needless to point out, however, that whether this was attempted at all and how successful it was in forcing a gift of *kesa* depended more upon the general quality of the personal relationship between the parties than upon the kin relation itself.

The Choiseulese also looked to assistance from other than human beings in the acquisition of *kesa*. The *sinipi*, which some people still claim exist, is a kind of *manuru* or "spirit," but a "good" one. (Not all *manuru* are ghosts of deceased ancestors; some are more or less evil spirits living "wild" in the bush.) The *sinipi* are "good" in that they are said to reveal lost *kesa* to those who befriend them. They are said to be tall and bald, generally pleasing in appearance, and especially narrow in the hips. There are two ways of befriending a *sinipi*. One requires capturing his taro knife and returning it to him only upon promise of being shown a hoard of *kesa*. The other is that a *sinipi* may wish to "marry" a person and may reveal himself (or herself) to that person. Then, it is said, the person goes to live with the *sinipi* in their village, perhaps for a year, and finally reappears in his own village and explains where he (or she) has been. The *sinipi* are visible only to those who have befriended them; therefore, some argue, it is possible to see them and capture their taro knives only when they want to be captured. The *kesa* that they reveal hidden in the ground is said to be *kesa* that has been "lost" by other men. Men often die without revealing to others where they have hidden their *kesa*, and it becomes lost to men. Only the *sinipi* know where it is, but they never reveal the hiding places of *kesa* belonging to living men. I met no one who had personally "gone with the *sinipi*," but some of my informants claimed that they had met such persons, and there were stories circulating during 1961 about a man in the Babatana area then associating with a *sinipi*. Men who uncovered hoards of *kesa* belonging to others may have claimed the *sinipi* led them to it, or men who acquired it by participating in a "pulling" transaction may have explained their acquisitions by reference to *sinipi* if their possession of new *kesa* became known. But the Choiseulese did not make such suggestions, and I have no idea of what men who "went to live with the *sinipi*" actually did with themselves during their periods of absence.

Loans sometimes were not means of acquiring *kesa* but rather means of paying debts. Rather than become victim to *sake* (certain sanctions, see p. 206), one man could persuade another to pay the debt for him, thus in effect "transferring" the indebtedness. One could also come into the presumably temporary possession of another man's *kesa* by exchanging it for one's own as when one had only "large *kesa*" and did not wish to part with it but needed to meet a debt. A person, then, looked for someone he could trust and who would "change" it for him, that is, give him an equivalent in small *kesa*. The understanding was that the original owner of the "large *kesa*" would reclaim it later with small *kesa*. There was no concept of charging for such a service; "friends" did these things for one another. However, difficulties sometimes arose when the "large *kesa*" was reclaimed but its return refused.

Reconciliation following some offenses could be accomplished by payment of a fine in *kesa*, usually only a small amount. Men who already had some power could manufacture situations so that an offense was committed inadvertently and cause was given for a claim to a fine, or they could make a false accusation of offense and rely upon intimidation to extract a fine. For instance, it was forbidden for a woman to "step over" a man's spear or shield. Should she do so he could claim *kesa* in compensation. If payment were refused, then he could legitimately claim the girl as his hostage (*sake*), and he could "marry" her or "sell" her in marriage to another man. The effectiveness of the threat depended upon the ability of the claimant to back up with self-help what he took to be his rights. A young man with little power in his own right could depend upon the strength of a notable kinsman. The Choiseulese mentioned men who had tarnished their reputations with such "tricks."

Taking "hostages" in order to acquire *kesa* had many forms— hostages were not necessarily persons—and one form was noted earlier in connection with the payment of "fines." There *sake* appeared as a form of sanction, as it was in general—a sanction for payments rather than an independent means of getting *kesa*. However, *sake* could be complex and amount to a means for parties not directly implicated in the initial dispute.

For instance, *sake* is also applied to the impounding of a grove of a debtor in order to enforce payment of a debt. If A owed B *kesa* for an offense or for services rendered and did not pay, B could call upon C to extract payment. C then went to a grove belonging to A and erected a sign—some pieces of twine and leaf— on one of the trees. This act was called *zaki midiki*, to "forbid" by erecting such a sign. For A to use the grove was then an offense against C, and A had to pay the debt owing to B, but he paid it to C who kept the payment in full. B got the satisfaction of knowing that A had to pay, or at least was out so much *kesa*, and B also maintained his own reputation as a man not to be trifled with. (Cf. Thurnwald 1912: 45.)

The sanction of *sake* could not be used arbitrarily, for if C came to believe that A was innocent of an offense or owed no debt he could impound one of B's groves and extract an equivalent payment from him. The *sake* was said to "climb back in." C could do this because B had to choose as his agent a man of repute whose actions were to be feared, not a "nobody." In that choice resided the effectiveness of *sake*. A might staunchly maintain his innocence of offense or indebtedness and destroy the warning sign and continue to use the grove. This would amount to a challenge against C—B would be no longer involved—who then had to maintain his prestige by mobilizing his forces and marching against A and his group, destroying homes and gardens and killing all and sundry in the village without regard to their affiliation with that descent group or kinship to A. Thus there was considerable pressure upon A from his kinsmen and others to pay his legitimate debts, but in the final analysis "right" and "wrong" were not the important issues. The actions taken depended largely upon the relative powers of the groups. Before initiating any action or taking vengeance everyone "counted his *kesa*." *Sake* could be done also by a kinsman who had paid a debt for one in order to rescue one's groves from possible *sake* by another and perhaps unrelated party. The rescuer then established a lien on the grove; technically it was "his" until the debt was repaid, but the true owner could continue to use it. The understanding was that the rescuer would not force his claim to the grove, but he could do so to force payment, in which case the debtor had presumably little choice but to pay.

This discussion of *sake* has been somewhat digressive from the original issue—means of acquiring *kesa*—but it has been a suitable point at which to demonstrate the significance of having *kesa*. The Choiseulese talk as though *kesa* were the be-all and end-all of personal significance. A man without *kesa* was a "nobody," a "poor" man, not just *pela* or "weak," but *sarakutu*, "weak" in the most derogatory sense, without a relatively independent means of livelihood and without defense, prey to all, a man who had to be "fed" by others. A descent group without *kesa* was in a similar position. One with *kesa* was wealthy and, therefore, powerful, capable of self-defense, not to be "downed" by others anxious to exact revenge or to "elevate" themselves by taking advantage of the weaknesses of others. A group's fate is seen as having been closely bound up with the waxing and waning of its wealth in *kesa*, which had always to be maintained—or at least a reputation for wealth had to be maintained. A descent group that had been recently wealthy still retained a form of wealth in its reputation, and a man or a group could live on his or its reputation for a time. It was sometimes known that a descent group had met heavy expenditures recently and could not then have had much *kesa* in reserve, but the exact amount was generally kept secret as a part of the strategy of group defense and prestige. Fear that there could be unknown *kesa* in reserve, or that it could be acquired easily, was sometimes as good a deterrent as knowledge of the exact amount held. A group that had been wealthy in the recent past had an important reserve in the willingness of others to extend credit with the expectation that "clever" men could always earn more and repay the debt with interest.

Kelo Transactions

Kelo was the most important and prestigious form of giving or receiving *kesa*, and preparing for and executing *kelo* were among the most important tasks of a manager. *Kelo*—or feast-giving— originated and proceeded in various ways, but they were always competitive and relative prestige was always an issue. Some were conceived of as exchanges between managers as two men in competition for relative prestige, each trying to "down" the other. These often began with a challenge to compete in the reciprocal exchange of increasingly larger feasts and sums of *kesa*, and there were a number of specified ways in which the challenge could be made. It might or might not be accepted, and no special stigma was thought to attach to refusal to compete. Other *kelo* began in formal transactions between two men or groups such as, in the case of two groups, an agreement to assist in a raid in return for so much *kesa*, the *kesa* being conceived of as obligatory payment for services rendered. The feast at which the *kesa* was presented was a form of ceremony marking the transaction, not a part of the payment itself. On these occasions managers acted as the representatives of their groups and took the *kesa* into their own custody, but the distinction between group and individual activity is not maintainable when one considers the long-run effects of *kelo* exchange. Even in the short-run it made little difference whether the exchange was undertaken in the name of an individual or a group; the manager was "assisted" by his allies in either event, and any glory he gained was to the benefit of the group while any glory the group gained was to his benefit as well. The "power" of the *kesa* in either event was at the disposal of the man or his descent group.

Many incidents could be taken as pretexts for beginning an exchange of *kelo*, and there were few formal limits to who could challenge or be challenged. However, in some instances only kinsmen could challenge one another, as when the *kelo* began with the death of a kinsman of the challenger. If man A were bitten by a centipede or a wasp, another man, B, might kill it, and A then gave B a *ziku* (a shell ring). B then gave A a baked pig and a *ziku*, and so on until they exchanged *kelo*. Or A might make a canoe for B and receive *kesa* at a *kelo* in payment for the service.

One example will illustrate the general form of *kelo* exchanges regardless of their "origin." When a person died his descent-group mates cremated the body after a short period in which other kinsmen visited the body. The ashes and bones were gathered, placed in a pot, and deposited temporarily at an ancestral shrine. Later the ashes were deposited permanently at another place according to the deceased's status in life. Sometimes a special resting place, called a *sara*, was constructed of flat slabs of stone. The *sara* was "built" by the descent group of the deceased, but anyone could participate in the construction, and all kinsmen of the deceased who were living in the vicinity were expected to attend at least as spectators. It was the responsibility of the immediate family of the deceased, assisted by descent-group mates, to provide food for the visitors. A kinsman of the deceased who was not his group mate could ask to be allowed to "erect the *sara*." The immediate kin of the deceased were known collectively as "the bottom people of the death," but they were represented by one man, perhaps a son of the deceased. He could accept or reject the request of the other party who was known, along with his kinsmen who assisted him, as the "ally people." If he were accepted he provided additional food, and especially pig, for the visitors and workers. Later the "bottom people" were required to present the "allies" several *kesa* in return for their services. This was done formally at a large feast given in their honor. At least three *kesa* were given: "one *kesa* 'changed' the purchase price of the pig, one *kesa* paid for the work of making the *sara*, and at least one *kesa* 'went with' the *kelo*."

The whole thing could terminate at this point, but it was not a matter for prior formal agreement even though an informal understanding might have been reached before the exchange. If the transaction had been undertaken by the "allies" just to earn *kesa*, they would have been anxious to stop then, but it could have been "made difficult" for them to quit by the presentation of what was considered an excessive amount of *kesa* to "go with" the *kelo* given by the "bottom people." The "allies" were thereby forced to reciprocate or lose prestige. Thus if the aim were only to earn *kesa*, it was wise then not to offer one's services to persons of too high a status. But this might have been difficult to judge. The "allies" would reciprocate with another *kelo*, perhaps giving only a few *kesa* to the "bottom people," thus retaining some "profit" and at the same time signifying a desire to terminate the transaction. Or they could attempt to outdo the "bottom people." This forced another *kelo* by the "bottom people" to "even" the transaction with an even larger amount of *kesa* equivalent to the amount previously received by them plus just enough more to allow the "allies" to come out ahead, but not so much as to signal a desire for further competition unless, of course, they wished to continue.

Another way in which a *kelo* might grow out of the death of someone was for a related party living in another place to bring a baked pig and present it to the immediate kin of the deceased who were required to reciprocate with another pig and one *ziku*. The "ally" then baked another pig and took another *ziku* to the "bottom," saying, "Here is the hair of the *boko robe*. Eat it." This signaled a desire to "make the *sara*" and to exchange *kelo* and was considered somewhat more obligatory than the method described above.

A number of relatively imponderable factors entered into termination of a series of *kelo* exchanges. Most important was probably the extent of other debts contracted by those concerned. Continued participation meant increasing debts, since help was received from other persons and groups, and it meant increasing the difficulty of meeting those debts. If a man or descent group had given extensive assistance to other men or groups in the past, however, he might have had considerable credit to draw upon, but it might not have been easy to extract payment of the debts. He could turn to threat of *sake*, but even this could have been difficult because it would have meant running the risk of even further indebtedness. Also important was the amount of uncommitted *kesa* available from one's own descent group or from others who might have been willing to help with loans. The strength of desire for prestige on the part of the principals was also important, and this could vary from man to man and time to time. To one man a particular transaction may have been crucial, to another it may have been more or less incidental. Few groups were resourceful enough to carry out an extended series of *kelo* without some help. Therefore, while *kelo* brought prestige and renown they also brought indebtedness in many forms, whether in *kesa* or simply in obligations to provide food to others when they made *kelo*. All these factors added up to make it impossible to prolong *kelo* exchanges indefinitely. Indeed, simple transactions of one or two *kelo* seem to have been the most common, and only rarely did a series ever run to three or four *kelo*. Much depended upon the size of each *kelo*. It was patently easier to participate in a lengthy series of relatively small exchanges than in a short series of large ones. Thus the amount of *kesa*, the size of the groups, and interests were all critical factors in determining how prolonged any series of exchanges was. Furthermore, *kelo* required a considerable amount of time to organize and execute. Large stocks of food had to be prepared, and one's supply of *kesa* may have needed replenishing. Since the major foodstuff was taro, which was nonstorable, huge gardens had to be prepared for harvesting on one occasion. All this required labor, time, and planning.

Sometimes a principal to a transaction died before he could complete his "end" of it. The debts of fathers were inherited by their sons, but sons sometimes refused to recognize their fathers' debts. They would claim ignorance of them, denying that they had ever existed, or they would claim that they had been paid. Men sometimes postponed paying their debts or meeting their obligations, trusting that they would die before forced to pay, despite the fact that their sons would then have to meet those obligations. The temptation to do this was particularly great when a man had no sons who could be made responsible. In that case the creditor could call upon another close kinsman to meet the debt, but again he could have met refusal, then on the grounds that it was none of the refuser's business. *Sake* or threat of violence was the creditor's only sanction.

However, while the debtor was still alive another sanction was available. The "bottom" party, that is, the person or group owing the debt, was obligated to *kelo* first, but if this were delayed too long (there was no formal recognition of how long was "too long"), then the "ally" could threaten to *kelo* first, and he might have had to go through with it. This worked a considerable hardship upon the "bottom" party because it enabled the "ally" to extract more *kesa* than he would have obtained otherwise. For that reason it was wise for "bottom" parties to pay their debts as quickly as possible and also to avoid any other complications. Also "allies" might not have feared nonpayment, but this did not prevent them from manipulating the situation to get more out of it.

Let us take a hypothetical case of the strategy of *kelo*-making as described to me by informants. Let us say B had done a job for A, for example, killed someone in revenge. A was the "bottom," and B the "ally." After the killing, B and his men reported to A in person and gave him the news of what they had done. A then "fed" B and his men "pig for bringing home the kill," but that is all he did at that time. Then B returned home and waited for his *kelo* and *kesa* from A. A eventually sent word to B that he wished to discuss the amount of *kesa* to be given, which presumably was agreed upon earlier anyway when the request for assistance was first made. Upon receipt of A's message, B prepared the "pig that makes the *kesa* go out," which he tried to give to A's messengers along with some *kesa*. But if A's messengers were shrewd they would take only one *ziku*, of very little value, along with the pig. B later went to visit A and discussed the amount of *kesa* he would take at the *kelo* to be given by A. If he had succeeded in persuading A's messengers to take some *kesa* when they brought A's invitation to the discussion he was in a good position to "talk forcefully" in regard to the amount he wanted, for not only had he to be compensated for his services but the amount given to the messengers had to be repaid too. Since *kelo* is now a thing of the past I did not witness any of these transactions, and I cannot say from personal experience what a man said when he "talked forcefully." However, if the general demeanor of managers is any indication of what was said, and if informants' accounts are accurate, it would seem that managers would have stressed the good relations that already existed with the "bottom" people, the difficulty of the job that had been done, the risks involved, the value of it, and so on, with eloquence playing an important part. They would play up the status of the "bottom" people, implying wealth and great ability to make lavish payments. The "bottom" party, on the other hand, usually pleaded that the demands of the "allies" were excessive, not because the service rendered was negligible but because of the temporary poverty of the "bottom" party himself. Without overdoing it and thereby making himself appear destitute, he pleaded that his *kesa* and supporters were depleted and that he was in debt. After much haggling, an amount was agreed upon and the date set for the *kelo*.

Now if the "bottom," A, was too slow in setting an amount to be paid and the date of the *kelo*, the "ally," B, could take things into his own hands and issue an invitation to A to come discuss a *kelo* to be given by B to A. A might have been in a position such that he could not *kelo* immediately and would then have had to submit to B's request. When A came to discuss the matter, B attempted to give him *kesa* and baked pig. A was more or less obliged to accept some *kesa* at this point, though exactly *why* my informants could not say, except that it was, of course, not really proper to give or receive pig without accompanying *kesa*; A attempted to take as little as possible while B attempted to give as much as possible. They agreed upon an additional amount of *kesa* to be given to A by B at a *kelo* and also set a date. After the *kelo*, A had to prepare one for B, and when B received the invitation to discuss the *kelo* he again tried to give *kesa* to A's messengers. When B went to the discussion he was then in a good position to talk forcefully about his demands. He demanded what he felt his services were worth, and in addition he demanded complete repayment of what he had previously given to A in *kelo* and to A's messengers on related occasions. The same pleas and claims were made once again, an amount eventually set after more haggling, the *kelo* made, and the transaction ended.

However, a further complication could arise. At the time of the *kelo* itself A may have pleaded that he had been unable to raise the total amount and asked B to take less, whatever A then had on hand. While this plea might have been true, it might also have been a deception, and A might have had more *kesa* in reserve in case he was refused and B got angry. Finally, if B were not content with the amount of *kesa* he had been able to extract he could "up the ante" even further by giving A another *kelo*! The obvious disadvantage in allowing the "ally" to *kelo* first was that the ante in each *kelo* was thereby made relatively larger and the difficulty of accumulating it relatively increased. Furthermore, much prestige was lost when one had to be forced to meet one's obligations. This despite the fact that there was generally much effort to escape meeting the payment of debts.

Men were generally concerned to come out ahead, with a profit, in all *kesa* exchanges. However, it was not absolutely necessary to profit on every occasion, for some prestige derived from the exchange itself. It was better to have participated in *kelo* without profit in *kesa* than to be a "no account" man or group and not have participated at all. One's wealth or power was not measured solely in the amount of *kesa* on hand but also in terms of one's past activities and the extent of one's debts, which indicated activity and ability, and the extent of one's credit, which indicated great potential through the obligations of others to one.

The *kelo* themselves were interesting but not particularly relevant to this discussion, and are therefore described here only in general terms. *Kelo* were lavish affairs, occasions for show of many sorts. The hosts invited the guest or guests of honor and "friends" from neighboring and allied descent groups. There was much display of individual and group wealth in food and personal ornaments, and many laudatory and self-elevating speeches were made by managers, particularly the principals. Dancing and the competitive playing of panpipes preceded the chopping down of the *kangge*, a large conical structure of leaf and lath set on its tip and filled with taro and nut pudding. During the dancing and panpipe playing there was a mock battle between the hosts and guests for possession of the *kangge* which the guests eventually won only after the intercession of the women of both groups. Afterwards the food was distributed by groups and later taken home to be consumed. The high point of the *kelo* occurred when the *kesa* to be presented to the guests was exposed and "stood up" to be examined for its quality and value. The food distributed at a *kelo* had to be plentiful, and it came from many sources. Much of it was grown by the manager himself with the aid of his descent group, and much was either purchased outright for *ziku* and *kesa* or received in donations from group members, affinal kin, and other kin in neighboring descent groups. All food "donated" had to be returned in kind or compensated for in *kesa*. It is said that no exact "account" was kept of amounts given by kinsmen, and it did not have to be reciprocated unit for unit. Much was given with "no strings attached," but there was always the understanding that a similar service would be rendered in return. Everyone within the descent group was obliged to assist in a *kelo*, but other kinsmen assisted as kinsmen, not as particular "types of kin" specifically obligated to assist in particular situations.

As noted earlier, there was no particular season for feasting, but there had to be a large supply of nuts on hand as one of the principal ingredients in the *taoga* pudding that was considered essential. A *kelo* was simply not a *kelo*, and for that matter could not take place, without *taoga*. Nuts could be bought and sold, but a man was principally dependent upon his own supply, and it was therefore extremely important for men to have their own groves and to have them unencumbered by the rights of others or *sake*. In this necessity resided much of the effectiveness of the *sake* sanction plus, of course, the shame of being "downed."

The Choiseulese considered making *kelo*, along with the possession of *kesa*, the fundamental "mark" of a manager. Men could gain repute in other ways, but none were so effective as participating in *kelo* exchanges. For each *kelo* one man was basically responsible whether it was given in his own name or that of his descent group. A *kelo* demonstrated a man's strength, "made him go up" relative to other men, "elevated" him and his group. *Kelo* were made by men and groups "to make their names heard all about," to make them famous as "makers of *kelo*," "killers of men," and "bakers of pigs." It is said that competitors wished to go on exchanging *kelo* until it "hurt" or until it "made them tired," until they were incapacitated or depleted of resources. Actually, they do not seem to have acted in this way, although they may have fostered the impression, deliberately, of having done so in order to postpone the payment of debts or to facilitate arguing that debtors meet their obligations.

A manager made himself by making *kelo* and by participating in those activities which required him to *kelo*. He was assisted in this process by his followers and those who hoped to benefit from his renown, and they too gained in repute and prestige in the process by being able to promote such a big-man and by receiving the protection of his name. In the process he contracted debts and acquired debtors, both among his followers who assisted with pigs, food, and their labors or even lives, and among other managers and big-men who had their own followings. These debts and credits gradually drew him and his followers in a web of obligations and interests which may be shown to have been among the primary constraints upon conflict and competition within a society that appears to have been organized more for sustaining than for resolving or restraining conflict and competition. Descent groups and their managers not only stopped short of incapacity to act further; they often avoided competition in favor of peace and coöperation, as clearly they had to if there were to be that "modicum of peace over a certain area, which is necessary if men are to live in any kind of security, and produce food, marry into one another's families, or deal with one another" (Gluckman 1955: 19).

Before these last remarks are elaborated, it is important to be clear about the relationship between making *kelo* or gift exchanges and being a big-man. It was not simply feasting and the exchanges of valuables that made a big-man but rather the activities which gave rise to the feasting and exchanges. The exchanges, even though they could be undertaken largely as exercises in the raising of the prestige of the participants, were more usually the terminal points in series of transactions involving alliances between individuals and groups and their resources. The essential attributes of a manager were not simply the abilities of making exchanges but rather to initiate and manipulate those transactions which eventually resulted in exchanges of valuables. Exchanges that did not stem from a previous contractual alliance were thought of as secondary forms of *kelo*-making, participated in largely by those who were already big-men.

THE GENESIS AND REPRESSION OF CONFLICT

We now come to consider some of the ways in which conflict was generated, enlarged, and finally repressed—I hesitate to say that it was ever terminated—within the general social situation already described. By implying that conflict between groups was never "terminated," I do not mean to imply that the usual mode of relations between groups was one of feud. Although they were not always such, it was expected that cognate groups (constituent units of the same major *sinangge*) would be "friendly." Other groups could be "friends" too, and it was expected that groups of the same region would be; ideally, they should have acted as "one big *sinangge*." But with other groups no such expectations prevailed. Still, peace was always a possibility for any two Choiseulese groups who might have become opposed to one another. However, sometimes it was difficult to establish and came about only through the disabling of one party, in which case one could speak of a state of continuing feud, but only between isolated segments.

On the other hand, the Choiseulese did form alliances with groups from other islands, especially Vella Lavella, to fight other Choiseulese, and they also fought, but only rarely, against peoples of other islands. While Choiseulese could usually establish a formal peace, though perhaps not a long-lasting one, among themselves, peace was never the result of formal settlement in interisland fighting. In this sense, one might speak of interisland relations as typically those of feud.

We may make an analytical distinction between interpersonal and intergroup conflict. This would correspond to the Choiseulese distinction between relatively minor and isolated quarrels and disputes that might lead to vengeance (*velo*), and the larger-scale acts of vengeance or war (*kana*) involving the concerted actions of groups or groups in alliance. This distinction cannot always be maintained, however, for ultimately groups were always involved. The Choiseulese note that only a fool would have taken revenge for an offense without at least the tacit support of a group to help restrain counter-vengeance, and groups were careful to restrain their members from initiating vengeance that would have been disasterous.

Disputes may be divided into two broad classes with regard to their origins: those over property and those over prestige. But these were intertwined. War often grew out of property disputes but quickly became more concerned with the reputations of the groups or persons involved. War was never undertaken for conquest, for political domination of other groups, or for control of their lands, and because of the nature of political control, conquest and domination would have been impossible.

Almost all offenses could be construed or magnified as cause for revenge, because not the offense itself but the relative status of the offended mattered most in determining sanctions. The "poor" and "weak" were offended with impunity unless they had powerful friends willing to take up their causes in order to expand their own repute. The most serious offenses, that is, those with the greatest assurance of retaliation, were against managers or their immediate families. Of course, some offenses did lead to vengeance more readily than others, and especially the death of the offender or his kinsmen, and some "went straight to war"; but the relative political status of the disputants was still the crucial variable in determining the scope of the dispute. This being so, offenses are not discussed here in detail. The most serious and most frequent causes of violence as classified by the Choiseulese are noted briefly.

Adultery, sexual relations with the wife of another man, was a very grave personal offense to that man. If caught in the act, the culprit could have been executed by the husband on the spot, and the wife too could legitimately be killed. It was not necessary to catch them in the act, however, and the offended husband could under other circumstances either demand *kesa* in compensation or the life of the offender. An unimportant man might not have been able to get either one.

"Lying about sorcery" was commonly done to magnify some lesser offense or series of offenses—or no offense at all—into a pretext for revenge. The Choiseulese thus distinguish between the "legitimate" slaying of a sorcerer and the use of a sorcery accusation to score off a party for some other reason. A legitimate accusation and slaying could follow only after a complex divination process executed by a man adept at such things. Counter-vengeance then would have been "wrong," for it was "right" to kill a demonstrated sorcerer. But it was also recognized that divinations could be rigged or "false" or simply proclaimed but not done in fact. It may have been that here, as in many African societies, sorcery divinations were only a means of legitimizing what people already "knew" and wanted to do. The Choiseulese, however, maintain that any "good" person would not make false accusations; he wanted only to do the "proper" thing. But divination was undertaken in private and for the party who thought that he or a close kinsman had been "poisoned." The parties eventually accused seldom witnessed the divination. Thus they could usually find cause to maintain their innocence or the innocence of the accused and if they were strong enough could seek to avenge the "injustice" of the accusation or any action taken on the basis of it. In the nature of the event, then, it was practically impossible for all parties to agree about a "right" or "wrong" slaying in regard to sorcery; an accusation against a man reflected upon the moral quality of his kinsmen too, for "only a bad line produces sorcerers." Within descent groups, where sorcery was thought to be most common anyway, it was thought to be possible to establish guilt for sorcery, to have the guilt accepted and for the issue to be settled by payment of a fine, which in the case of sorcery was paid in *kesa* and called *sioro*. But when such accusations were made the accused parties frequently sought to disassociate themselves from the group.

Disputes over property rights and interests could lead to a progressive degeneration of relations between two parties, and one party would eventually seize upon some pretext to have the other killed. Again, to those who actually did the killing it was not a matter of "right" or "wrong" but simply an occasion to "show strength" and "take *kesa*."

To "refuse a woman" in marriage to a powerful man was an offense to his pride, and it was not unknown for a man so wronged to have the woman's father or some other kinsman killed in revenge. Some wars are said to have begun when a manager offended in this fashion launched an attack upon the village of the offenders.

"Stealing" (*siko*) property of any sort, especially *kesa*, was an offense. Misappropriation of garden produce was not taken lightly, and a fine in *kesa* could be demanded, and if it were not paid it could lead to the execution of the thief. It was not so much the gravity of the offense itself that justified killing but rather the refusal to pay the fine. It is as though the offender were saying to the offended, "You are a man of no account, and I can do as I please with regard to your property."

To the above we must add homicide. To the slayer, who usually worked through agents, the murder of an offender was always justified or at least justifiable, and others might have agreed with him. On the other hand, kinsmen of the victim seldom saw it that way unless he had the reputation of a trouble maker among them too. Even so, they were free to see the occasion as one upon which to show their strength. Counter-vengeance was almost always a necessity, for murder of a group member represented a challenge to the life of the group itself.

Upon discovery of an offense the wronged party usually put on an impressive show of anger, some of which was probably genuine, but more would have been simulated. He raged about, shouting and gesticulating; he would kill the offender, or so he said. But this usually took some time to arrange even if he intended to do it. Thus there was usually a little time in which to arrange a more peaceful solution, and advantage could be taken of it. Of course, when a person had a grievance which he kept to himself, others, not knowing about it, could do nothing to pacify him, and he might eventually have taken some action which implicated them all in violence.

Conflict within the descent group seldom attained violent form, not because of some mystical concordance among kinsmen, as should be apparent by now, but because the considerations favoring the repression of conflict were most strongly operative within such groups. Descent-group members were united by their interests in some resources and in one another's services. But this "unity," perhaps better called "association," was also a cause of enmity which often led them to disputing. There were, however, practical considerations for not creating or maintaining an open breach with kinsmen or group mates. Kinsmen built and sustained binding obligations through the establishment of vested interests in one another's services and properties; they turned to one another for aid and they owed debts to each other. A manager and his followers, a disputant and his descent group mates or other kinsmen, were united by similar interests in their shared resources, and these interests were expressed in the idioms of kinship. A basic "capital" resource consisted in the obligations one had managed to impose upon others through the exchange of services (cf. Barnes 1962), and those obligations were most intense within, though not confined to, one's own descent group. Furthermore, schisms within the group reduced its strength vis-à-vis other descent groups, a fact of which the Choiseulese are aware and frequently discuss even today.

The web of kinship was most tightly knit within the descent group, and persons could not easily align themselves wholly with one faction or the other, having interests in both parties, as they frequently did. In such cases, it was usually to the advantage of all concerned, or at least to the advantage of a substantial number, to press for peace rather than a breach or retribution. They found their agent, as they still do today, in the manager of the group who acted as a "go-between." He did this in the name of group solidarity, which was important to him above all since his strength was directly dependent upon the unity of his following.

A dispute did not have to erupt into the "public" domain before a manager could intervene; sensing the possibility of a dispute, he could act to keep it from developing further. In the early stages he did not bring disputing parties together, for indeed if they met fact to face any discussion would have been likely to become a quarrel. He went from man to man urging moderation and then reported to each that some compromise could be reached. At first the offended party was unlikely to consider modifying his demands. If he had said he would kill the offender then he would stick to this intention for some time. If he had demanded a large amount of *kesa* as a fine he would refuse to consider less. The accused would probably deny at first any guilt or responsibility whatsoever. Unless one side was clearly at fault, and perhaps even then, it was not the manager's job to suggest or impose an exact settlement but merely to bring the two sides closer to some agreement. He did not assess guilt; he only arbitrated with the intent of reëstablishing peaceful relationships. As initial anger cooled, the manager was able to persuade the disputants to reduce their claims against one another, and if the dispute was a relatively minor one—perhaps over the destruction of part of a garden by a pig—the manager was able to arrange an exchange of shell rings, an expression of desire for peaceful relations. The displays of ferocity and indifference to the threats of others were then taken as sufficient to maintain the prestige of the disputants. Some men were anxious to maintain the appearances of someone to be reckoned with but not anxious to have those appearances tested. They readily agreed to arbitration so long as it was not inferred that they submitted out of weakness. The manager's task was to find ways in which the disputants could regard the demands of pride as satisfied without having to resort to violence. There were occasions upon which he had to pass judgment and then be ready to implement it with self-help, but it was virtually impossible to do this arbitrarily and still maintain a following.

Pressure to settle disputes peacefully came from descent group mates as well as the manager. Kinsmen who would have been implicated in the dispute, like it or not, and other associates of either "end" to the dispute were unlikely to argue that their "end" was in the wrong and should, therefore, give in, but they too could press for a peaceful solution. While they gained in prestige by "winning," no "win" within a descent group was without some penalty to the group as a whole and to the individual welfare of its members. Internal disputes could lead to situations in which members had to ally with one or the other principal, thereby creating factions within the group. Such disputes could serve political ends, but when they did not it was clearly better to press for peace rather than for a "win."

Few disputes were "simple" or concerned only a particular event. Minor differences often blew over after some initial flurry of words, but they became part of a stock of grievances to be brought to the fore on any particular occasion. This complicated a settlement, for it meant resolving many issues at once. The stock of grievances contributed further to the imponderable but important factor of individual anger. Some men are said to have been "inclined to anger" and difficult to pacify. They saw prestige only in aggression. The higher a man's status, the greater his repute, the more likely he was to be able to maintain such a position.

Disputes between members of different descent groups also could be settled peacefully, the likelihood of peaceful settlement being directly related to the closeness of the kin ties between them or the existence of a manager closely related to both "ends" of the dispute. The greater the overlap of the personal kinship circles of the disputants, the larger was the body of persons sharing an interest in resolution of the dispute. Again, managers offered their services unsolicited and were not compensated for them except through the prestige to be earned as keepers of the peace. Only managers related to both "ends" could take an interest in disputes between members of different descent groups. Indeed, only those related to both "ends" were thought to have an interest in peace between them. Again, the principal appeal was to the dogma that kinsmen should not fight, and a man who was a kinsman to both parties could use this argument most forcefully. The managers of the disputing groups were expected to side with their group mates and thus were in no position to act as go-betweens, but there was nothing to prevent one's manager from supporting one publicly while privately urging peaceful settlement.

Despite their avowed emphasis upon taking revenge for wrongs, the Choiseulese generally preferred to settle disputes peacefully when possible. It was probably true, as they say, that some men "wanted only to fight" and that no man admitted that he never wanted to fight. But it was probably true also that men often found it to their advantage not to fight. It was better to settle things peacefully with fines, exchanges of *ziku* or *kesa*, "because then no one was killed." This is not to be construed to mean that each man feared death, and so urged peace only to save his own life. That sentiment may have been operative, even though it would have been a source of shame, but another important consideration was that one's supportive sphere dwindled through violent conflict, thereby limiting one's potential for further actions. Peace was also valued for itself and for what it enabled men to do, for only in time of peace could men perform daily activities without anxiety, and only in time of peace could they make *kelo*. Peace was necessary to enable men to pay their debts and extract payments from other men.

When arbitration broke down or never got going because of an impulsive action by an offended party, for lack of a manager to act as go-between, or for other reasons, if feelings still ran high and if support could be found, vengeance took the form of homicide. There was no limit to the time within which vengeance had to take place, and a grievance could lie dormant for some time, at least as long as it took to gather support. The period between offense and retaliation varied inversely with the status of the offended party. A wealthy manager asked no advice and acted on his own if his wife had committed adultery, but in other cases he marked time and determined the extent of his support.

The strategy of conflict could be complex, but it resembled a readily recognizable model. There were several courses which could have been taken by an offended party: It was inconceivable that "nothing" would be done, but it was, of course, possible that preparations were only a "fronting" movement designed to intimidate the opposition and to save face when no action was immediately intended. Any offense constituted a challenge to the prestige of the injured party and had to be avenged if prestige were to be maintained. Not to retaliate or at least to make a show of readying one's forces was to admit weakness and to invite further abuse from others, or so it was thought.

When revenge was necessary first one had to "count one's *kesa*," which is a way of saying that a careful assessment of the situation had to be made to determine the course of action most propitious. The immediate allies of the offended party held a discussion to determine the sentiments for or against action and how extensive that action should be. They had two choices: to kill the offender or someone in his stead, or to launch a sneak raid upon the offender's village. Both possibilities had their advantages and disadvantages. An all-out attack could result in annihilation of the enemy and his followers or so effectively disperse them that further conflict would have been more or less precluded. On the other hand, if the attack failed then continued warfare was a certainty. The murder of the culprit or his substitute required considerably less effort and expenditure of resources, and was less likely to result in retaliation or at least retaliation on the scale that followed raids. In short, it was a matter of costs measured against resources—one's own *kesa*, debts and credits due, and the resources of those likely to have come to one's aid. An important aspect of the cost of revenge was the relative power of the group to be challenged, though it was sometimes difficult to assess just how large or how wealthy that group may have been. If such things were not already generally known, discrete enquiries were made as to the amount of *kesa* in the possession of the enemy, the extent of the debts and credits due them, and the likelihood of help from other quarters. If such enquiries were not made carefully enough the information was almost certain to leak out that some sort of attack was in the offing, and the enemy would have been forewarned by a third party. If it were decided that the enemy was relatively weak, that is, that counter-vengeance was relatively unlikely or, if it did occur, could be coped with effectively and without loss of prestige, it was then decided to act immediately. On the other hand, if the enemy were relatively strong the decision was not to forego vengeance altogether but rather to wait until a more propitious occasion. That vengeance might never be extracted was beside the point, because no group wished to admit that it was not always a possibility.

Relative power, so far as could be determined, seems to have been the crucial variable in determining whether vengeance would be extracted, how soon it would occur, and the form it would take. Let us assume for the moment that it had been decided to seek only the death of the offender or of an alternative party. If a dispute were between two particular persons, the wronged party often did not participate in the revenge killing. It could be done by his descent group mates who wished to gain repute as killers and men to be feared, or it could be done by wholly unrelated third parties whose services were hired. Two considerations favored the latter alternative: If counter-vengeance were feared, hiring killers from a distant group could divert attention from oneself and thus afford some secrecy; on the other hand, hired killers had to be paid in *kesa*, which meant a *kelo* and further fame for the offended party. These two considerations seem mutually incompatible, but if secrecy were desired the *kesa* could be presented without a *kelo*. This was not the "custom," but it was possible even if undesirable from some points of view. After all, there was really nothing to prevent it if the agents were agreeable. More usually, however, there was no attempt at secrecy, and the killers made a point of spreading the news of what they had done and why they had done it in order to make the names of all concerned "go out."

With regard to any counter-vengeance the same considerations were operative. Technically speaking, there should have been no question of whether counter-vengeance would be taken, only when it was propitious and how extensive it would be. Occasions did occur when the kinsmen of the offender felt that he only got what was coming to him, and did not wish to carry the issue any further. They did not argue that counter-vengeance was not necessary but only that it was difficult at the time. Since it was not necessary to kill the offender himself—any one of his kinsmen would have done—it was sometimes necessary to exact counter-vengeance for a party relatively innocent in the original issue. Furthermore, the Choiseulese conception of revenge was not simply "an eye for an eye" but rather to inflict a more grievous injury than had been received. Therefore, if the opportunity presented itself, the killers taking vengeance would kill several persons rather than one. There was always the danger that they would get carried away by the spirit of the thing and go too far. In that case, counter-vengeance became all the more necessary.

Warfare could come about through the escalation of vengeance and counter-vengeance or it could be chosen as the initial form of retaliation. In warfare, and the *kelo* exchanges that followed, descent group allegiances became most clearly defined and the statuses and boundaries of descent groups became most clearly defined. Warfare and its responsibilities required the mobilization of considerably more resources, personal and corporate, than any other activity, and its consequences were highly disruptive of daily life and individual ambitions. Therefore, it was not lightly undertaken nor the responsibilities easily assumed. The considerations were much the same as in lesser vengeance; the costs and risks were greater, but the possible rewards in repute and prestige were greater too.

Groups were sometimes precipitated into war more or less against their wills, as when the impetuous act of a member brought an attack upon the group which had to be avenged. Then it was not an issue of "Shall we attack in return?" but of when and under what circumstances counter-attack was best executed. If the initial attack were largely successful and considerably reduced descent-group personnel, causing the group to disperse, counter-attack was likely to be postponed for some time, perhaps a few years or until the next generation. There was also the possibility that the group might never be able to reorganize itself, and then vengeance never took place. On the other hand, some men who had lost their allies through an attack but retained their *kesa* had little difficulty in getting others to fight battles for them. Whether forced into war or choosing that course deliberately, a group went about organizing its offense and defense in much the same way.

Rather than describe warfare alliances in the abstract, their operation is here illustrated by a case history which is related to Case V, presented in chapter 6. The war took place probably some time during the 1880's, but in some ways it is still being worked out today.

Case III:

Pinggolo of the Gabili descent group in the Tepazaka region invited Monggo and Zale, two of his kinsmen from the Kubongava descent group in the same region (see Fig. 7, p. 90) to come "see his *kesa*." Monggo and Zale were related to Pinggolo through persons who had been adopted into Gabili some time before, and the exact genealogical connections are now unknown (see Fig. 10) and a matter of some dispute. Both resided at one time with Pinggolo and his group, but Monggo "returned" to Kubongava, his mother's "origin group." Zale appears to have married a close kinsman of Monggo and gone with him. Both were powerful and able men, but while Monggo used his powers to befriend others, Zale seems to have been more adept at making enemies. From the Choiseulese point of view, he was, like too many managers, an overly jealous and spiteful man. Monggo clearly was recognized as a member of Gabili descent group when he wanted to be and even later returned there, but Zale's status in respect of Gabili is a debatable subject today. In any event, Pinggolo invited them to see his *kesa* because, it is now said, he considered them both to be "of his *sinangge*," and he thought that should anything happen to Gabili these two men might be able to use the *kesa* to avenge it. He apparently had a change of heart about Zale; it is said that someone reminded him that Zale's grandfather had made trouble about a Gabili grove by claiming it as his own, suggesting that Zale might do something similar if encouraged. So Pinggolo revealed his *kesa* only to Monggo.

Now "properly" Monggo and Zale should have been given a small gift of pig and pudding at the time Pinggolo revealed his *kesa* to them, but Pinggolo presented pig and pudding to both. Zale was no fool and realized that Pinggolo was up to something. He guessed Monggo had been shown the *kesa* already, and he was properly insulted; his pride had been injured and his rights in Gabili in effect denied by Pinggolo's actions. He took his gift and hung it from a tree limb near the Gabili village. It was seen hanging there and taken as a sign of Zale's anger, but he made no threats and demanded no compensation.

However, Zale, it seems, began quietly to organize revenge. Exactly how he went about it is unknown today, but he did

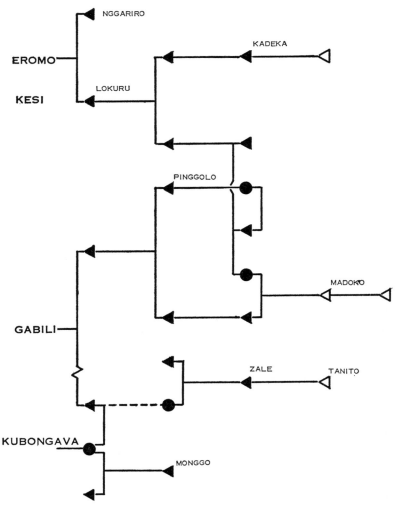

Fig. 10. Principals in the Pinggolo-Zale War

solicit the aid of another nearby group, Subavalu, that had a
grievance against a small descent group, Nggolunggolu, a segment of the major *sinangge* Korasokana, temporarily residing
with Gabili. Vatukosi of Subavalu had hoped to marry a woman
who had been taken by a Nggolunggolu man instead. Apparently
there had been some understanding between Vatukosi and the

woman's kinsmen, but they broke the "contract." Vatukosi had another grievance against Nggolunggolu too and took the opportunity to side with Zale, and since Vatukosi had his own reasons for entering into the fight, Zale did not have to promise him any *kesa*. Zale solicited additional aid from the Babatana area, his mother's home; they in turn got allies from Vella Lavella. Altogether, with the exception of Zale who stayed behind, as was his privilege—if he were to be killed, who would pay his debts?— this large war party went up the coast in canoes at night, landed near the Gabili village, and at dawn attacked it. (Attacks were always at dawn when the light was fair but villagers were still asleep.) The village was not fortified and presented no difficulty; everyone in sight was slain, but a few escaped. It is said, though with how much accuracy I cannot say, that some seventy persons, men, women, and children, were killed in the attack. Houses were burned, nearby gardens uprooted, pigs slain, and any valuables lying about carried off.

Pinggolo, his daughter, and her husband managed to escape to Kesi seeking refuge with Lokuru, the manager there. Pinggolo's brother's son had recently married Lokuru's son's daughter, and Lokuru, noting the smoke from the burning village, had readied his people to chase the attackers, fearing that they had killed his granddaughter. But Pinggolo appeared before they got very far and informed Lokuru that his granddaughter had escaped too. Lokuru agreed to give him refuge and, furthermore, to seek a means of revenge. Pinggolo gave Lokuru five *kesa* (*zapaka*, security against losses that might be sustained in Pinggolo's behalf) and promised more later. Zale meanwhile ran off to Babatana and only much later returned to Tepazaka. He had acted in secrecy so as to foster the impression that the attack had been organized solely by Vatukosi and the Subavalu group.

Later Lokuru conferred with Nggariro, reputedly Lokuru's brother and manager of the Eromo branch descent group of major *sinangge* Kesi. Nggariro was then living with his followers in the village of Subavalu, the attackers in the raid on Gabili. The estates of Subavalu and Eromo are near one another, and the two groups appear to have been on friendly terms. Lokuru sent word to Nggariro to "gather some nuts and make ready; I will come, and we will eat a pudding," a sure sign that some proposition was about to be made. When Lokuru appeared they

began to eat the pudding, but Nggariro had only begun to eat
his share when Lokuru said, "You do not eat pudding, you eat
Vatukosi's feces." Nggariro replied, "You see all these taro and
nuts, for I am about to make a *kelo*, but you bring me this thing;
you *buli* me." (*Buli* is a form of "swear" whereby one indicates
to another that he wishes his assistance in taking revenge against
the party mentioned.) Nggariro then surmised what it was that
Lokuru wanted; his plan was to attack Subavalu with Nggariro
and his forces already on the inside to assist, and he asked Lokuru
how much *kesa* he would get for assisting. Lokuru produced a
section of the midrib of an ivory nut leaf and indicated that the
kesa he would give would be that long—of that much value—
and told him the name of the particular *kesa*. Its value was
great—ten *kesa*—and Nggariro agreed to help. Actually he was
in no position to refuse. Branches of the same major *sinangge*
were obliged to assist one another; they "could not" refuse to
help, or so it is said, but they too could demand *kesa* for their
services, and they could quibble over how much their services
were worth. Otherwise, as previously noted, the various branches
of a major *sinangge* were independent of one another in their
affairs and not necessarily closely allied.

The assistance of other groups could be solicited this way or
by formal contract (*ruata*). The manager sent his agents with a
ziku or small *kesa* to call upon those from whom he wished assistance. Again, they would *buli* the manager of that group and
promise him *kesa* (also called *ruata*) if he would assist. He was
not obliged to accept their offer, but if he did he took the valuables
they brought. His acceptance was binding. It is said that truly
outstanding managers would give the total *ruata* before the fight
itself, but most often it was promised for a later date. When looking for groups to contract one went to those who were powerful
and also "good friends." It was important not to pick good friends
of the enemy lest they refuse and warn the enemy too, who
would take the opportunity to attack first or prepare for the
attack or disperse to other regions. One also looked for groups
who could "join the *ruata*" by soliciting aid from yet other
groups. In the ideal (most favored) situation A would contract B
who would contract C who would contract D, E, and F, and so on.
In this way a large war party was formed consisting of persons

only remotely related to the principals to the conflict. A "chain of *kelo*" resulted. If *kesa* was to be given after the fight, as was the "custom," ideally the process began with A and then proceeded through to F, and so on. If A gave five *kesa*, B would take one from the five, add one of his own, and so on down the line. In this way each group would get one of the *kesa* in the original *ruata*. But situations seldom worked out so orderly, and no particular stigma attached if they did not. By participating in a war for *kesa* a group would thereby contract debts as well as debtors, and this was a good enough reason for staying out of the affair. Furthermore, each party was individually responsible for its debts, having no claim upon the "bottom" or "originating" party unless promised *kesa* from him or them. Each was also liable to claims of compensation for excessive loss of life, especially important men, from groups it contracted.

Any two groups could form an alliance regardless of the type of kin tie between their representatives and even if no such ties existed. Aid could also come from any region within Choiseul and from other islands. Lokuru was the manager of a large major *sinangge*, and he solicited aid only from several of its branch descent groups. Some appear to have given their assistance without promise of *kesa* because, it is said, Lokuru had helped them in various ways before, and this was a way of meeting the obligations thereby incurred. Nggariro, however, had only recently separated from the truncal group and was just beginning to establish himself as a manager. Thus the demand for *kesa*. He was in no position to extend the contract by soliciting aid from other groups, but he was in a strategic position to help in the attack itself.

After preparing his attackers, Lokuru set a time for the raid. Nggariro continued to reside at Subavalu, and his people continued to go to their gardens daily. But each taro shoot planted was split first so it would not take root! Finally the attack came, and Subavalu was decimated. The major fighting came to an end there with no one ready to avenge Subavalu, a branch descent group apparently on poor terms with its truncal segment, Barokasa. Lokuru went to Pinggolo, who had since returned to his own land, with the news of what he had accomplished. He danced about and chanted his exploits, and he was given baked pig and promised a *kelo* later. But both Pinggolo and Lokuru were old men and soon died without having "straightened out" their debts to one another.

The *kelo*-making was left to their descendants, Madoko and Kadeka, who were young men when the old men died. Kadeka, although he was the "bottom," made his *kelo* first, but Madoko managed to take only one *kesa* from him. Finally Madoko made his *kelo* and gave five *kesa* to Kadeka. No one knows of any *kelo* made to settle with Nggariro, so it would seem that Lokuru probably gave him the *kesa* without a *kelo*. Thus Kesi lost at least one *kesa* in all these transactions. Pinggolo gave five *kesa* to Lokuru and Lokuru gave ten to Nggariro. Kadeka gave one to Madoko to force final settlement, and Madoko gave five to Kadeka in return. All in all, Gabili gave ten *kesa*, but Kesi gave eleven. The transaction would have come out even if Madoko had given Kadeka six *kesa* in return, but he pleaded that he had no more than five. Since the principals were closely related—Kadeka was Madoko's mother's first cousin—they considered the transaction closed at this point. Relations between Gabili and Kesi have remained good over the years, and the issue has not arisen again. Kadeka is said to have "forced" settlement of the debts by making his *kelo* first in order to eliminate a potential source of disputing.

But more violence was to result. Zale remained uninjured and perhaps even anonymous in the fighting that followed the attack on Gabili, and a few years later he returned to Kubongava. Shortly after his return he was accused of sorcery by Barokasa, the truncal segment of the major *sinangge* with which Subavalu was affiliated. The representatives of Barokasa were given assurances of assistance if needed by Gabili and Kesi, and they killed Zale as a sorcerer. Zale was avenged by his mother's kinsmen from Babatana, with whom he sometimes resided. They recruited a large force and intimidated the kinsmen of Zale's killers, who made it known that they would not interfere any further. But Zale's killers sought refuge with Kesi, and only one was later caught and killed. He was not a close kinsman of the principals to the conflict—he was from the Babatana region— and it was thought that too many people had already been killed because of Zale. No further revenge was sought, and the matter ended there. But not quite, for in recent years Zale's son, Tanito, has become a thorn in the side of Gabili and Kubongava, and the troubles of his father have taken on a renewed significance. This matter is discussed in detail in Chapter 6.[7]

Much more could be said about warfare and vengeance in general, and numerous and more complex examples could be given. The case cited here was actually more complex than I have made it seem. The reasons certain persons or groups did or did not involve themselves and the forms that their actions took were often not as simple as I have pictured them. However, even this much is enough to make an important point: Vengeance and warfare were not simple matters; their ramifications were often wide-ranging and protracted, the costs high, and the rewards dubious. This case allows us to see some of the factors that made for peace within this society, the factors which restrained conflict, and, if conflict had arisen, the factors which would have helped to bring it to an end.

Where private vengeance and self-help are the principal overt sanctions against injury by others, and where the exercise of those sanctions is likely to lead to further vengeance and eventually warfare, as on Choiseul, some means must be developed to mediate or prevent conflict if the society is to survive. Ethnohistorical evidence indicates that Choiseulese society clearly did survive for at least 400 years in such a situation, and it is simple enough to formulate a hypothesis to suggest how this was accomplished, in view of what we know about the maintenance of order in similar situations (cf. Colson 1953; Gluckman 1955; Glasse 1959).

The argument is simple: Simultaneous membership in more than one group clearly led to conflicts of allegiance, especially when those groups came into conflict as well as in the more mundane situations of daily life. But in daily life the kinds of relations that individuals and groups sustained with one another were divisible; the resources with which those relationships were sustained were allotable over a fairly wide range, and great expenditures of resources were not generally required. On the other hand,

---

[7] All data on this case derive from one side to the dispute, the descendants of Pinggolo and to some extent from the descendants of interested parties less closely related to him. Zale's son denies any knowledge of the affair, and Zale's kinsmen in Babatana were thoroughly evasive when I questioned them. Other cases will be cited in a further study, now in preparation, of social change consequent to pacification of the island.

in situations of vengeance allegiance was not divisible; clear lines had to be drawn at least between the two "ends" of the dispute; resources had to be committed wholly and solely to one party or the other; no one within the regions of the principals, and even many from without, could remain neutral for long. Conflicts of allegiance, phrased in the idiom of cognatic descent, and the system of redress both gave rise to efforts to repress or terminate disputes (see also chap. 3).

Some aspects of this argument have been mentioned earlier, but perhaps it is best to begin here with fundamentals.

The fact that a man's kinsmen, and especially his descent group mates, were ultimately responsible with their lives for his behavior meant that not only did they make efforts to keep a known trouble maker in line—they could kill him themselves if it became necessary—but also that they restrained him from impulsive action when he was offended.

The causes of conflict were such that it was kinsmen who perhaps most often found something to dispute about, despite the injunctions against conflict between kinsmen. There were supernatural sanctions against killing kinsmen (see chap. 5), and there were also some practical considerations for not creating or maintaining an open breach with kinsmen. But their unity was divided by kinship with other people and vested interests in their resources. Fighting with kinsmen meant encumbering one's ties and interests with them, and this division of allegiance and interest could link people directly or indirectly with their enemies, or potential enemies, in relationships other than revenge. Cognatic descent operated then as an element of social control. By constraining men from violence against kin or the kin of kinsmen, cognatic descent as an idiom of kinship was a fundamental covert sanction expressive of the constraints imposed by various conflicts of interest and allegiance. Many conflicts were nipped in the bud when a group refused a proffered contract and warned the other "end," who then fled until tempers cooled and a peace could be arranged. Those related to both "ends" of a conflict sometimes found it more expedient to assume the alternative role of peacemaker rather than disputant, and such persons were not necessarily the immediate descent group mates of the principals. They could have been other kinsmen who saw the possibility of implication if a breach occurred or if the conflict went further.

The responsibility of many for the actions of one man, even though he was not necessarily a descent group mate, involved many people in a dispute who were not really interested in revenge. Their motives for participating varied, but they were seldom as strong as those of the offended party, and as the conflict grew they sometimes found that their principal interest was simply to keep alive. They were likely to prove more reluctant to commit themselves to the expenditure of their resources as it became more apparent that they had little to gain.

The system of revenge itself thus contained a built-in ambivalence. It brought into a conflict parties who participated for motives peripheral to the central dispute itself. Generally they participated for gains in repute and wealth or to settle earlier obligations they felt binding. But they were likely to find that participation was costly—perhaps too costly—and that they could not sustain interest in continuation of the dispute. They came to feel that the needs of revenge had been satisfied and to press for moderation or termination of the conflict when cost began to appear to exceed probable profit. Once involved they could not simply "quit," but they could help to find an honorable way out for all concerned.

Besides, every conflict had to be "straightened out." It could "come to rest," but it was not "terminated" until the last debt or obligation contracted through it was finally extinguished. The *kelo* had to be given and the *ruata* and *toka* paid. The principals were therefore constrained by their ability to meet growing obligations, and helpers were constrained by the desire to see the principals emerge in a condition in which they could meet those debts. Any vengeance could go too far! It is said that any one who did not meet his contractual obligations could be turned upon by his helpers—and creditors—who could *sake* or even slay him for that reason. One doubts that the latter was ever done, no instance being given by informants, but the "right" gives evidence for the sentiment that debts were not to be taken lightly and for the recognition that every alliance sowed the seeds of further conflict or at least competition.

There was no jural obligation to refrain from initiating or participating in another conflict until an earlier one had been "settled" completely. There was, however, considerable practical advantage to doing so if possible. In the war case cited above, Nggariro made it clear that he was about to *kelo*, and helping Lokuru would be a considerable hardship. This fact, too, probably contributed to Nggariro's demand for *kesa* for his services. Technically he could not have refused his help because of the obligation of his group as a cognate unit, yet any other group in a similar position could have refused on the grounds of previous commitments.

The economy also played an important role in mitigating conflict. Each group was the producer of the staples that it required for its normal needs, and so long as it or any of its neighboring groups was engaged in a war it was not wholly safe to work in the gardens. Work proceeded only with difficulty and anxiety. Groups that had been attacked had to be supported by others until they could begin to produce again, upwards of six months, and the principals had to supply food for war parties. Since conflict disrupted normal life, it disrupted production as well, which could not continue for long.

At times none of these considerations were sufficient to prevent conflict. The desire for revenge or to gain from assistance was strong, and men did act impulsively, forcing others to follow suit. Interest might not have been strong enough to constrain passion, for the whole system involving pride and the need for revenge demanded that individual passions run high. The strain for peace was strongest within each descent group and within each region where the web of kinship ties was more tightly knit and where interpersonal and intergroup obligations and interests beyond those theoretically imposed by kinship were most strongly established. Disputes were more likely to erupt into violence and to be more difficult to resolve when they were inter-regional. However, even inter-regional disputes could be resolved and a formal peace established, for although the restraints imposed by the "kinship system" were less likely to be operative, those imposed by the system of revenge were still at work. As the conflict grew, debts increased, and more lives were lost, there were fewer disputants who stood to gain from continuation of the conflict. The pressures for settlement mounted.

It was possible for a manager to act as go-between in a dispute between two descent groups and arrange a formal peace. He is said to have done this because the disputants were his kinsmen and he did not like to see kinsmen fight. However, he may have had other reasons; he may have feared implication of himself perhaps against his will, or one or the other party might have been indebted to him and it would have been to his disadvantage to let the conflict continue, but his effectiveness depended upon how well he maintained a show of disinterested peacemaking. A man with too much interest in one party was not likely to be trusted by the other. Persons without much status in their own right but with an interest in settling a dispute could call upon a man of status to intervene in their behalf. The go-between had no power to impose a settlement—he could only suggest—but he was sometimes useful to make public the private anxieties of all concerned who could not speak for themselves without losing prestige. He may have been able to persuade the disputants not to fight or to discontinue fighting, arguing that there were good reasons why both parties should find it advantageous to make a settlement or pointing out ways in which they could view the demands of revenge as already satisfied.

If the go-between were able to arbitrate a settlement, perhaps an exchange of *kesa* rather than more revenge, he arranged a formal peacemaking ceremony which was known simply as "breaking the spear." In this ceremony the principals met together with their supporters, and each took one end of a spear which was grasped in the middle by the go-between who then pressed upon it and broke it in two. The former disputants then exchanged one *ziku* each, and that is all there was to the ceremony. It is said that if they agreed to exchange *kesa*, as they could, or if one party agreed to give the other *kesa* in order to even the score, then a *kelo* could be held. Again, informants could cite no specific instance. Some mentioned the possibility of a marriage between disputants "settling" the conflict, but this was not a matter for formal arrangement. In the one instance that came to my attention, some years after the formal peacemaking the son of one disputant married the daughter of the other, and one argument given in favor of the marriage was that it would secure the peaceful relations between the two "ends," but the marriage was not arranged specifically for that purpose. Not all conflicts were settled formally. Some met a "natural death" when one party became too disabled to continue, abandoned the fight, and fled to another area to live quietly. Of course, a great deal of prestige was lost, and it was best to agree to a truce before one was reduced to such a state. Furthermore, there was always the possibility that if a formal truce were not made then the "other end" would continue to harbor its grievance and entertain the possibility of further violence when it had managed to regain its strength. Even in a truce there was always the same possibility, and it is said that if the spear split rather than broke clean one side still retained a "small anger." This was "only a saying," but it expressed the knowledge that both "ends" made a truce only when they found it mutually advantageous, not when they could be persuaded that they really had no dispute.

Finally, it is important to note a concomitant feature of the system of revenge alliances. The economy and ecology placed limits upon the size of permanent local groups, and the vengeance system insured that the alliances between local groups did not endure beyond the accomplishment of the task for which they were formed (with the possible exception of some alliances between cognate branches) because, thereafter, members of the alliance entered into relations of opposition among themselves in the exchange of *kelo* and *kesa*. Alliances between cognate branches could suffer the same fate. In the war case cited above, Lokuru was assisted by Nggariro and his branch for a consideration in *kesa*, but other cognate branches assisted without compensation because they were already in his debt. Their alliance with Lokuru persisted precisely because they remained in his debt, but their assistance contributed to the annulment of the debt as a basis of continued alliance. As the Choiseulese put it, it helped to "kill" the debts. Future alliances between cognate branches remained more likely than other alliances, but they were never simply "automatic."

Despite the advantages in peace which might have ensued, the region could not become a solidary unit without internal competition. Within the region no one manager "stood out" over all others. There were always several men of considerable power and prestige, and it is said that they had to "trust one another," meaning that they should have been ever ready to coöperate and lend assistance to one another, but this did not lessen the responsibility to meet obligations incurred in time of conflict or upon any other occasion. Affinal and cognatic ties drew the groups of one region "close together" and often created considerable overlap in their cognatic descent categories. They were traditionally "close," but, as we have seen, kinship and marriage divided as well as allied.

To summarize: War was a considerable drain upon all of a group's resources and could lead to the end of the group as an active political unit. Such considerations led men to take simple revenge when they would rather have had massive retaliation; since no manager could go to war without the consent of his followers they were able to dissuade him from the more drastic course of action, and the followers and would-be allies could exert similar pressures and thus keep the conflict from ramifying. But as in any vengeance system, there was always the danger of counter-vengeance and the possibility of escalation into warfare. Furthermore, since secrecy with regard to actual strength was a major stratagem, miscalculation was always possible and sometimes the relative strengths of the parties could only be determined in conflict itself, so that, in effect, conflict had to be enlarged before it could be resolved. Warring occurred then, but not as often as it might have if pride and prestige were the only considerations. When war did eventuate, its organization entailed its resolution. The organization of warfare involved expansion of the conflict through a multiplication of the number of parties; and as the number of parties increased, so did the likelihood of conflicts of allegiance, and in these resided the possibility of peace.

Chapter 5

Ghosts, Gods
and Groups

The following outline of the relationship between religious and kin-group structure shows how the system of ancestor worship "reflected" or was coördinate with Choiseulese concepts and norms of descent group structure. It has some comparative value in that Hogbin's (1939) study of the To'ambaita of Malaita Island, to the east of Choiseul in the Central Solomons, reports a complex relationship between the observation and maintenance of religious obligations and group affiliation quite unlike that of the Choiseulese, yet the groups and their interrelations seem otherwise similar to those of the Choiseulese.[1] For comparative purposes, then, a brief statement of Choiseulese religious concepts and practices is in order here.

The Choiseulese have been, almost to a man, at least nominal Christians for thirty to forty years, and the aboriginal religion is nowhere practiced today. A few people told me of others who still persist in certain activities, but those persons staunchly denied it and frequently professed total disinterest in or ignorance of the subject in any detail.

As we would expect of such a fragmented society, the Choiseulese had few concepts of other than human beings whose interests or concerns transcended those of particular descent groups.

---

[1] Materials forthcoming from a study just completed in the Kwaio area of Malaita by Roger Keesing again reveal similarities to the Choiseul situation but also some striking differences, especially with respect to the role of religious phenomena.

Many *bangara*, or "gods", were not associated with particular groups; nor were the *sinipi* (see pp. 204–205); nor were various other "wild" beings such as the evil and malicious *manuru piru* ("wild spirits" as opposed to *manuru basoe* or "ghosts of the dead"); nor was *manggota Nabonabo*, a huge "woman" who roamed the bush and captured men for her sexual pleasures; nor was Porana, the trickster-orphan-hero so well known in Solomon Islands mythology who introduced the delights of sexual intercourse. There were no cults organized to propitiate these beings, and they did nothing to transcend group differences. Their actions mainly accounted for a number of events and they are of no great significance for this discussion.

Few descent groups attempted in any way to account for their origins by reference to other than human beings or events. A few men related myths associated with the origins of their groups; the following story is typical:

> A long time ago—not so long that there were not already people on Choiseul—a snake gave birth to a baby girl. Later a man passed by the village of the snake and saw the girl and decided he wanted to marry her. The girl said, "I am the child of a snake, and so it cannot be." But the man wanted her very much, and she finally relented. Later she gave birth to a baby boy. The man worked in the gardens, and the woman tended the baby. One day the man went down to the sea and left the woman and child in the village. She then went off to the gardens leaving the child in the care of its snake-grandmother. This happened on several occasions, and the man began to be suspicious, for the wife always had garden produce at the end of the day, yet she was supposed to be tending the child in the village. "Who was watching the child?" he asked himself. So one day he decided to deceive her, and he did not go to the sea. He went only a short way down the path and then returned to the village. There he found his child seated in the coils of the snake. He snatched up the child and slew the snake with his club, breaking it into several pieces. Some rolled into the sea and became the sharks and rays; others rolled into the streams and became eels. The Kubongava people descended from that child, and that is why sharks, rays, and eels are tabu to them.

But this story hardly accounts for the "origin" of the Kubongava descent group, for where did the man come from? Nor did my informant mean it to be taken as an account of Kubongava origins;

it accounts rather for some restrictions observed by these people. (See chap. 2 for further comment on "origins.")

Each descent group had such tabus, though the Varisi generic term for them is *mamanggila* in this context. Most are accounted for in similar terms, though many were acquired through the actions of particularly notable managers who imposed certain restrictions on their followers. Sometimes these restrictions were sanctioned only by the power of the manager and did not "carry over" to other generations, but others, in some unknown way, became accepted as part of the group's culture and distinctiveness and remained. For instance, the people of Kesi could not use a particular type of tree for firewood because Bose, their most notable manager, made his slit-drum from that wood. Many *mamanggila* were not, however, restricted to particular descent groups but were common to whole regions or perhaps the whole of the island. For instance, the numerous restrictions placed on women in general, pregnant women, and new mothers were also known as *mamanggila* and with minor variations seem to have been practiced over the whole of Choiseul. The observance of restrictions on conduct peculiar to a particular descent group was demanded only of participating members of the group or of those who considered themselves only temporarily dissociated from it. The restrictions were not incumbent upon those who were only members of the group's cognatic descent category. In this sense the Choiseulese were somewhat relativistic about such matters, and those who considered themselves "close" to the group could observe its *mamanggila* if they so chose. Personal observation of these restrictions was probably indicative of a person's self-identification as a descent-group member.

"Misfortune" or "bad luck" was the principal sanction against the violation of these restrictions. A person who violated them was likely to become ill and would not succeed at his tasks or enterprises, such as gardening, pig-raising, and child care. To succeed at all enterprises was to demonstrate the gift of *mana*. *Mana* was given by the gods (*bangara*) and spirits or ghosts of the dead (*manuru*) to those persons who regularly observed all restrictions and customs and who fed the gods and ghosts at the proper times. *Mana* gave *makaulo*, general good fortune and success, which in particular realms had more particular names (e.g., *rakisi* in productive and reproductive endeavors; *siakale* in vengeance activities). The opposite of *makaulo* was *situ*, "bad luck" or "misfortune," which also had more particular names in specified realms of activity. *Situ* was the product of the anger of the *bangara* or *manuru*, who disliked some conduct or who had been neglected, that is, had not been "fed" frequently enough or on the proper occasions.

When angered, the *manuru* or *bangara* did not warn the incautious parties but scared them or made them sick or impeded their activities. Such events, especially if protracted or recurrent, aroused suspicions, and then those men who had the talent of being able to "speak" to the *manuru* or *bangara* were called upon for assistance. These men discovered the cause of the misfortune and recommended sacrifices or the use of "medicines" (*sumuku*) to cure an illness. Various symptoms or empirical manifestations are said to have been characteristic of the effects of the *manuru* or *bangara* as opposed to sorcery or other forms of "magic," and only those men who "spoke" to the *manuru* or *bangara* are said to have been able to discern them and then confirm their knowledge by talking to the *manuru* or *bangara*. Again, one suspects, with confirmation from the Choiseulese themselves, they only told the parties what those parties already "knew" and wanted to hear confirmed, but since I was unable to investigate these events empirically, I cannot describe the processes in detail. My informants professed to no detailed knowledge of these things, and the one well known "curer" with whom I was more or less friendly refused to discuss his knowledge or activities in detail too; these were frowned upon by the missionaries in particular, and some Choiseulese were openly opposed to his activities which, they argued, "only made trouble." (See Case V, chap. 6, for an instance of this.)

Bangara were more powerful, "stronger," than the *manuru*. They were also considerably less numerous and of greater strategic significance in intergroup relations. One indication of their greater strength, and an acknowledgement of it, was that they received the first offerings of the smoked nuts ready for storage at the end of the nutting season. Offerings were made at all shrines at that time, but the *bangara* got the first and largest share.

Bangara were of various sorts and forms. Some had the appearance of men, others had the bodies of animals, such as snakes

Most of them resided in the sea but a few in the bush. Some were associated with descent groups, others were independent. *Bangara Laena*, who created and introduced *kesa*, resided in the sea and was not connected with any particular descent group. He was of human or quasi-human form, and he is reputed to have died in a contest of wit and strength with *bangara Nggola* who was a bush *bangara* with a snake body. Other *bangara* are said to have appeared in quasi-human form sitting on the surface of the sea or at their sacred places. Such appearances rendered their viewers deathly ill, though they could be cured by some "medicines" unless they had deliberately violated the restrictions. To avoid seeing them, their "keepers" are said to have looked away from their shrines when making offerings.

Ideally, each descent group maintained at least one *bangara*, and some maintained several, each belonging to a branch even though that branch might not have been separate in other ways. Each branch in the latter instance "fed" or gave sacrifices to its own *bangara*. But not just anyone could do this; feeding the *bangara* was the responsibility of only one man who "cared" for it, and that man was not necessarily the *batu*. As *bangara* proved themselves more or less powerful, they were said to care for the whole descent group, and requests could be made by other branches for the keeper to ask the *bangara* for assistance. In any event, whatever a *bangara* did for its branch affected the whole group more or less directly. Independent branches also maintained *bangara* of their own, and if they were temporarily without one they had to depend solely upon their ancestral spirits.

Each *bangara* had a "sacred place," and usually some representation of the *bangara* was kept there. The place itself was in the bush away from settlements and paths, and was strictly out of bounds to all but the keeper of the *bangara*. Some such shrines were based on natural boulders, others contained mounds of coral slabs as altars. The representation of the *bangara* was placed upon this along with a receptacle, perhaps only an open clam shell, for the sacrifices offered to it. In some cases the representation consisted of an idol of quasi-human form decorated with the various ornaments most appropriate to a manager. In others the representation was an object of, for instance, crossed sticks also profusely decorated. Some sacrificial or sacred places contained nothing, and the sacrificial offerings were merely thrown into the bush or a nearby stream in offering.

It was the duty of the keeper to feed the *bangara* regularly and also to make it offerings of *ziku* (shell rings) or miniature imitations of them. At the same time he asked the *bangara* to give his group good fortune in the form of health, wealth, and success in all endeavors, enumerating them at length. On special occasions further sacrifices and prayers were made, and advice was asked of the *bangara* and his answer read in various signs. Thus when the group was about to undertake a raid, for instance, the keeper went out in a canoe (if the *bangara* resided in the sea) and threw offerings into the sea while asking the *bangara* if the raid were advisable. The answer was given by the rocking of the canoe from side to side or a failure to rock, indicating a negative answer.

The *bangara* was also asked to inflict injury on the enemy. Each *bangara* had a number of animals that "went with" or "followed" it, and these were forbidden as food to the keepers (the whole group) of that *bangara*. *Bangara* who came from the sea typically were "followed" by sharks, crocodiles, and squid; bush *bangara* by the eagle, owl, a few other birds, and sometimes snakes. These animals did the bidding of their *bangara* and sometimes served as oracles. The keepers could ask the *bangara* to send them against the enemy bearing misfortune of all sorts. Thus, before a raid, they might have been sent to fly over the enemy village bearing *situ* (ill fortune). They could appear to the keepers as oracles foretelling the death of a group member or some other disaster about to befall them.

Bangara were acquired by descent groups in various ways, but always by the choice of the *bangara* itself. The people of Nggolunggolu *sinangge*, a dependent branch of Korasokana, were chosen by a sea *bangara* who manifest himself as a floating slab of stone. The story tells how they and other *sinangge* saw this peculiar phenomenon in the sea and went to where it had washed ashore. A man who "talked" to *manuru* and *bangara* claimed it was obviously a *bangara* and reported that he had been told it had come to Nggolunggolu and wished to be worshiped at a certain place on their land. The people of other groups were jealous and tried to lift the stone and carry it off, but all failed because despite its relatively small size it proved too heavy for them to move. The

Nggolunggolu people tried, and the stone was as light as a feather to them. Another group acquired its *bangara* when an old man dying in great pain asked for some *bangara* to come carry him off to death. That night, so goes the story, a *bangara* came and said he would be taken away, but first he had to instruct his kinsmen about the *bangara* and request them to feed the *bangara*. The people were happy to accept and chose the old man's brother as its keeper. In yet another instance, *bangara* were bought and then shared by several groups. *Kesa* was given in exchange for a share in the *bangara*, but the *bangara* was not then obliged to accept the situation. To determine whether he had, a coconut was taken from a palm sacred to the *bangara* and planted at the would-be new shrine. If it grew, this was taken as evidence that the *bangara* had "crossed over," but he did not surrender his allegiance to the first group. In one such instance the groups concerned were not of the same religion, but they were traditionally "friendly" groups.

None of my information indicates that the keeper of the *bangara* played more than a sacred or religious role. The keeper merely acted as the group's representative vis-à-vis the dangerous person of the *bangara*, and this role conferred upon him a degree of respect but no further formal powers. Anyone who could speak to *bangara* and *manuru* could occupy such a position, and though the keeper's son was the most eligible successor he could be succeeded by any member of the group. Managers sometimes "kept" *bangara*, and some managers were thought to derive much power from particular ones, but a manager could be strong even without a *bangara*.

The *bangara* do not seem to have played a significant role in sanctioning conduct other than that due to themselves. The *manuru*, on the other hand, sanctioned the bulk of customary norms and expectations and were the continuing source of *mana*, power, and general success.

The *manuru*, as already indicated, fell into two classes—"wild" and "ghosts" of human beings. Some "wild" ones were propitiated too, especially those which were the motivating force in the various medicinal and magical plants known collectively as *manuru leba* or "*manuru* plants." The plants used in making "medicine" were sometimes cultivated in small quantities near dwellings, and the spirits of the plants were occasionally propitiated with small offerings of food put near them. Other *manuru* plants were used for such things as warding off enemy spears or the "poison" of sorcerers. The leaves of the plants were rubbed on one's body. The plants used in sorcery concoctions are also *manuru* plants, but these were, or are, planted in secrecy. Some men are believed to know other "medicines," as the Choiseulese now call them, that can kill the *manuru* of the plant if it is inadvertently discovered. All these "medicines" get their powers, for good or ill, from their *manuru* who in some unknown way effect cures or inflict injuries. The *manuru* of the plant is also called its *madau*, the word for the human "soul." This *madau* could also appear in animal form. For instance, the *madau* of *siakale*, the *manuru* plant for averting enemy spears, could manifest itself as a particular snake and enter a house in order to indicate it wanted to be propitiated.

Other wild *manuru* were believed to do no particular good, and they frequently appeared to people in the bush or alone, and severely frightened them. Some informants thought these were ghosts who through neglect had lost the attention of men and were seeking revenge. People sometimes saw them, or so they say; they have an "ugly" appearance, though much like ordinary men in general body form. Glimpses of them are only fleeting. Otherwise they make their presence known only by moving about and making noises.

Of far greater social and sociological significance were the *manuru* who were ghosts. My informants were not sure how men became ghosts, unless a person's *madau* or "soul," which was his motivating force in life and resided in the region behind his sternum, became his *manuru* at death. Others were not so sure of the connection, but all were sure that all men became ghosts just as they were sure that ghosts retained the general physical and social characteristics of their former living selves. Thus some were "strong" and others "weak," and some were inclined to anger easily while others did not take offense readily. Their strength varied also with the amount of attention paid to them by their living kinsmen, but all had the power to sanction inattention to themselves or customary conduct by inflicting illness or other forms of misfortune.

The *manuru* given most attention were those of managers, and they were, as might be expected, the strongest of all *manuru*. They were the objects of group cults. Particular individuals were concerned mostly with the ghosts of their own recent ancestors, such as a father or mother or mother's brother or grandparent. They could sacrifice and pray to them at the descent-group shrine, but they could also throw bits of food into the family hearth and call out the ancestors' names and ask them for a blessing. They did this especially when the family had made a good catch of fish, or wild pig, or had been given a portion of a pig from a feast. Other *manuru* continued to exist but were not singled out as individuals and instead were referred to collectively as the "dead ones" of the group in prayers and offerings.

At death a person's *manuru* stayed about for a short time, and, if sorcery was suspected, helped to point out the sorcerer. After that it could reside in a number of places and perhaps return to visit the living from time to time, especially in the months following death. Such visits were considered ominous and frightening, for only the malcontent *manuru* would bother the living. At the time of the death all *manuru* of a group, good and bad, returned to its village to escort the new *manuru* to Ungana, the land of the dead somewhere high on Bougainville Island. Thus this was a dangerous time, and immediately after the cremation of the corpse a ceremony had to be performed to drive the *manuru* back to Ungana. The *manuru* at Ungana led an idyllic life with little work and much happiness. As conceived, it was otherwise much like the life of the living but had no effect upon the latter.

After a brief period in which the corpse was viewed by relatives from near and far, it was usually cremated, but a few *sinangge* had as one of their *mamanggila* that the dead were buried and later exhumed instead. The responsibility for carrying out the cremation devolved upon no particular persons, that is, no specific classes of kinsmen, but rather upon the descent group of the deceased, less his immediate kinsmen who were too grief-stricken to do any more than sit and wail, and others of his kinsmen who had come to mourn. Informants knew of no special ritual accompanying the cremation itself. Shortly after the cremation the ashes and bone fragments were gathered into an earthen pot and left for a time at the site of the cremation. Offerings and prayers could be made there until the later stage of the funeral. Meanwhile, various mourning restrictions were observed by the immediate coresident kinsmen of the deceased and by others who had felt a particularly close attachment to him, but in the strictest sense they were incumbent only upon the members of his immediate family. They were not, however, restricted to particular classes of kinsmen nor to members of the descent group with which he had been affiliated.

The second stage of the funeral, called "the setting of the bones," marked the end of the mourning period and could take place any time after an undefined decent interval and whenever the kinsmen of the deceased had managed to provision the necessary feast or to get someone to do it for them (see chap. 4). At this time the bones and ashes were removed to the ancestral shrine of the descent group concerned, or the remains of a "visitor" or "guest" were removed to his "own" and "proper" place. The remains of an established *tamazira* stayed where he had died. Some groups kept the remains of managers in a separate place, for example, a *dolo* or large stone urn, and all groups maintained separate shrines for the remains of men and women, though usually nearby one another. The work at this point was carried out by the immediate kinsmen, their descent group mates, and other friends and kinsmen of the deceased, and again no specific kinsmen were delegated the responsibility. If the same pattern was followed in the past as is today, and informants said it was, then the immediate kinsmen did little more than observe the proceedings and supply food for the feast that followed. Again, there was no special ritual for such occasions. The remains were deposited in their final place with the usual prayer to the *manuru* already there to care for the recently deceased and not to be angry with the people and to give them success and welfare in general. Small offerings from the feast were made too.

The generic term for ancestral shrines was *tuangga*. The small temporary one constructed at the site of the cremation was the *pinoma*, and after the second stage of the funeral it was ignored. The commonest type of *tuangga* was made of slabs of coral built up into an altar-like structure. Remains were concealed inside. Others made use of small rock shelters, and the urns were placed inside "boxes" of coral slabs for protection. Managers were, of course, treated with greater dignity and set apart in death as in life. The monolithic *dolo* were used only by a few descent groups and were confined to the northwest half of the island beginning at the Ririo and Varisi regions. Some groups took great care to preserve the skulls of their managers (those groups who did not cremate their dead), and these were placed in special shrines, "ghost's houses," which were merely small, A-shaped structures made of reeds and profusely decorated with arm rings and other ornaments.

Any man having ancestors residing at a particular shrine could go there and make small offerings of food and prayers to the *manuru* of that place. He did not have to be a permanent and full-fledged member of the descent group to do so, nor was it necessary for him to do this in order to be able to claim membership in the descent group if he were not already resident with it. Usually one made offerings wherever one was living and had ancestors in the group concerned, and it was not necessary to make an effort to go to other places just for the purpose of propitiating one's ancestors there. Men residing as *tamazira* could propitiate the ancestors of their wives' groups, and men resident with their mothers' descent groups could and did propitiate their mothers' ancestors as well as their fathers' ancestors. When traveling about or visiting, a person could propitiate his ancestors at various places, but there was no formal obligation for him to do so. When a person left one group and took membership in another he left the care of the *manuru* of the former group to those persons remaining there and assumed an interest in maintaining the *manuru* of the new group.

A person devoted his attentions to the *manuru* of the descent group with which he was affiliated at the time and gave minor attention to others when the occasion presented itself. This did not mean, however, that more immediate ancestors were ignored by him if he was not resident near their shrine. As already noted, he could make minor sacrifices on his own family hearth. In fact, people seem to have avoided the ancestral shrines, since they were "dangerous" places, and left their care to the elder men or to those who could "speak" to the *manuru*. Again, as for the *bangara*, the "prayers" were simple, announcing the presentation of the offering and asking for *mana* for oneself and one's kinsmen or for a more particular form of assistance.

The deceased *batu* were by far the most important ancestors, and the person with the most immediate and continuing interest in them was the living *batu*. He derived much of his power in the form of *mana* from them, and the more powerful they were in life the more *mana* they could confer as ancestors. They favored their own descendants, especially lineal ones, but they would confer *mana* upon "anyone who was good for the group" too. They sanctioned constraint on the part of the manager in relation to other group members, for their role was to aid him in caring for the group. Thus he could expect retaliation from them if he abused his position.

The recognition of the status of the living manager, especially if he were a *batu ununa pua* rather than a *batu sokele*, was sustained by the presentation of first-fruits, and this presentation was sanctioned by his relation to the ancestors of the land. These had to be presented to the manager or the ancestral ghosts of the group would not sustain the productivity of the land. Upon receipt of the first-fruits the manager made an offering to the ancestors and asked them to "bless" the garden concerned. The significance of these presentations for land tenure matters was noted earlier (p. 121).

We have also noted (p. 187) the ways in which ancestral managers were believed to assist their groups. Their strategic importance demanded for them special forms of attention, and each living manager kept a special shrine for an ancestral manager, perhaps his immediate predecessor. This shrine, called a *lopo*, consisted of a small structure made from an ivory nut frond shaped so as to form a cup with a hood over it. This was tied to a tree or post near the general ancestral shrine of the group. The *lopo* held fragments of the remains, especially teeth or jaw fragments, or small personal possessions of the ancestral manager, and small offerings were put into it "as though the manager were eating them." The *lopo* contained also a kind of "medicine" which drew its power from the ancestral manager. Whenever the keeper undertook some endeavor of importance he took the "medicine" out of the *lopo* and carried it with him on his person so that the strength of the ancestral manager would go with him and assist him. The teeth inside the *lopo* represented the "strong, straight" speech of the ancestral manager, and small shell rings were put there to represent his eyes which saw through many deceptions and which could help to evaluate the size and quality of *kesa* that might be exchanged. Although such "customs" as first-fruits were sanctioned by the ancestors, other forms of conduct, such as restrictions established by an ancestral manager himself, were not. Each manager had various personal possessions, such as his string bag, his lime box, and his pudding mortar, which others were forbidden to use or even touch. He could also *tabu* his nut trees or restrict the use of groves and reefs for a period to commemorate the death of a close kinsman. Violations of these restrictions constituted a grave offense to the person of the manager, and climbing such a tree, for instance, was "like climbing the body of his wife," that is, equivalent to adultery with her. Such offenses "downed" the manager, and thus their observance was probably symbolic of allegiance to him and recognition of his powers. Their only sanction was his strength, and the offender did not fall ill as a consequence, though managers and lesser men could protect their groves from others by using a *manuru* plant that would injure thieves.

Informants said that each descent group worshiped its own ancestral managers and other ancestral ghosts. Each branch could maintain its own ancestral shrine regardless of its political or residential status. But, although branches that had not formally established their separateness or autonomy could continue to do so, independent branches did not go to the shrines of the truncal segment and offer sacrifices to the more remote ancestral managers of both units. However, these ancestors could still be appealed to by throwing bits of food or shell rings into the bush and calling out their names. The establishment of separate *bangara* and ancestor shrines probably followed the establishment of separate residence and these were stages in the development of separate political identity. I could not observe these events in process and can only infer that this was so.

A final note on the subjects of cannibalism and head-hunting. This diversion may be superfluous, but it is a point about which the Choiseulese feel greatly abused. Early European observers (e.g., de Tolna 1905) were inclined to see a cannibal behind every bush and to interpret the most innocuous practices as cannibalistic. There can be no doubt that many Solomon Islanders practiced cannibalism and head-hunting on a lavish scale. The peoples of the islands of New Georgia, Vella Lavella, and Simbo were rightly notorious in this respect, and skull houses, which were important religious shrines, are still to be seen in these places. The Choiseulese at first, as was to be expected, denied such practices, though they could describe these customs on other islands in some detail. Later my more intimate and knowledgeable friends described the only "cannibalistic" practices of the Choiseulese themselves.

Just as other Solomon Islanders took the heads of slain enemies and placed them in shrines in order to acquire their *mana*, and also ate bits of their flesh to accomplish the same end, so the Choiseulese also took small strips of flesh and muscle from the calves of the legs of slain enemies, mixed them with taro and a bit of "bush medicine," and ate it. In this way they too acquired some of the enemies' *mana*. Such concoctions were also kept in small packets and consumed just before a battle in order to make the warrior full of rage and unafraid of his enemies of the moment. As far as my informants knew, this practice was not the subject of a public ritual but was purely private. Nor were these concoctions offered to the *manuru*. De Tolna (1905), however, claimed to have accompanied a raid upon a bush village on Choiseul around 1903 or 1904. According to him, these "cannibals" ate only human flesh, fruit, and vegetables during the course of their campaign, and he claimed they took earlier captives with them, who were killed and eaten during the preparations for the raid itself. They were not killed before his eyes, he said, for the natives "observed the classical precept of tragedy and did not murder before an audience." My informants denied that the Choiseulese had ever done such things and suggested that de Tolna may have accompanied a party of hired killers from Vella Lavella or New Georgia, that is, if he had not made up the whole story.

The children taken as *mate bangara* (see p. 102) in order to christen or inaugurate a new ancestral shrine or a new war canoe or to honor a recently deceased manager were slain and their blood spilled over the object in order to placate the *bangara* and ancestral spirits. However, there was no cannibalism on these occasions, and the child could be saved if some woman of the group, especially the wife of a manager, intervened and offered to adopt it.

Chapter 6

The Particular
and the General

The following analysis of detailed case histories is designed to give substance to the foregoing abstract discussion and also to demonstrate further the complexity of the issues in changes of affiliation. Presentation of these cases has been deferred to this point because understanding of them requires a general knowledge of Choiseulese social structure. These cases have not been chosen because of any typicality, for changes of affiliation are not particularly typical, but rather for the processes and motives they reveal, and these are not unusual. In particular they illustrate something of the interaction between the formal ideology and the social situations within which people have recourse to various aspects of the former.

Case IV: The Evolution of a Descent Group

Sinangge Votuae, already referred to in the war case of the previous chapter, had a complex history. For a long time it apparently was not an organized group but rather only a descent-group segment consisting of people sharing interests in a segment or "share" of the estate of the major *sinangge* Kesi. The manager of Kesi descent group is said to have allotted it to his son Sodabangara, who did not then form a separate descent group but remained affiliated with the truncal segment, descent-group Kesi. According to one of his descendants, he married *tamazira* to Nggolunggolu, a dependent branch of Korasokana descent group, but according to another of his descendants he sometimes coöperated closely with the

Nggolunggolu people and only resided among them from time to time. However, he was killed in a battle on the estate of yet another and neighboring descent group (Singgotu) from which he had taken another wife and with which he was resident at the time. He had refused the demand of an influential man from Babatana region for one of his daughters in marriage, and that man then attacked the village and Sodabangara was killed. After his death, his wives did not return to Kesi but remained with their respective natal groups. Thus his sons became affiliated with two different descent groups, and none of them ever resided upon their father's share of the Kesi estate. One of them later returned to Kesi on the strength of his father's previous affiliation and took two of his sisters with him. Later, some of Sodabangara's descendants realigned themselves into a separate hamlet and effectively established a descent group, though again not on his share of Kesi estate.

In any event, the descendants of Sodabangara are now widely scattered throughout the Tepazaka region and affiliated with several different groups. Their movements were influenced somewhat by "traditional" considerations (e.g., cognatic-descent-category membership, "filiation," and *tamazira* marriages) and others by factors arising from the disturbance of the settlement pattern, principally by the missions (e.g., need for schooling in the early days when there was not a school in each village). Figure 11 illustrates their dispersion today as well as some of the genealogical ties between them. (See also Fig. 7, p. 90.) All of them at times refer to themselves as Votuae people, or Kesi people, or as members of the descent groups with which they are now affiliated.

The following account concentrates on Sodabangara's descendants who finally formed a descent group which took the name of his portion of the Kesi estate, Votuae, though apparently they never have resided at Votuae itself. This account illustrates, among other things, how some men despite their status as non-agnates may come to occupy an important and perhaps even dominant position in descent-group affairs. It illustrates too the ambiguity and possible multiplicity of group affiliation or allegiance.

Monggo, who had been adopted into Gabili descent group, had a daughter, Sara. Monggo, even though he was an adoptee, had earned a reputation as a big-man, ambitious and able. His daugh-

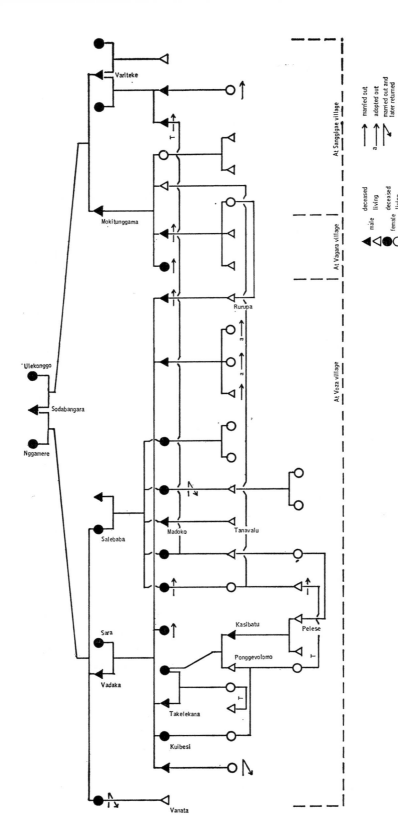

Fig. 11. Sodabangara's Descendants

ter fell in love with Vadaka, Sodabangara's son who was then the manager of Votuae's estate and resident at Kesi, having "returned" from Singgotu, his mother's group, and activated his interests in his father's share of the Kesi estate. Sara ran off with Vadaka to Kesi; this greatly angered Monggo, who put on such a show of ferocity that Vadaka offered him a brideprice of ten *kesa*, an extraordinary amount under the circumstances. Monggo had to consider, too, that one of Vadaka's sisters was already married to the manager of *sinangge* Gabili. In the end, to show that he was not really so angry and to compensate Vadaka for the large brideprice, Gabili allowed Monggo to allot a grove to Sara and Vadaka. There was yet another motive behind this; Gabili, and especially its manager, wished to strengthen its ties with Votuae people and ultimately Kesi. Sara and Vadaka took up residence on that grove, which is known as Kubanakesa, and raised a large family there (four sons and two daughters). The grove is right in the center of the Gabili estate and on the coast. It contains exceptionally good land for coconut plantations and is well planted today.

Vadaka's children continued to reside either at Kubanakesa or, from time to time, with their kinsmen of the Gabili descent group in its village. Gradually they all married. Three of the sons and one of the daughters (who took a husband from the Nggolunggolu group by *tamazira* marriage) stayed together at Kubanakesa as a group, one of the sons married *tamazira* to a nearby group, and one of the daughters married a man in another region. These descendants of Sodabangara and Vadaka continued to use the original grove of Votuae deeper inland (for gardens and the gathering of nuts, leaf, and so on) and allowed others to use the land too, but did not assume residence there.

Vadaka's daughter Kuibesi married Vavasa, who came to live with Vadaka as his *tamazira*. Later Vadaka's son Takelekana married a cousin (FFBDD), Likungguana, a Kesi woman who had previously been married to a man from Subavalu, the branch of Barokasa descent group, also mentioned in the war case of Chapter 5. Likungguana's first husband had died, leaving her with two small sons to care for, and she had "returned" to live with her mother's brother who had married a sister of the manager of Gabili. Subavalu was in the process of disintegrating, only partly as a consequence of its role in the war. Thus she could not stay with it. Nor were there evidently any close patrilateral kinsmen who could have claimed the boys at the time. Takelekana assumed the care of her sons and is said to have adopted them as his own. He had no other sons, though he eventually did have a daughter by Likungguana. Later, some of the boys' patrilateral kinsmen did argue that the boys should go with them, but Takelekana refused to discuss the matter and said they were his sons and now members of the Votuae group. The two brothers, Ponggevolomo and Kasibatu, then considered themselves to be Votuae people and the rightful heirs of Takelekana's interests in that group's estate. To make sure of Ponggevolomo's status in Votuae, Takelekana arranged for him to marry Polosokiu, the daughter of his sister who had brought a *tamazira* to Vadaka. Thus Ponggevolomo became linked to Votuae as the adopted son of Takelekana and as his *tamazira* too. He was also related to it through his mother who had been a Kesi woman. Kasibatu married Oivavene, the daughter of an adopted son of Monggo and then a recognized member of Gabili descent group. In neither instance was brideprice paid, and so both marriages may be regarded as *tamazira*. However, the situation is not so clear-cut since both marriages took place after the mission had become established and banned brideprice payments, so that both may be considered "nothing marriages" (*busi volomo*) too. However these marriages may be construed, the brothers always stayed together whether or not the Votuae people happened to be coresident with Gabili.

Since World War II, Votuae and Gabili have been coresident in the same village. The people of Votuae have freely used the lands of Gabili, for the manager of Gabili regards them all as members of Gabili or at least as "very close kinsmen" of it. They have found it difficult to maintain any form of residential segregation since further intermarriage has even more greatly confused their distinctiveness. They are almost completely "coresident" (*vari kapakapa*). Ponggevolomo has become the principal and certainly the most active claimant to interests in Kubanakesa and the chief contender with Tanavalu, the present manager of Gabili, for prestige and leadership within the community. It happened this way:

Vadaka's eldest son had only one daughter who married elsewhere, was widowed, and left her one daughter by that marriage in the care of Ponggevolomo and her husband's brother who lives in an adjacent village. She has remarried into yet another village.

THE PARTICULAR AND THE GENERAL

Ponggevolomo declined to take a brideprice for her, though he was offered one, for he said he wanted any of her children to feel free to "return" any time they wanted to do so. Vadaka's second son had a son and two daughters. His wife died in childbirth while the other children were still small. They were cared for by her sister who was living in an adjacent village. Their father died many years later without ever having reclaimed possession of his children and without having remarried. The daughters are now grown but unmarried and still live with their mother's sister. Ponggevolomo as their closest living patrilateral kinsman has discussed marriage for them and will probably get the lion's share of their brideprice if one is paid, though some will have to go to their mother's sister and her husband since they have reared the girls. The son has married as a *tamazira* and lives nearby. He still maintains an interest in Kubanakesa and has a few coconut palms there. He claims he would reside with Ponggevolomo if he could, but his wife's father refuses to let her go elsewhere. He says he wants his children to "keep" *sinangge* Votuae because his wife's group has little to offer them; his wife's father's group is Eromo, another branch of Kesi, which is living off its own estate, which is deep in the bush, and as "guests" on the land of Gabili too.

Vadaka's third son was Takelelana, whose daughter by Likung-gguana was married during World War II to a man who is now dead. She returned to the coast with Ponggevolomo after the war, has since remarried, and brought her husband to live near Ponggevolomo as his *tamazira*. Vadaka's fourth son married *tamazira* to a group in the same region and had one son, Rurupa, who is now married and lives in the same village into which his father married, some miles from Kubanakesa. Ponggevolomo says Rurupa has an interest in the Votuae estate and tries to persuade him to "return." He was particularly active in this respect during 1959 when Rurupa's wife was party to an adultery case, and Ponggevolomo tried to convince him that if he stayed where he was he would only have more trouble. But Rurupa claims that he is settled in the other place, and his mother's group, and he has no need to move. However, he occasionally uses the coconuts at Kubanakesa with Ponggevolomo's permission.

Ponggevolomo is himself married to Vadaka's eldest daughter's daughter (also an only child), and the children of Vadaka's other daughter live with their father's group on the other side of the is-

land. The only other active claimant to an interest in Kubanakesa is Vanata, an elderly man who is the son of Vadaka's second
sister who married to a Singgotu man but was widowed and "returned" bringing Vanata to live with Vadaka and his sons. Vanata
also has active interests in his father's share of the Singgotu estate,
especially a section to which he is the sole heir and claimant. It too
is well planted with coconuts, and Vanata has tended to cultivate
his interests in this holding, which is nearby, and has left Kubanakesa pretty much to Ponggevolomo. He has also allowed Ponggevolomo to plant coconuts on it. The coconuts on Kubanakesa
were planted by Takelekana, Ponggevolomo's wife's father, and
Ponggevolomo himself. The other men of Votuae reportedly
planted very few there, and so their sons must ask Ponggevolomo
for permission to use more than those few. A few have also been
set aside for the use of Ponggevolomo's half-sister's husband who
is his *tamazira*.

Ponggevolomo's elder brother and his wife died some years ago,
and their children were adopted by Ponggevolomo and his wife.
Their position is particularly ambiguous, for they can claim membership in both Votuae and Gabili—in Votuae through their
father who was adopted by Takelekana and through their father's
brother who is now the acknowledged manager of the Votuae
estates, and in Gabili through their mother, for whom a brideprice
was not paid. Tanavalu, the present manager of Gabili, says they
are members of Gabili, that is, they owe their principal allegiance
to that group, or him, because their father was a *tamazira* of that
group; but Ponggevolomo says they are clearly members of
Votuae. They can, of course, be and are in fact members of both;
the disputes that arise when there is animosity between Ponggevolomo and Tanavalu tend to bring the issue into the open. But
the issue is not so much to which group they "belong" as it is with
whom they should side in the petty squabbles. Kasibatu's two
older sons, who are now married, tend to side with Ponggevolomo,
but although he has at times refused to speak to Tanavalu for a
few weeks they have always maintained respectful relations with
him. Both men are anxious to do what they can for the boys, and
Tanavalu has allotted them small parcels of Gabili land on which
to plant coconuts, and they garden freely upon all of it.

Kasibatu's eldest son, Pelese, has recently married the daughter
of a Gabili man and is living temporarily with him, says Pongge-

volomo, because Ponggevolomo's house is already overcrowded. Besides, says Ponggevolomo, it makes the other man happy to think that he has a *tamazira*. Kasibatu's other son married the daughter of a Kesi man who had been adopted after his death by one of his kinsmen who is a member of Gabili too. This son lives in his own house adjoining that of Ponggevolomo. Finally, Ponggevolomo has recently acquired another *tamazira* through the marriage of his eldest daughter. The young man did not want to marry as a *tamazira*, or for that matter to marry at all, but he was caught sleeping with the girl twice, and on the second occasion Ponggevolomo effectively forced a "custom" marriage by restraining the young man and putting on such a show of indignation that the young man's father capitulated to Ponggevolomo's demands for a marriage rather than face the certain gossip and possible litigation that was threatened. Later the young man's father attempted to talk Ponggevolomo into taking a brideprice, but he would have none of it although he did make a show of reasonableness and let the father go through a protracted process of negotiation before turning him down.

Sodabangara's other descendants have all established themselves elsewhere, but in any event they would have had no direct interest in Kubanakesa for it was "given" to Sara and Vadaka and their descendants, and it is, technically speaking, still Gabili land anyway. Thus to Tanavalu, they are "all Gabili people." Ponggevolomo prefers to see the situation somewhat differently. He is not too clear about the custom whereby such divisions or gifts of land took place, that is, whether the land itself changed hands. But, as he says, it really does not matter much anyway. The important thing today is the coconuts, and those are clearly his. Nor does Tanavalu ever claim the land itself but rather the allegiances of the people he feels "belong" to his group. He wants to keep on good terms with them and so does not assert Gabili's claim to the land, which he has enough of elsewhere. Thus Ponggevolomo retains effective and unchallenged control of the land at Kubanakesa, and this is an important issue for him since it enables him to think of himself as a *batu* with land to control.

Here, then, a man who has no true descent status within a particular group is the acknowledged head of it. True, he owes much to the circumstances that have substantially reduced other claimants and made the "group" consist largely of his own extended family. And the other possible claimants to the land are little interested in it because its primary value would be as plantation land; Ponggevolomo has inherited most trees on it, and the unplanted land is not suitable for further planting. These facts might lead the observer to belittle Ponggevolomo's accomplishments, yet he is an able and ambitious man who has been able to acquire *tamazira*, and the status he has gained is important in his and the eyes of others who, even though they may do so grudgingly, have to regard him as a manager. He has plans to go even further and to establish a separate hamlet at Kubanakesa. He has been cutting timber for a house for several years now and is saving to buy corrugated iron for a roof. He hopes to pull away from Tanavalu and set himself up in an independent residential unit, taking his brother's sons and his *tamazira* with him. Tanavalu, of course, resents this, reminds Ponggevolomo of their long-standing "friendship," and argues that he ought to stay with him and help to build up the present village. I doubt that Ponggevolomo will ever accomplish his great aim, for although it might not require an open breach with Tanavalu it would require that his brother's sons and *tamazira* go with him, and these younger men prefer, for now at least, the social life of the larger village. They are also less than enthusiastic about the effort required to establish a new village.

Case V: An Affiliation History

Several generations ago, Riringini of Kivilae descent group in the Varisi region committed adultery with the wife of a reputed elder brother who then threatened to take Riringini's life (see Fig. 12). Riringini fled to a distant group in the Taula (Vagua-speaking) region where he died some years later. His son, Vazingo, got into difficulty there after his first wife died and sought refuge with the manager of Gabili descent group in the Tepazaka region. A brother, Visuru, remained behind in Taula. Vazingo got into yet another dispute concerning a sacred grove which he attempted to use without the manager's permission. He was allowed to stay on at Gabili, and he eventually married again to Daengguana, reputedly a sister of Monggo who had been adopted into Gabili when a Gabili man, probably Kisara, married a widow, Mabengguana, who had originated from Kubongava descent group, also in the Tepazaka region, but who had been married to a man from

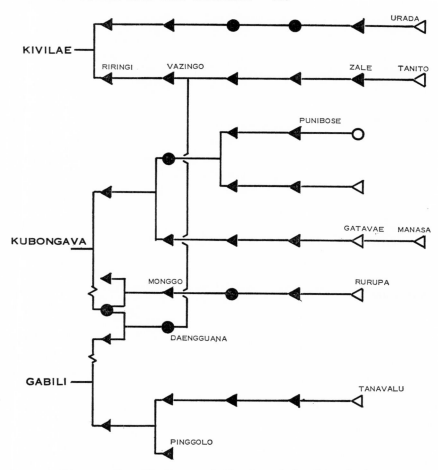

Fig. 12. Case V: Gatavae's Version of the Genealogies

the Taula region. Monggo is "known" to have been her son by the
Taula man, but Daengguana's status in this respect is not certain
to informants today. At any rate, she is generally referred to as
Monggo's "sister." Monggo later decided to go live on his mother's
land at Kubongava. Immediately adjoining the Kubongava
estate is a tract of land known as Sarepota, no more than one
square mile in area. Although about six miles from the rest of
Gabili estate, Sarepota is Gabili land, and at that time it was in
Monggo's care. (See map, Fig. 7, p. 90.)

    At Kubongava, Monggo was joined by his "sister's son," Zale.
(This relationship seems hardly possible as there would appear to

have been at least three genealogical generations separating
Monggo from Zale, both adults. Nevertheless, Zale was considerably younger than Monggo, whom he is said to have called *bubue*,
"mother's brother," and more of an age mate with Monggo's children.) It is uncertain where Zale came from: Tanito, his son
and a man of about sixty today, denies that he ever lived elsewhere, but others say that he came from his mother's group in the
nearby Babatana region. Since Zale and his ancestors, and his son,
have all been married to Babatana women, it is likely that Zale
did come from there. Furthermore, he seems to have earned a
reputation in that region, but it was a mixed one. Zale had ambitions, but he was in a poor position to realize them. He attempted
to make claims upon lands in Babatana, but he was rebuked and
put in his place. He did manage to gain fame as an assassin (often
hired by other men), and he did ingratiate others to himself by
helping them with their debts. He is said to have left Babatana
because of "some big trouble," but no one now seems to know, or
cares to admit, what it was.

Then the troubles began. Monggo's son and daughter-in-law
died, and it was rumored that Zale had killed them by sorcery so
he could acquire Monggo's interests in Kubongava and Sarepota.
But Zale was not directly accused and no action was taken,
partly because he had a reputation as a big-man and people were
afraid of the possible consequences. Zale also precipitated the war
described in the preceding chapter. To recapitulate briefly:
Pinggolo, then manager of Gabili, invited Monggo and Zale to
"see his *kesa*," because, it is said, he considered them both to be
Gabili men and thought that should anything happen to Gabili
the two men might use the *kesa* to avenge them. Pinggolo apparently had a change of heart about Zale and revealed his *kesa*
only to Monggo. Zale, his pride injured, felt he had been insulted
and his rights in Gabili denied, so he arranged for an attack upon
Gabili in which all but a handful of the Gabili people and many
others were killed. Zale remained uninjured in the fighting that
followed, but a few years later he was again accused of sorcery,
this time by some people of Barokasa, the truncal segment of the
branch descent group (Subavalu) which had sided with Zale in the
war against Gabili. Zale was killed, and his mother's descent
group avenged his death. Zale's wife was killed at the same time—
about 1900—and their children were adopted by a kinsman of

Zale (Kodu) who had moved onto the land of Kubongava some time before and lived there peacefully with the other Kubongava people, only two families at that time. Those kinsmen Zale had brought from his mother's region did not attempt to avenge his death, for it seems that they too had agreed to it. Most people thought Zale got what he deserved.

The troubles of Zale and his ancestors might have ended then if it were not for his son. Tanito lived for a short while at Kubongava, but later he was taken to his father's mother's descent group in Babatana. As a young man he got into disputes there over the use of some groves, and he went to the then manager of *sinangge* Gabili, Tanavalu, Pinggolo's brother's son's son. Tanavalu and Tanito are reputed cognates and are said by others, playing on the ambiguity of the term, to be of "one *sinangge*" on the basis of Vazingo's earlier marriage to the woman adopted into Gabili. Tanavalu and his supporters now say that marriage "brought Tanito's line close to Gabili" but did not make his ancestors or him members of Gabili descent group or give them any particular rights over it. In other words, they are kin and that is all it amounts to. In any event, Tanavalu now reports that Tanito said at that time, about 1925, if he could not stay at Gabili he would go to his mother's descent group, Kalekubo, on the other side of the island in the Varisi region. Zale had four wives (some were consecutive), usually Babatana women, but one was a Varisi woman and Tanito is her son. She had a daughter by an earlier marriage who remained with Kodu for a time in Babatana but was then returned to Varisi and her mother's natal group where she still resides today. Tanito had not had much to do with Kalekubo people before his trouble in Babatana, and he did not know how he would be received. Furthermore, they are Catholics and he is a Methodist, as is Tanavalu. This was the heyday of mission influence, and Tanavalu was full of "brotherly love." He and the other "important men" of Gabili decided to let Tanito stay at Gabili, but only as a guest. There Tanito married a woman from Babatana also living there as a guest. An earlier marriage, also to a Babatana woman while Tanito was living in Babatana, resulted in divorce because, says Tanito, the woman was lazy and disobedient. In the late 1920's Tanito tried to sell some Gabili land to some "friends" in Babatana. He said that Vazingo had kept the grove, and so it was his own to do with as he pleased. Because of his reputation in Babatana the "friends" checked first with the men of Gabili and learned Tanito was lying. The Gabili people wanted to ouster Tanito, but he acted contrite, admitted to having made a "mistake," and was allowed to stay on. About 1930 he moved to the village where the Kubongava people were then living, though not on Kubongava land. He lived there for some time, quietly using a grove that his father had used and the coconuts that his father's kinsmen had planted there long ago. With the permission of Punibose, then manager of Kubongava, he planted more coconuts and also made gardens there. When World War II came Tanito, like everyone else, fled into the bush. He lived with his father's brother's son, Ngganggurae, who had remained affiliated with their fathers' mother's descent group, and he stayed on in Babatana with Ngganggurae after the war until about 1950. Tanito then announced to Punibose that he intended to return to Kubongava and resume his and his father's property there. Some say that he quarreled with Ngganggurae and was under pressure to leave Babatana, but Ngganggurae himself refuses to say anything about it (to me, at least). Tanito then argued that his father had been the primary right-holder in a segment of Kubongava's estate, or as he stated his case somewhat more strongly, the manager of an autonomous branch of that major *sinangge*. Punibose is reported to have countered that Kubongava had never been more than one unit nor had the land ever been subdivided. According to accounts of Punibose's argument, Zale had established himself at Kubongava with Monggo's permission and on the basis of a rather tenuous genealogical tie. Zale had planted some groves there, which belonged to Tanito, but that was the total extent of Tanito's interest in Kubongava. Punibose, who died a few years later, was supported by his "brother's son," Gatavae, but Gatavae's young son, Manasa, just returned from the Methodist mission school in Roviana, and still very much under its influence, intervened in Tanito's behalf. Since then Manasa's attitude has changed somewhat—he has grown older and more jealous of his property interests—but he then argued that since Tanito did have property there and also a tie with the group they should, as good kinsmen and true Christians, allow him to rejoin the group and live there. Mission influence does seem to have affected the recognition of Tanito's rights. However, in the past there might have been factors which would have led someone in Kubongava to espouse Tanito's cause. Some parties who are more or less disinterested in the case claim that Zale had "straightened out" some debts for Kubongava, which had never been repaid. Manasa's counsel prevailed, and Tanito returned to Kubongava and now lives there. He established a hamlet on the beach at a place called Zarepe. Gatavae continued to live in the nearby village of Sanggigae but later, when he wanted to open a "store" of sorts there, he met some opposition from the people who "owned" the land—some of whom already had stores and wanted no competition [1] from Gatavae—and he too moved to Zarepe, taking the remainder of the Kubongava people with him. He established a hamlet only a couple of hundred yards away from Tanito.

Meanwhile Tanavalu had, on various occasions, disputes over Sarepota, a section of Gabili land lying adjacent to the Kubongava estate. Sarepota has for many generations been regarded as Gabili land, but no one knows how they got hold of it, and it is unusual for a group to have land in two places. Neighboring descent groups use this land with Tanavalu's permission, but he has always insisted that before planting coconuts there they should make a specific request of him. They may garden freely, for, as Tanavalu puts it, he and they are "all one big *sinangge*," and the land, being so far away, is of little use to Gabili. Their arguments were always based solely on past use; they would point out that their fathers had used the land freely so it must have been "theirs." Meetings of the local "important men" were held to discuss each dispute, and the issue was always resolved in favor of Gabili on the basis of common knowledge of Gabili's possession and that other groups have used it as a privilege of "friendship" and not as a right. In 1958 the issue arose again and was settled in the usual way. Tanavalu continued to allow free use for gardening but not for planting coconuts.

Immediately after the meeting in 1958 Tanito came to Tanavalu and asked if his son-in-law, then living with Tanito as a *tamazira*, could plant coconuts on a portion of Sarepota immediately adjacent to the land of Kubongava. Tanavalu refused Tanito's request, for he had already promised to let Isivikesa of the neighboring Kubobangara descent group and his own fifth cousin plant

---

[1] The competition would have been for prestige and not for economic goals. These "stores" are shoestring operations, sometimes five or ten to a village with only a few more families than that number.

coconuts there. Isivikesa returned from Honiara, where he had been a policeman, early in 1959 and began to clear the land. Tanito approached him and said he should not work there for the land belonged to Tanito and Isivikesa had not asked permission to work it. Isivikesa reported this to Tanavalu who advised him to go on working the land, but when Tanito repeated his earlier performance Isivikesa quit altogether. He told me that he knows the land belongs to Tanavalu but he is afraid of sorcery and so quit his work. I pressed for an explanation, but he did not want to elaborate.

Tanavalu, who is also the assistant district headman of Tepazaka, called a meeting of the local "important men" to discuss Tanito's claims in June of 1959, and I attended as Tanavalu's guest—I was residing in one of his houses. Everyone of any importance in Tepazaka was there, and Tanito brought his father's brother's son, Ngganggurae, and some other men from Babatana to support him. He had no apparent support from within the Tepazaka district, and even his Babatana kinsmen said little. The atmosphere was charged with tension, for they were also to discuss a complaint by Tanito against Gatavae and a well-known local curer-cum-sorcerer whom Tanito said had killed some medicinal plants near his house. In so doing they had obliquely accused Tanito of sorcery—the implication was that they would not have killed the plants unless it was suspected they were being kept for some nefarious purpose—but neither Tanito nor anyone else would say this in so many words. The meeting, a kind of "preliminary hearing," was called to consider the grounds for formal court proceedings since both parties had requested them. Actually, such hearings are more the old-style "discussions" in which managers try to arbitrate a settlement, but they are usually unsuccessful in terminating land disputes, and a formal court often follows. Such meetings have the curious effect of allowing disputants to hear each other's evidence more or less in full and to prepare to meet it in court.

The dispute between Tanito and Gatavae was heard first. It quickly became apparent that most people agreed that Gatavae and his friend were wrong in destroying Tanito's plants, though Tanito was evasive in talking about his plants, and more than one man came away with the suspicion that Tanito had indeed kept them for a disreputable purpose. Gatavae claimed that he had not been near the plants, but a boy living with Tanito had seen him and his friend in the act, and they changed their story to say that their "medicine," designed to rid the area of evil spirits that had been making Gatavae's family ill, must have touched Tanito's plants accidentally. It was agreed that Tanito had cause for a court-hearing and that it would be held later along with some other cases from the district.

Then they heard the land dispute between Tanavalu and Tanito. Tanito claimed the disputed land was not part of Sarepota but part of the land of Kubongava, that it had belonged to his father and now belonged to him. Others pointed out that Tanito had always supported Tanavalu in the past in disputes over Sarepota, and they had always included this portion within its boundaries. But Tanito was adamant, arguing that mistakes had been made in the past and that they ought to be corrected. Tanito thereby raised once again the issue of his own position in Kubongava and this thoroughly confused the situation. The discussion continued for several hours with a review of every dispute that had ever been aired about Sarepota or Tanito's rights in Kubongava. However, Gatavae and his supporters were not prepared to argue the latter point or to straighten it out then and there, and all agreed, in the best Choiseulese style, to "leave it" temporarily. They would retire to summon more evidence.

In the ensuing lull—which was not really a lull for Tanito and Gatavae managed to get into several additional petty squabbles— Tanito began to arrange a neat story, containing all the details conventionally asked for by a land court, to support his claims. He was assisted largely by his son-in-law who is literate as he is not. Many times during the next ten months Tanavalu said he was going to call a further meeting, and he and his supporters did get together to arrange their facts. One of their principal acts of defense was to call the manager of Kivilae descent group, whence Tanito's remote patrilineal ancestors had originated, from the other side of the island to find out what they could about Tanito's ancestry. From this man, Urada, they heard for the first time a detailed history of the movements of Tanito's ancestors out of Kivilae and around the island until Zale finally settled at Kubongava. Urada declared Tanito to be a Kivilae man through his patrilineal connections; "Kivilae is Tanito's true *sinangge*," he said, "but we are crowded, and there is no room for him at

Kivilae now. So should he threaten to return to Kivilae when you confront him with these facts, you must tell him that we do not want him either." Actually Kivilae is no more "crowded" than any other group, and there is enough land to go around. Urada's contribution was to confirm that "Tanito's line" had always been disreputable and since Riringini's departure from Kivilae had not had a place it could call home.

No general meeting had been called by the time I left Choiseul in March of 1960, and the land in dispute remained in disuse, as does much other land with similar status. I was to learn the rest of the story, as told below, when I returned to Choiseul in February of 1961.

Tanito, tired of waiting on Tanavalu, who is a procrastinator, went to the district headman of the island and requested that he hold court over the land. Court was held in December of 1960. Following the "rule book" devised by the Protectorate Government regarding the relevant evidence in land cases, the district headman asked both sides to tell what they knew of the land— who lived on it in the past, who planted on it, who took first-fruits, who had been cremated and his bones deposited there, what shrines were there, and so on. Tanavalu recited the boundaries and said it is common knowledge that this land is a part of Sarepota and that very little had happened upon it. The sacred places of Gabili were elsewhere, and there had never been a village or hamlet on the land except for short periods during nutting seasons. He admitted to not knowing how Gabili got the land. Tanito admitted the Gabili title to Sarepota but reiterated his argument that the land under dispute was not a part of Sarepota. He said it was a part of Kubongava land and that it had always belonged to his ancestors; his father had a grove on it, and, furthermore, several of his ancestors and kinsmen—his father's children by other wives, it turned out—had been cremated and their bones deposited there. He took the court around the land and pointed out the reputed sites, which Tanavalu says were no more than meaningless piles of old rocks such as abound throughout the jungle. Gatavae and his son, Manasa, testified that Tanito had no right "to speak about" the land of Kubongava even if the disputed section were a part of it, which they denied, for Tanito was there only by their grace and his claims upon the Kubongava estate were of debatable validity. The district headman is re-

ported (by Tanavalu, Gatavae, and Manasa)[2] to have replied
that Gatavae and Manasa had brought up an "unrelated" issue,
for the court's concern was the ownership of a small section of
land and not relative rights in Kubongava. He advised Gatavae to
request another court should he wish to contest Tanito's right to
speak. If true, it is indeed difficult to imagine the grounds for this
remark. The district headman then awarded the land to Tanito
because "he knows about the land and Tanavalu does not."
Tanavalu refused to appeal, although Gatavae urged him to do
so. Tanavalu told me that he was tired of the litigation and quarreling, which had gone on for more than two years, and, anyway,
he had lost nothing as he did not use the land. Some Gabili people
protested the decision and urged Tanavalu to appeal, but the land
itself means little to them. Tanavalu took the viewpoint that the
court had not been "straight"—the implication was that the district headman is Tanito's kinsman and so biased in favor of him—
and the best tactic thereafter would be to contest Tanito's right
to speak about Kubongava land. He and others urged this course
to Gatavae.

When I returned to Choiseul in February of 1961 Gatavae was
still considering his possible course of action. He soon came to me,
thinking I might help him to clarify the issues as well as give him
advice. He did not know Tanito's brief in detail, for although he
and Tanito live only about two hundred yards apart they do not
talk to one another and hear each other's claims only through
third parties. Since he was not allowed to make an issue of
Tanito's Kubongava status during the court with Tanavalu, he
had no substantial idea of the basis of Tanito's claims. These two
men have quarreled over several issues in recent years, and Tanito's land claim was until then only the most recent bone of contention.

I had been on Choiseul only about six weeks when I was first
visited by Tanito. I had been recording *sinangge* genealogies, and
he came to ask if I wanted to record his. He was obviously anxious
to have it done, but I thought nothing of it because so were many
other men. Tanavalu acted as interpreter since Tanito speaks
neither Pidgin nor English. According to Tanito at that time,
Kubongava has two segments, and each has its share of the land.

---

[2] I have no reason to doubt their statements. They suggested I check the
court records at council headquarters, but I was unable to get there.

One part, that of Gatavae, is the truncal segment and the other part, Votakolo, a branch belonging to Tanito. Tanito said it is unknown how the founding ancestor of the branch was related to the truncal segment. He also "knew" that the founding ancestor had a daughter who married Vazingo, who remained at Votakolo as a *tamazira*. Vazingo came from Kivilae, said Tanito, but after his marriage to the founder's daughter all his lineal descendants lived at Votakolo and thus Tanito has succeeded to the primary rights in that segment. Tanavalu made no protests at this story then or later, and when I asked him about it after the dispute had arisen he told me that he had not discussed genealogies with Gatavae before and did not know until after Tanito began to extend his claims in the open that Tanito was lying. This may well be true because neither did Tanavalu know much about Zale or his war with Pinggolo until the present dispute arose, and he seems to have accepted Tanito's story that his earlier claims on Gabili land were a "mistake" for which he was sorry. Indeed, they seemed to be on good terms until Tanito made his claims to that portion of Sarepota.

When I discussed Tanito's story of the Kubongava situation with Gatavae he countered by saying that there was no Votakolo segment of Kubongava, although there was a place within the Kubongava estate that bears that name and Zale did have a hamlet there where he resided with his kinsmen from Babatana. Zale had done so, said Gatavae, only with the permission of Monggo and others.

Gatavae contended that the only basis Tanito had for claims on the land of Kubongava was his descent from Monggo's "sister" and no one is quite sure how good a claim that is. Monggo was related to Kubongava through his mother, but all knowledge of her genealogical link with Kubongava is lost today. Nonetheless, Monggo's status is common and accepted knowledge, and no one has ever challenged it as far as Gatavae knows, but even Monggo's descendants, of whom there are still a few, are not affiliated with Kubongava today, although they could be if they wanted to, said Gatavae. He argued that by marrying Monggo's "step-sister," as he chose to consider her, Vazingo "came close" to Kubongava but this did not make him a member of Kubongava nor did it necessarily make his descendants Kubongava people other than in the broad sense of making them cognatic kinsmen of the present

Kubongava people. It was on the basis of this marriage that Zale
was allowed to affiliate with Kubongava. None of this would mean
much if Tanito were a "good man," but he is not; he is trying to
establish himself over the legitimate primary right-holders, said
Gatavae. Tanito now considers that the court against Tanavalu
established his right to "talk strong" about Kubongava land, and
he has circulated the information that Gatavae and his son must
in the future ask him for permission to garden on his land—
something which even legitimate managers are not permitted to
demand of members of their own descent group and, furthermore,
a sure sign of aggrandizing behavior.

It seems clear that Vazingo married a woman associated in
some way with Kubongava descent group and that he and his
descendants have at times been associated with that group too.
But they also spent much time in the Babatana area and had close
ties there. Zale had probably established himself with Kubongava
too, but he was a trouble maker, and his status remained somewhat ambiguous.

Tanito's conduct seemed demonstrative of an insecure position,
and at this point I was convinced of the validity of the case
against his strongest claims, even though it was apparent that his
opponents may have been stretching a few points in their favor.
Tanito's conduct conforms to a pattern that was by then well
known to me from other property disputes I had recorded. I had
heard often of this sort of conduct—a man gradually working his
way into a fairly secure position in a group and then attempting
to consolidate that position by making claims to primary rights,
often to the exclusion of others with long-established rights and
interests in the group's estate. Furthermore, everyone I spoke to
agreed either that Tanito had no rights or was attempting to extend too far those limited ones he had. A few pleaded ignorance of
the "facts," but they argued that Tanito and the others should
not fight because they are "one *sinangge*." I learned from Rurupa
who is commonly recognized to have claims on Kubongava land
as a descendant of Monggo that Tanito had been attempting to
solicit his backing. He told Rurupa that when Gatavae gave me
the Kubongava genealogy he omitted Rurupa's name, thereby
denying Rurupa's commonly acknowledged rights. Tanito assured Rurupa that he was included in Tanito's version of that
genealogy, as he was in fact, thereby implying that only Tanito

had Rurupa's interests at heart. However, Tanito had no way of knowing, from me at least, what Gatavae had included in his genealogy. I determined to get Tanito's version of the dispute and went to see him. He was hospitable to me even though he knew that I had discussed the case with Gatavae and Tanavalu.

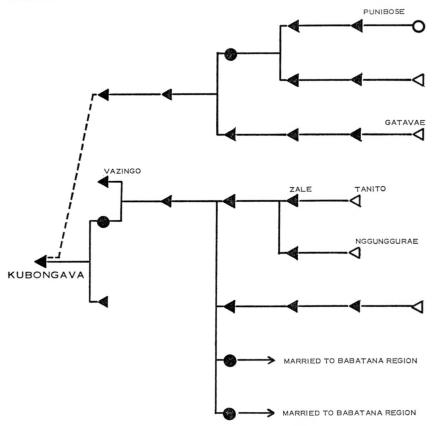

Fig. 13. Case V: Tanito's Later Version

According to Tanito, he is the innocent victim of selfishness on the part of Gatavae who would do him out of his primary rights and take "everything for himself." He showed me a genealogy (see Fig. 13) that he and his son-in-law had drawn on a large sheet of paper. It consisted only of that part of Kubongava that two years previously he had called a branch, but this time he said it was the whole of Kubongava. Detail was added to the earlier version: the founding ancestor had a son and a daughter. The daughter married Vazingo who had come from the other side of the island and was living then at Gabili. The son died without issue, and the founder then recalled his daughter's son to be his heir and the primary right-holder in Kubongava. Tanito is an agnatic descendant of this son, and therefore, he argues, the primary right-holder now. When I asked how Punibose, Gatavae, and others came to be at Kubongava, though not in this version of the genealogy, Tanito said that the founder had adopted a boy when his own son died, and Punibose and others are descendants of that boy. Therefore, they have only secondary rights in Kubongava. According to Tanito, he has lived there minding his own business and allowing them to do the same, but just recently they have begun to be aggressive, and now he is forced to defend his rights. He went on to tell of his ancestor's bones deposited on the land and how his father had been a big-man and had done so much for the other Kubongava people and their neighbors. But Gatavae and his son and their neighbors are all selfish and ungrateful, he said. Tanito said he wanted to cause no trouble for Gatavae, but it was being pushed upon him. "We could all live together in peace," said Tanito, "if only Gatavae were not so selfish like big-men used to be."

Gatavae's case seemed ironclad, so I asked him why he did not go ahead and contest Tanito's claims in court. He would only say that he did not trust the local courts and cited how Tanavalu had lost his land. He suggested again that the kinship between Tanito and the district headman might operate in his disfavor. I suspected that another source of hesitancy was fear of sorcery, and so I made some discrete inquiries among my friends about Tanito's reputation. Most of them quickly changed the subject to Tanito's father who, they pointed out, had been a notorious sorcerer. Finally one informant replied to an exasperated direct question, "Maybe he is and maybe he isn't—after all, that is why his father was killed," which is no more than the Choiseulese way of saying, "Of course he is, but I'm not fool enough to say so openly or to tell you, so you can go home and put it in your book." And so the case stood when I left Choiseul in April of 1961. Gatavae, afraid of injustice in the courts and also of Tanito's sorcery, was doing nothing, and probably nothing will happen until one of them starts clearing garden land in what the other considers the wrong place. Then the district commissioner will probably hear the case, for he has tired of hearing appeals from the native courts on land cases and has decreed that they can no longer try them. Some prediction: Tanito is not likely to leave the area even if he should lose to Gatavae, for he has nowhere else to go, and he now has a piece of Tanavalu's land at Sarepota. If Gatavae loses on the basis of the issues as Tanito now sees them, he will still have certain but limited rights to remain where he is. Even if he should become legally deprived of those rights he would not be likely to leave. In other cases involving long-term "squatters," the courts have either recognized that displacement would be a considerable hardship and refused to order it, pleading for tolerance by the disputants, or they have not followed through with enforcement of their decisions. In any event, Gatavae and Tanito are sure to go on quarreling for a long while.

The essential issues of this case are clear. It demonstrates the contingent nature of jural principles concerning rights in a descent group and the activities of a man with contingent rights attempting to consolidate them. That Tanito has a tie with Kubongava is generally accepted; neither Gatavae nor anyone else has ever denied that much. It is the nature and the value of that tie that are questioned now that Tanito is extending his claims. Zale was able to establish affiliation through Monggo. When Zale came to Kubongava he was already a big-man in his mother's region, so he was probably welcomed as an addition to Kubongava's forces. A few relatively disinterested parties, as I have already noted, argued that when Zale came to Kubongava that group was in serious debt from some earlier transactions, and Zale helped to liquidate those debts. This, they thought, ought to entitle Tanito to some say-so in Kubongava, but as far as I know no one openly supported Tanito's full claims. Even his father's brother's son, Ngganggurae, argued against him in 1950 when he wanted to return to Kubongava. Ngganggurae is reputed to have said then that Tanito ought not to talk too forcefully about his rights for he could hardly be sure of what they are. Zale died when Tanito was only a baby, and who could have taught him all that he professes to know, asked Ngganggurae at that time. Tanito's latest version of the basis of his rights is a rather transparent amalgam of bits and pieces of various and isolated tales that are common knowledge in the region bound together by the also common knowledge of the typical behavior of big-men in the past, all of which gives it an air of historical truth.

Zale had also made enemies in and around Kubongava. Sorcery, when it was said to be the reason for a killing, was probably only a pretext. Adultery or a property dispute was frequently at the bottom of it, and the Choiseulese are aware of this. Zale is said to have been just like his son today in that he too made extravagant claims upon the property of Kubongava, and although no one in Kubongava was directly responsible for his death, they are known to have agreed to it. It was an easy resolution of his claims and of any debts Kubongava might have owed him.

Whatever the basis of Zale's claims on Kubongava, he was and is generally known as a Kubongava man, but he had a brother who was identified, and whose sons are now affiliated, with their (Zale's and his brother's) mother's descent group in Babatana. Zale brought kinsmen from Babatana to support him, and some of them became known, however impermanently, as Kubongava men too. This is generally admitted even by Gatavae. Zale's somewhat ambiguous and tenuous tie to Kubongava was strengthened by his status as an influential man. His activities in the name of the group secured that identification for him. The difficulties with him were glossed over in the heyday of mission influence during the 1920's and 1930's, and Tanito was allowed to re-activate his father's prior affiliation and the tenuous genealogical tie through Vazingo. As long as Tanito confined himself to the use of his father's grove and used only a small part of the land he was no trouble to Kubongava, for the demise of the old social and economic order has acquitted them of any personal or corporate responsibility for or to him. When he attempted to extend his interests in 1950 he was met with stiff opposition and seemed to allow himself to be convinced that he had "misunderstood" the exact nature of his father's position in Kubongava. When Manasa intervened in his behalf he accepted his past position. But Tanito is now an elderly man and, as he has no sons, is no doubt concerned about his daughter's future. She has married a young man who lives on land owned by the Methodist mission which he has been told he will soon have to vacate. Tanito's son-in-law helps him with his case to the extent of drawing genealogies and maps for him. He is urged to reside with Tanito, which he sometimes does. If Tanito should be able to consolidate his claims, his son-in-law could take over in his daughter's name.

In 1930 when Tanito first re-activated his father's claims to Kubongava Zale's troubles were not emphasized, but they could have been to his detriment. Neither were they emphasized in 1950 when the only concern was an unjustified claim to primary interests in a presumed segment of Kubongava land. But finally when Tanito became excessively aggressive in 1959 every available disadvantageous fact was brought out against him. The dispute over the segment of Sarepota provided a good opportunity for Tanito to develop the whole Kubongava issue once again. Furthermore, since several knowledgeable old men from Kubongava and related groups had died in the preceding ten years, there were fewer generally respectable opponents to controvert Tanito's presumed "facts." This "waiting until all the old men are dead" is a well-known tactic in such disputes. Kivilae representatives argued that an ancestor of Tanito had committed adultery with his "elder brother's" wife and so Tanito's line was "no good" and not wanted. Furthermore, Tanito's line had "gone out" so long ago and so many generations had "covered up" his link with Kivilae that they could no longer allow him to reactivate it. All this plus the fact that Kivilae is already "too full"! Gabili representatives argued that Tanito was not welcome there because his father had made war on them and thereby "severed forever" the genealogical tie that bound them and surrendered all rights in respect of Gabili. Gatavae and others cast suspicion upon the quality and value of Tanito's tie to Kubongava by stressing the dubious nature of the relationship between Monggo and his presumed "sister." A narrow interpretation of brideprice payments was made by some who argued that Vazingo had bought the woman and therefore his descendants had no claims over Kubongava even if she had been a legitimate member of that group. The Kubongava people and their supporters denied that Zale had ever done anything for Kubongava and recounted only his bad deeds—cheating them of *kesa* that should have been theirs in payment for a vengeance-killing, making claims to primary rights over their land, killing Monggo's son and daughter-in-law by sorcery, and so on. Tanito's excessive claims have, in the eyes of Gatavae and his supporters, mitigated any legitimate claim he might have had.

Now that he is behaving exactly as his father behaved, they say, there is only one thing to be done—get rid of him. But this is proving difficult. They can no longer dispose of him by the same means used on his father, and their fear of injustice or sorcery prevents them from using the only means now at their disposal, the court.

One further comment. Tanito's actions seem to me thoroughly explainable in terms of the analysis of Choiseulese society presented in the preceding chapters. It should not be necessary, if my analysis has been at all clear, to go over his case point by point demonstrating its relevance to that analysis. However, I would emphasize once more that in addition to illustrating the contingent or conditional nature of jural principles, the way in which they are subject to different interpretation to meet the needs of a particular situation (e.g., the argument about brideprice), this case also shows how strong is the need to secure and maintain an identification with a particular group, not only by each man but by each man through his parent or parents. Whether Tanito is agnatically affiliated with Kubongava was never an issue. Both sides used agnatic status to buttress their arguments, although Tanito did not claim to be an agnatic descendant of the founder, only an agnatic descendant of his immediate heir, nor did the Kubongava people maintain the necessity for Tanito to show a consistent line of ancestral affiliations with the Kubongava descent group. The basic issue remained, for Kubongava at least, the extent to which Zale had earned interests in Kubongava after Monggo had recognized his entitlement to membership. To the extent that they recognized what Zale had earned for himself thereafter, they did not deny limited recognition of his son's rights. But his son was not satisfied with only that much; he recognized the tenuous nature of his rights, which he has helped to maintain in that state by waiting until so late in his career to re-activate them. His actions show too the lengths to which some men will go to acquire and maintain secure rights. To be sure, he has been aided and abetted in his actions by the modern situation.

In the past Tanito would have been a liability to Kubongava. Not only do his actions cause internal strife, but he is the kind of man who would have earned enemies outside of his own descent group. His group mates would have had to coöperate with him in daily activities and would have been responsible for his actions towards "outsiders" by implication as his kinsmen and coresidents. If they would not take the responsibility for killing him, then sooner or later someone from "outside" would. But today all of that is changed. The *pax Britannica* and the Christian ethic prohibit killing, but, happily, from their point of view, most people do not have to coöperate with Tanito from day to day, nor are they responsible for his actions against "outsiders." The modern economic situation encouraging nuclear family production has freed them of the former responsibility, for they need Tanito no more than he needs them, and not faced with external conflict as a reality or a possibility as a result of his actions or otherwise, they can afford to dispute internally. There is no pressing necessity to settle the dispute. Each party has plenty of garden lands and some coconuts, and so long as each party feels he may lose either property or prestige in a final settlement it is to the advantage of both to maintain the *status quo*.

Case VI: More Land Troubles

This case concerns a major *sinangge* within which several landtenure disputes are developing along with a dispute over who shall bear the prestigeful title of manager of the major unit as well as hold title to the truncal segment. We can begin with the residential history of one of the contenders.

Nggisonggiso, who is an agnatic descendant of the founder of the major *sinangge* Singgotu and therefore a member of its truncal segment at least as a cognatic descent category, now lives at Vagara village in the Tepazaka region (see map, Fig. 7, p. 90). He is the son of Sovala of Singgotu and Eluvavene of Tabukaro descent group in the Varisi region and was born at Singgotu. Sovala apparently paid no brideprice for his wife, but his is not considered a *tamazira* marriage. Eluvavene was murdered by Valoda of Singgotu (Sovala's father's brother's son), who was then manager of the truncal segment and the major *sinangge*, ostensibly because she was a sorceress. Nggisonggiso denies that she was, but he admittedly knows little about the event for he was still nursing when she was killed. Sovala went off to his kinsmen in the Varisi region in a rage to recruit allies for revenge, but other kinsmen intervened and got Valoda to offer Sovala *kesa* in compensation. Sovala called off the fight, but he refused to return to Singgotu and stayed on in the Varisi region and died there.

When his mother was killed, some of the hired killers wanted to kill Nggisonggiso too, but Zule of Nggolunggolu segment of Korasokana descent group (and Singgotu on his mother's side) intervened and took Nggisonggiso as his "son" (he had none of his own). Zule took Nggisonggiso back to Nggolunggolu and later went to live at Gabili with the powerful manager Madoko (some of his kinsmen had married there already). Zule died at Gabili, and Nggisonggiso was then cared for by Vavasa (Zule's brother's son). Nggisonggiso was the sole successor to Zule's interests in Nggolunggolu and now retains them.

When he was a young man and still unmarried, Nggisonggiso went to Vagara village to live with the Singgotu people and also near his interests in Nggolunggolu. He was then able to care for himself and lived with no one in particular. He went to work as a deckhand on a trading ship for six months and then settled for a year with his mother's kinsmen in the Varisi region. Later, he left them for a visit among his mother's father's kinsmen in the bush village of Baukolo, the residence of an autonomous branch of major *sinangge* Kesi. There he married *tamazira* to the daughter of a man who was also a visitor. Then Baukolo split, some people moving to the coast and others to Tagatagara, an Eromo (another branch of Kesi) village also in the bush. Nggisonggiso went there with his wife's father, who was following his Baukolo kinsmen. Around 1945 the Tagatagara people moved down to the beach at the present village of Voza. Voza is on Gabili land, and the former Tagatagara people live there as guests of Gabili. They are close enough to it to garden on Eromo land, though they use Gabili and Singgotu land, which is also nearby. A segment of Voza is composed largely of Eromo and Baukolo people and their affines.

After living at Voza for fourteen years and marrying off a couple of his daughters and a son, Nggisonggiso decided it was time to return to Singgotu at Vagara village. Lamukesa, his wife's brother, argued that Nggisonggiso was still his *tamazira*, but there was little Lamukesa could do about the move. Nggisonggiso said there was no ill-feeling, but he had been a good, helpful, coöperative *tamazira* long enough. When questioned, he insisted that he had never renounced or lost his interests in Singgotu or Nggolunggolu; that he had gardened, planted coconuts, or used the groves in those places all along; that he had been only a "visitor" among kinsmen in the various places he had lived; that he had moved about not because quarrels or disputes had driven him from place to place; that the reason for moving to Vagara was that he wanted "to return to my 'origin land' and make things straight." He also wanted his children "to know their own land." So in 1959 he began to build a house at Vagara and moved there shortly thereafter to live with his Singgotu kinsman Pitakamuki until the house was finished. Nggisonggiso's married son who also lives in Voza had not yet gone to live in Vagara in 1961 but says he will in due time.

Nggisonggiso says he did not have to ask permission of anyone to "return" to Vagara since Singgotu was his father's *sinangge* and had been his "proper" group all along. Furthermore, he is now the only living adult agnatic descendant of the Singgotu founder within the truncal segment; there are two other agnates, but they are only small boys. I asked who "kept" the land and people in his absence, and he replied Pitakamuki. Pitakamuki is his father's sister's son, whose father was a Singgotu *tamazira*, more specifically the *tamazira* of Valoda (see genealogy, Fig. 14, for details of the relationships). He added that Pogolo of the Panggaratuetue branch of Singgotu had tried recently to claim some of the truncal segment's land as his own, but that Pitakamuki had kept him off it. Nggisonggiso apparently regards himself as the legitimate manager of Singgotu, but he has some competition.

On earlier occasions I had been told that Vadalo, now an elderly man living in a hamlet (Biavoru) halfway between Voza and Vagara, was the manager of the major *sinangge* and its truncal segment. Vadalo is the son of a Singgotu woman, the sister of Valoda, who was once the generally recognized manager of Singgotu and the man who had Nggisonggiso's mother murdered. Valoda had only two daughters and no sons. His sister had married an Eromo man, and Valoda had taken a brideprice for her. When Vadalo was about fifteen years old, Valoda reportedly asked him to return to Singgotu to be his heir and successor. Thus Vadalo "returned" to his mother's side and lived with Valoda and eventually "kept his property and his *sinangge*." Valoda and Vadalo were joined at Singgotu by Vadalo's father and mother. Valoda lived until about 1922, and Vadalo has been the generally recognized manager of Singgotu ever since, according to relatively disinterested third parties as well as Vadalo himself.

He has spoken for Singgotu in various court cases affecting its lands. He married the widow of a Subavalu man, herself a Singgotu woman with tangled lines of adoption and descent in her ancestry. They have lived at various times with the Gabili and Votuae people with whom she has ties, and with the Eromo and Singgotu people with whom he has ties. Vadalo, however, is a quiet man and disinclined to disputing, so he prefers to live in a hamlet by himself. His wife's daughters and their husbands, and

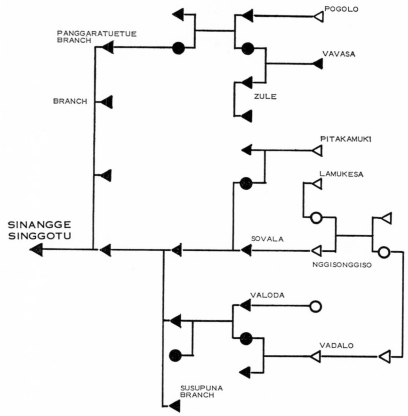

Fig. 14. Case VI: Skeleton Genealogy of *Sinangge*
Singgotu and Associated Parties

also some adopted children, live with him. His own son has recently married Nggisonggiso's daughter and taken up residence temporarily with his young wife's sister's Eromo husband in Voza village, although he had just finished building a new house in his father's hamlet. Vadalo says this is because he is about to give up living in his own hamlet and will probably move to Voza too. There has been much sickness and trouble over adultery within his hamlet, usual causes of residential realignment. In 1961 his wife fell ill and went to the mission hospital, and he moved into the men's house in Voza; he probably will not return to his own hamlet. Only one of his wife's daughters and her husband remain there now, and they probably will not stay for long.

When I asked Nggisonggiso about Vadalo's status, he argued that Vadalo is really an Eromo man since a brideprice was paid for his mother (a peculiar argument for a Singgotu man, but understandable under the circumstances). If Vadalo tried to advance any claims on Singgotu land they would chase him out. Admittedly, says Nggisonggiso, Vadalo has been their spokesman for some time, but only in the temporary absence of a more legitimate claimant. However, Vadalo is evidently giving Nggisonggiso no trouble, since their children married without protest. Vadalo is little concerned with managerial politics. He seems to have filled a vacuum that existed for a time, and now that Nggisonggiso is becoming active he is not going to make a fuss. He did not object when Pitakamuki spoke up about Singgotu affairs and he has a more disinterested attitude towards his managerial role than many other men would.

This giving way to a qualified agnate is not an automatic procedure. Vadalo could, if he wished, choose to argue that Nggisonggiso had taken little interest in Singgotu affairs up to now and so should be welcome back as anyone else would be but not accorded managerial status. There are other descent groups in which a nonagnate is manager even in the presence of agnates, and there are agnates living in other than their own agnatic groups which are without agnatic members. I know that in one case the man has been asked by his kinsmen to return but he has not been with the group since childhood and has no need or desire to return. But Nggisonggiso's agnatic status was yielded to by Vadalo more for personal than formal or jural reasons. Nggisonggiso could afford to stay away from Vagara as long as Vadalo was quiet and unpretentious and still associated with the group, but when other parties began to be obstreperous he had to go back to defend his and Pitakamuki's interests.

Singgotu has been wrought internally with squabbles over land for many years, few of which, however, have reached court. Those with other groups have gone to court and Singgotu has always won. Most recently, as already noted, Pogolo has been pressing claims and attempting to consolidate and separate his and his brother's interests in the Panggaratuetue branch of the Singgotu estate and, according to Nggisonggiso, Pitakamuki, and others, to alienate portions of the truncal segment's estate as well. One of the consistently recurrent issues concerns the nature of the division of the rights and interests in the segmentation or division of an estate. According to some people, and apparently according to "custom," the estate as land always remained a unitary whole and only rights of usufruct were divided, and even these were not absolutely exclusive. Members of branch segments should continue to let others use the land freely. This at least was the ideal condition, but it seems that most men regarded their custodial prerogatives with jealousy and took offense if kinsmen did not "tell" them first. Today many men are attempting to interpret the divisions in somewhat more definite terms and refusing to recognize the rights of others to use their shares. They argue that the land itself was divided and that holders of "shares" can do with them as they please. Thus Pitakamuki started to plant on Panggaratuetue land a few years ago and was ordered off by Pogolo. According to the "unity" interpretation, the land as a whole belongs to the manager of the major *sinangge*, and each branch merely controls certain "groves." According to the "separatist" parties, each branch has its own manager and its own lands. The "unity" people say the others care not for the integrity of the major *sinangge* and "think only of themselves"—"they want to be big-men with their own land." The "separtists" argue that others are trying to steal their lands or do them out of what little they have. Despite his "separatist" leanings, Pogolo has at times been accused of intimating that he should be the manager of the whole of Singgotu. This suggestion is generally scoffed by others who point out that Pogolo is not even an agnate in his own branch of Singgotu and that his father was "merely one of Valoda's hands" and not a big-man himself.

And so the controversies go on. Nggisonggiso seems likely to come out ahead in the end, if ever there is an end, but he is not yet pressing for more than a nominal recognition of his claim to the managership of Singgotu as a whole. At the moment his interests seem to lie in keeping Pogolo and others from pressing claims to segments of the lands of the truncal segment. These are all, of course, coastal flatlands, or there would not be so much fuss over them. Land-tenure matters are those which exercise the most interest today, and such matters are difficult to settle with finality. In the past managerial claims over land, groves, and other issues could be sanctioned not only by appeal to various "customs" or "rules" and genealogies but by sheer force as well. Thus the "rules" and the presumed facts were often only arguing points, elements in the rhetoric of politics. But self-help employing force or violence is no longer possible; thus the verbal battles rage and are likely to continue to do so as long as the courts and government are unable or unwilling to enforce decisions.

SUMMARY

There were, and are, at least three forms of structural unit in Choiseulese society, and all were known by the same term. Analytically we may distinguish cognatic descent categories, descent groups, and kin circles, and each of these forms was interdigitated with the others through the ideology of cognatic descent. Cognatic descent conferred membership in social categories, not in viable social groups. Filiation established membership and rights in a descent group consisting of a localized core of a cognatic descent category plus a number of spouses, guests, and others. To members of the cognatic descent category who had not become members of the descent group by filiation, cognatic descent conferred only conditional entitlement to membership in the group. That entitlement depended on several considerations besides the genealogical criterion. They included residence (or domicile) and the complex of interpersonal relations implied by it, the use made of potential rights by one's parents, and, perhaps most important, the *de facto* rights of those who had already consolidated their rights over, and established vested interests in, the corporate property of the group. Patrilineality was not a principle of recruitment to descent groups: it conferred a title, also contingent, to a more influential voice in group affairs and thereby provided one of the criteria for leadership status.

The corporate discreteness of descent groups (the discreteness of cognatic descent categories was minimal and of kin circles nonexistent) was not attained or maintained through formal organizational principles alone. The cognatic-descent idiom allowed persons to maintain interests in more than one descent group even to the extent that it may, under some conditions, be meaningful to speak of multiple membership in relation to descent groups as well as cognatic descent categories. The discreteness of descent groups, if measured in terms of the loyalties of members, remained always a relative matter, though at some times less so than at others. It was in the sphere of competitive transactions between groups, represented by managers, that a descent group gained its maximal discreteness, the strongest and most clear-cut allegiance of its members, and this was frequently in the form of allegiance to a big-man or manager as well as to the group. Crises situations, such as war, precipitated those allegiances most clearly, and especially for the two groups who were principals to a dispute. But since the discreteness of a descent group was contextual and dependent upon the group or groups to which it was opposed or with which it was allied, whatever discreteness a group may have achieved varied from time to time. New descent groups arose through the segmentation of older groups, big-men forming factions within truncal segments and splitting off to gain distinctiveness for themselves and discreteness for their groups by entering into competitive and coöperative transactions with other big-men and their descent groups.

Descent groups were the principal but only relatively enduring and discrete residential-proprietary segments of Choiseulese society. They related to one another and were thereby linked into a larger society in several ways.

Some were linked to one another, and alliance made more probable between them, as segments of a major *sinangge* or cognatic-descent category. However, the major *sinangge* as an operative unit was only a situational emergent, appearing as an alliance of its segments—and not necessarily of all of them—only in some crisis situations. Its permanent functions were minimal. Each branch was as dependent upon or independent of its cognate branches within the major unit as its political status vis-à-vis other groups necessitated.

Descent groups were also linked to one another through ties of kinship generated by intermarriage and the idiom of cognatic descent. However, it was not kinship per se that made genealogical ties effective but rather the rights and interests entitled by them and given strength as vested interests and secured rights through interpersonal transactions.

In addition to the genealogical ties or, more specifically, the ties of interest which bound descent groups or their members to one another, there were those relations of complementation and opposition which arose through vengeance, war, and gift exchange. Those relationships, arising from competition and conflict, contributed to the internal unity of descent groups and regions. No alliance between groups with comparable political status or ambitions could be more than temporary, thus preventing the formation, even within regions, of factions between whom no peace could prevail.

The network of overlapping cognatic and affinal ties, given meaning as described, was an important element of social control in Choiseulese society. In the absence of formal juridical institutions, the conflict of those interests and allegiances expressed by the web of intergroup kinship ties led to divided allegiance within groups already divided internally by jealousy over proprietary interests and individual political status. As an expression of the division of individual allegiances and the distribution of interests among possibly several groups, the cognatic-descent idiom reduced the possibility of violence between groups or their individual representatives and provided channels of arbitration through which disputes could be mediated and possibly resolved. Further order was generated within this society of self-seeking individuals and groups by the system of revenge and redress. The threat of self-help imposed some restraint through self-control and intragroup sanctions, but when this failed self-help tended to escalate into warfare. At that point the conflict of interests and allegiances became so aggravated and the responsibilities incurred by vengeance became so burdening that all parties began to seek termination of the conflict and found its possibility in the kinship ties between descent groups.

In some respects the social changes which have taken place within the past sixty years confirm the hypothesis that conflict between groups was essential to the attainment and maintenance of their distinctiveness and discreteness. Today, no longer faced with external conflict, and enjoying an economic situation that encourages production by nuclear families, the *sinangge*, in all aspects, have lost much of their significance. They perform few activities as corporate solidary units. Small and closely related groups of kin form task groups for certain activities—copra-making and gardening—but nuclear families show signs of becoming the basic independent and grudgingly coöperating economic units. Increasingly, the village and the district, entities imposed and maintained by external pressures, are the effective political units, but their effectiveness is lessened by the weakness of the sanctions made available and supported by outside authority. Quarreling over land arises largely from attempts by individuals or families to establish separate and exclusive rights over what was once corporate property and to deprive others of their rights of usage. Part of the motivation for such actions is economic—the desire for good coconut land with one's rights to it unimpaired—but another part comes from the unremitting pursuit of prestige and managerial status symbolized and made valid by control over land. Other forms of validation of claims to managerial status are no longer possible, because of *pax Britannica*, or desirable, because of the lack of necessity to distribute wealth or to be a party to its distribution in order to obtain security. The solidarity of kinsmen has become greatly impaired by self-interest unrestrained by obligation toward a larger social unit, and the recognition of kinship obligations has become considerably restricted through lack of formal or informal sanctions to enforce them. The Choiseulese of today have little to unite them either as kin groups or as a larger society, and they feel deprived of leadership. Their culture has been deprived of much of its meaning because the social situation which gave it significance is no more. As a result, their managers are powerless except for the minor powers delegated to a few of them by the protectorate government, which are inadequate for they lack the immediacy needed in such a small-scale society.

The argument presented in the preceding paragraph must be considered, for the time being, as no more than a hypothesis. It would take a more detailed discussion of the events of the past sixty years and of life on Choiseul today to validate the argument, but that is a task which must await another occasion (see Scheffler 1964d).

Chapter 7

Conclusions

Anthropologists have yet to build, and perhaps never will be able to build, models of "total" social structures (see Lèvi-Strauss 1953; Firth 1954; Nadel 1957). The best we can do is to describe one or more kinds of "order" within a society, conceptualizing the whole as an "order of orders" (Lèvi-Strauss 1953) within which there may be degrees of interdependence or degrees of freedom between the various "suborders" (cf. also Nadel 1957: 138–140).

"Order" has many referents, but in this context it is taken to refer to types and degrees of *interconnection* between phenomena and to the *qualitative features* of different types of phenomena. The qualitative phenomena and organizational forms we choose to study may be objectively or subjectively defined (that is, by us according to our scientific perception of problems or by our subjects); they may be, for instance, orders of events or orders of concepts, or the orderly way in which concepts are handled in the course of events. But the choices we make lead in different directions and require or prohibit some kinds of data (see e.g., Schneider 1963: 50–52).

Probably taking his cue from the distinction Lèvi-Strauss (1953) makes between "mechanical" and "statistical" models of social structure, Leach (1960: 124) argues that "social structures are sometimes best regarded as the statistical outcome of multiple individual choices rather than a direct reflection of jural rules." As I understand this, Leach argues that many ethnographic accounts of what social anthropologists have called social structure ought to be regarded in this way—as accounts of states of affairs which, presumably, may be phrased in numerical or quantitative terms, even though the ethnographer may not do so. Furthermore, these states of affairs cannot be understood simply as products of, or as principally constrained or determined by, the affective commitment of the actors to systems of norms and values, nor by self-maintenance or homeostatic mechanisms. The anthropologist should not confuse norms or rules *for* behavior, which may or may not have the affective commitment of the actors, with the normal patterns *of* behavior or "structural principles," which may well be no more than quasi-numerically derived characterizations of behavior and of no explanatory value. And norms or rules *for* behavior, which have psychological validity as constraints upon behavior, cannot be deduced from patterns of social transactions alone.

Neither Leach nor Lèvi-Strauss argues that anthropologists should confine themselves to the construction of "statistical models" of social structure, because such models, if they may properly be called such (see Harrè 1961), are only the first descriptive-analytical step, a statement of events which require explanation through the construction of mechanical models. These latter models postulate and allow testing for the phenomenal reality of specific mechanisms each of which partly constrains—I specifically avoid "determines"—and in their totality may be said to account for, the events observed. The anthropologist as a student of human behavior—rather than merely a student of social systems—may postulate whatever mechanisms he wishes provided he is willing to formulate tests of their existence and to gather the relevant data. Mechanisms such as affective commitment to norms and values and "the structure of the mind" have been suggested and used as explanatory variables. These are, presumably, important behavior-generating and -constraining mechanisms, as are such factors as the natural and man-made "material context" within which people order their social lives, but only for those who are willing to follow through with the implications of postulating them. In any event, these mechanisms as explanatory variables cannot be exhaustive; each explains only that much of social behavior which is dependent upon it, and not the whole, and there remain others to be explored.

In this view, structure is an emergent property of social systems. The structure is there in phenomenal reality, like a suicide rate (cf. Leach 1961b: 300), but fleeting, and we try to capture it and its causes, however imperfectly, in the models we built up after it. The models, of course, are not the same thing as the structure and its causes for they are made of concepts, not of real events and mechanisms. But the concepts should refer, as closely as present knowledge and language permits, to existent events and mechanisms. The emergence and continuation or persistence of a particular configuration of social transactions, which may be described with concepts and numbers, is to be explained through mechanical models which are not models of social structure but of behavior generating and constraining mechanisms. Some of those mechanisms may themselves be "structural" but they are causal mechanisms only through the intervening variable of personal or individual motivational systems. Social systems are sometimes ordered or structured in such a way and within a larger environment such that they do endure largely intact over long periods of time, but they are not structured thus *in order to* endure in that way. What endures is not a social structure, or a particular form of social order in all details, which people strive, either consciously or unconsciously, to uphold, but communities of individuals with some order, for better or for worse (cf. Leach 1961b: 300–301). Continuity or stability of a "total" system, once demonstrated, is a datum for study and must be seen as the adventitious by-product of multiple transactions rather than a postulated or assumed inherent dynamic of social systems (see also Stanner 1963 and Nadel 1957: 141–147).

To reconstruct the "sense" of Choiseulese society as it was and to reconcile seemingly conflicting statements about it, I have found it useless and debilitating to assume that the totality was ever any sort of "unity," and I have found it necessary to remain constantly aware of the fact that it was a society without "law" in our own naïve sense of the word. It was a society in which one could attain and maintain one's interests and goals only through other men and only on terms either of agreement or force (cf. Stanner 1959). An important corollary of this situation was that everyone's rights were contingent upon whatever he could himself either force or persuade other people to "agree" they were. It has also seemed important to realize that without specifically juridical institutions there were no relatively objective means available to test whether any segment of conduct was in conformity with the norms nor, for that matter, which norms were "really" relevant to any particular situation. These were matters for "agreement," and agreement could only be coerced or bargained for.

These issues have considerable relevance for understanding the significance of norms or rules in Choiseulese society. One of their functions may have been to constrain behavior directly through the affective commitment of actors to the modes of behavior recommended by the norms, but the meaning of norms or rules in this sense was problematic to and for the participants in social transactions as well as for analysis, precisely because of the absence of relatively objective means of testing the meanings of the norms or the conformity of conduct with them.

Therefore, an interesting problem is posed for sociological analysis: Rather than assume that the principal social function of norms or rules is the regulation of conduct through the intervening variable of affective commitment, examine the role played by norms or the operations performed with them, and the consequences of these operations, in the process of social organization (in Firth's [1954] sense). To do this, it is unnecessary and debilitating to assume that in the organizational process persons have either social order or the maintenance of a particular form of social structure as a goal, or that the organizational processes in a society are inherently productive of any particular form of order. The resultant social structure, again for better or for worse by *any* subjective or objective standards, is an emergent phenomenon. It is a distortion of the concept of social organization (as distinguished from social structure) to argue that the organizational processes "support" the social structure, nor can they be said to constitute the "working out" of the social structure in any sense other than in effect adventitiously producing it. The *principles* of social organization must have psychological validity for the actors, but organizational *processes*, like social structure, may have properties describable in general terms, and unknown to the actors, which are, in effect, the inherent properties of human social transactions.

Stated in terms of "orders," one could ask what are the relations between the "order of rules" and the "order of events" (where social transactions are taken as the events). It has been unnecessary to consider the question whether the Choiseulese are or were "really committed to" the norms or rules they talk about

—one form of relation between the two orders—for it has seemed to me the better procedure for an anthropologist without special psychological training to regard the introduction of norms or rules into social transactions as a form of social action in itself. In this view, norms or rules are not just static ideological entities, nor are their social functions exhausted when it is said of them that they serve as constraints upon or guides for behavior. They are also strategic rhetorical resources in the process of social organization.

I have assumed that although norms and other concepts do exist in people's heads, and perhaps have a logical and meaningful organization there, they are in that context a psychological datum. They become a social and sociological datum, and their logical order and meanings become socially and sociologically relevant, only when they enter into transactions between persons and groups. I have assumed that they have no sociological meaning outside of those transactions. Norms, for instance, may be dealt with sociologically without reference to the issue of whether the people who introduce them into situated transactions "really" believe in them or "really" are committed to them as modes of action for themselves. I do not say that this is the best, most interesting, or exhaustive way to deal with norms or rules, only that it is possible and fruitful as well as necessary in the absence of extensive and reliable psychological data.

One of the sociologically relevant facts about norms is that people "exchange" them in social transactions, and those "exchanges" have noticeable effects upon the conduct of the parties to those transactions.[1] The social anthropologist may observe the "functions," or operational consequences, of the "exchanges" and generalize about them. He may also ask if the exchanged norms form a logical system and how they are adjusted logically and meaningfully to their larger social and material contexts. *A priori* we may assume that they must be both, but the ways in which and the degrees to which they are must be empirical problems.

In Choiseulese society a person's rights, even in the ideal sense, were matters for agreement, and agreement could only be coerced

---

[1] This view is not new. It is basic to "symbolic interaction" analysis in American sociology. My most immediate references have been Mills (1940), Gerth and Mills (1954), Goffman (1958) and Rose (1962).

or bargained for. One of the elements in the coercive or bargaining process was the normative one. Those perceptive informants who remarked "Our customs are not firm; we look only for that which will help us to live well, and the rest is just talk" did not demean the significance of the ideological components of conduct by calling them, in Leachian fashion, "just talk," for "just talk" is a highly significant social process. They were also, in their own way, getting at the fact that "norms" or "customs" are not an independent system in themselves but are rather part of a larger system of social action. They exist not only as "guides to behavior" but also, and in this instance perhaps even more so, as rhetorical elements in behavior.

The norms or rules, if the Choiseulese concepts or ideological components of conduct about which I have written may be accurately described as such (see pp. 110–113), can be understood sociologically only by taking seriously the fact that they were and are meaningful only in their transactional contexts, the attributes of which were generally understood and usually left implicit. The "ideal" was, and still is, openness of the group to all legitimate descendants of the founder, and the implied context was "provided he is a good kinsman," "provided the group is not too full," "provided not too many generations have 'covered' the link," "provided it is in our interest," and so on. These were shared understandings and mutual expectations which constrained claims which were made, and the reactions to them. These loopholes or escape clauses protected the interests, or merely the prejudices, of those within whose power it was to exercise closure. They did not have to repudiate the norm that the group was always open, for they could question the legitimacy of any particular claim on genealogical grounds or upon other grounds as well. It was the interested parties who made the judgments, not outside, disinterested parties with juridical powers. Thus, what the "facts" were and, therefore, which aspects of the norms applied, were determined in the first instance by each party according, I would suppose, to his own needs and desires and his interpretation of the situation. But his interpretation was not *the* interpretation, nor was there any single "correct" interpretation against which any particular one could be measured or assessed. Therefore, in the final analysis there could be only a "working consensus" which defined the situation and the norms relevant to it for the moment and which evoked expectations about future conduct of the parties to the transactions.[2]

These processes are well revealed in the strategies of gift exchange or interpersonal and intergroup conflict. For instance, the Choiseulese who entered into transactions requiring the exchange of *kesa* had to agree, at least tacitly, to certain understandings (norms) about those transactions. But it was known that others did sometimes deliberately seek to avoid completing transactions to which they had either explicitly or tacitly agreed. Thus one party might have found cause to expect that he would have to invoke forceful sanctions to complete the exchanges "properly." Others may have found cause (by "reading" what they took to be critical signs) to expect that such sanctions could not be invoked and to expect to act with impunity. Parties could also attempt to convey the impression that they had completed transactions to the best of their current abilities and thereby preserve their reputations as reliable parties. Cleverness in such strategies was an admirable attribute, but all Choiseulese admit in the abstract that such "deceptions" were "bad." One must reckon, however, with the relativity of moral judgments which may be characteristic of such societies (see e.g. Read 1955). In the judgment of particular situations, what was "bad" was being deceived in one's expectations or, on the other side of the transaction, being revealed as a deceiver of those who could then justify, with their interpretation of the norms, the use of any sanctions at their disposal. None of these were "ideal" situations in Choiseulese terms—they were not "straight" or "proper," and people could get killed doing such things—but they were part of the normal course of life.

The party who reportedly reminded Pinggolo (see p. 227) that Zale's father had caused trouble and suggested that Zale might be expected to do the same did not have to appeal to any "normative" forms of conduct to get Pinggolo to act unfavorably towards Zale. In fact, Pinggolo was led to ignore some norms about the presentation of pig gifts and thus provoked Zale's ire by failing to meet his expectations that he would be treated as a big-man.

---

[2] It is not necessary to assume that the consensus was one of "identity." See, e.g., Nadel (1957: 55–57); Wallace (1961: 29–44); and for the "symbolic interaction" point of view Blumer (1962).

My informants suggested that Pinggolo made a gross miscalculation in regard to Zale's potential for counteraction and did not
realize that Zale might be able to find allies among the enemies of
Pinggolo's immediate allies. Zale reacted as expected of a man who
thought of himself as a big-man, and who had the means. He acted
in conformity with no jural norms, and in fact he too violated
those norms which were truly "ideal" norms by bringing injury
to his kinsmen. His actions were considered "normal," but no less
reprehensible, under the circumstances.

It might be objected that in concentrating on the rhetorical
functions of norms I ignore the fact that the effectiveness of rhetoric is at times dependent on the commitment of various actors
to those norms. I would not deny that this is true, only that the
effectiveness of norms is *necessarily* dependent upon that commitment. This may be demonstrated by reference to one type of situation that occurred, but no longer can occur, in Choiseulese
society. Kinship through common membership in a *sinangge*,
whether cognatic descent category or descent group, ideally required of parties to a transaction that they coöperate harmoni-
ously and without excessive self-interest. When kinsmen fell to
disputing and perhaps to violence, parties with vested interests
in both could get "caught in the middle" by formal kinship obligations and the possibility of vengeance being exercised against
them. The norms gave them no sure direction unless they were
coresident with one but not the other disputant, and perhaps not
even then. The norms were assertive, unqualified and yet ambiguous, as they had to be if they were to cover multiple situations. Thus without compromising either their interests or their
ideals, persons caught in such binds could argue that the disputants had no business fighting anyway since they were kinsmen.
The disputants could of course argue that one or the other had
violated the ideal canons of kinship harmony and was therefore
a "meaningless" or "nothing" kinsman. If the accusation could
be made to stick it stigmatized the other party and defined him
as not worthy of normative considerations. On the other hand, if
the disputants wanted, or were being forced, to compose their differences, they could find in the "ideals" common grounds for so
doing. Go-betweens appealed to these ideals, as they still do, and
in purporting to accept them as generally valid and relevant to
the immediate instance each disputant presented himself as a

"good kinsman" and saved face and prestige. Neither had to feel that the norm really was applicable, but both had to believe that there was some significant personal advantage to be gained in settling the dispute. Each could have had his own reasons, such as conserving strength for a latter offensive movement against the other, but many motives could find compatability in the norms.

The same might be noted about the formation of alliances between cognate descent groups. The considerations that led them to coöperate were numerous and perhaps diverse, but once together through contractual bonds there existed potential sources of cleavage (see page 238). However, even as cleavages developed, the potential for continued alliance could be maintained by appeal to the norms of common descent. In themselves, these norms were insufficiently strong to insure that there would be initial coöperation and then no violence between cognate groups; but perhaps only because men were sufficiently committed to life itself, the norms remained as a convenient basis upon which to transcend many dissimilar immediate concerns. It may have been a consequence of the possibility of using the norms of common descent in a rhetorical fashion that major *sinangge* composed of separate and independent descent groups were able to exist at all.

I find it grossly misleading to say or to imply that the course of these various transactions was governed by "norms" or "principles." In refusing to do so I am not trying to say that the "ideals" of Choiseulese society were "all things to all men," but simply that it was precisely" the manipulative, bargaining, transactional approach to life which [was] the system" in Choiseulese society (cf. Stanner 1959: 216). The norms must take their place in that context.

What can we say in general terms about that "place"? In any transaction or series of transactions, the "proper" mode of conduct was only one element, and possibly not an important one.[3] Norms and expectations, as well as past precedent, jural or otherwise—the totality of which the Choiseulese call, with convenient ambiguity, "our ways"—provided one basis for the possible initiation of transactions. Beyond that, each party contributed its own

---

[3] These observations are similar to those made by Gulliver (1963) in his study of social control in Arusha society. I am indebted to his study for assistance in the final clarification of my thoughts on Choiseulese society.

interpretations and its own powers to press for and sustain its own advantage. What happened was a consequence of the skillful or unskillful manipulation of the available social and material resources, the relative strengths of the parties, the degree to which each was able to influence or constrain the actions of others, and the degree to which it was in the interests of both, or others, for an accommodation to be reached. To say that in these transactions the norms served as "guides to behavior" or to "define the boundaries of 'legitimate' conduct" would be to miss an essential point. It is more to the point and closer to what the social anthropologist, with his conventional techniques, can observe to say that norms served as rhetorical elements with which persons defended their own actions and supported or condemned the actions of others. In so doing the actors themselves "decided" what was "legitimate" and so urged others to support them.

Such uses of the norms were not abuses nor were they an aberration of the "system." They were an integral part of it. They were forms of social action, but they were not, in any meaningful sense, designed to uphold any specific or general social "institutions." Such usages of the norms were designed, if at all, to uphold or to improve the positions, within "the system" as it was seen by them, of the participants to the various transactions. To be sure, certain "institutions" or recognizable social forms continued to exist as a consequence of the multiple and continued occurrence of such conduct, and the processes by which this happened may be described in terms of regularities and perhaps even "self-regulation," but the regularities are not meaningfully describable in terms of "principles."[4]

The use of ideals or norms as rhetorical elements occurs in any society, though it is perhaps more characteristic of some societies than others, and perhaps more characteristic of some kinds of situations in some societies than of other kinds of situations in the same societies. The ethnographic literature abounds with de-

---

[4] As Davis (1959) has noted, the most profound difficulties are introduced into social-science analysis by the necessity of describing and analyzing events in the terms of a language derived from everyday, predominantly "moralistic," discourse. Clearly there was much ambiguity in, for instance, Radcliffe-Brown's use of such terms as "integration" and "order." One cannot be sure whether he meant a "harmonious" and "happy" order or just "order . . . for better or for worse" (cf. Easton 1959).

scriptions of situated transactions which may be interpreted in such terms, and these are not only, nor even predominantly, "crisis" or dispute situations. They occur wherever the process of "social organization" takes place (see Firth 1951; 1954; 1955).[5] To recognize this "function" and to deal with it sociologically, it is not necessary to "reduce" ideology to "mere rhetoric," nor would it be defensible to do so, but rhetoric is, after all, one of the ways of "getting the work of society done," of organizing and "steering" action.

In the societies which social anthropologists have conventionally studied, norms or rules are usually, though not universally, phrased in terms of what we call kinship. Gluckman (1955; 1962), for instance, has done much to advance our understanding of why this should be. Kinship idioms are particularly useful as idioms of morality because social relations in relatively undifferentiated societies are usually "multiplex" and between kinsmen; indeed, this is what we usually mean when we describe a society as "simple" or "primitive." Thus kinship idioms may be fairly effectively used as sanctions for the fulfillment of one's duties in, say, the economic sphere because the parties to the transactions are also probably coparties to many other transactions and failure in one sphere could easily jeopardize the operation of all others. The introduction of kinship norms or rules into transactions may thus be a way of sanctioning expectations about those transactions. This, I take it, is what Leach means when he says, "What the social anthropologist calls kinship structure is just a way of *talking about* property relations which can also be talked about in other ways" (1961b: 305, my emphasis).

Whether "kinship structure" is just that and nothing more is a matter for empirical enquiry and need not detain us here, but a few points should be noted. First, I do not think that Leach

---

[5] To mention only a few: Firth (1936: 194–195) on sexual relations between kinsmen in Tikopia; Firth (1949) on the control of chiefs by commoners in Tikopia; Pehrson (1957: 22–23) on sexual relations between kinsmen among the Lapps; Best (1924: 247 ff.) on the rhetoric of "rank" and the manipulation of stigma in Maori society; Berreman (1962) on intercaste relations in northern India; Singh Uberoi (1962: 47) on "rank" in Trobriand society. I am indebted to Kelly and Rothschild (n.d.) for some of these examples and for some excellent observations on "kinship as ideology" which, however, I have not been able to use here.

would deny that kinship may be a way of "talking about" relations other than property relations, nor that it would be an un-
productive exercise to reduce those other, for example, political,
relations to property relations. Secondly, although people may discuss their economic, political, and other relations by means of
kinship norms or rules we should be careful not to imply that in
so doing they are attempting to attain or maintain an ideal state
of affairs, not even that seemingly implied by the norms or rules
themselves. Leach's statement that "It is only when we have observed the practice that the rule, as an ideal type, acquires meaning" (1961b: 4) would seem to imply that he shares this view.
Finally, the notion of "kinship structure" implies that not only do
kinship norms or rules serve as rhetorical elements in the social organization process but also that these rules are parts of ideological
systems which probably have a logical-meaningful structure which
is related to the larger environment within which they operate, including the material context within which social transactions take
place. Some aspects of that structure may enter into social transactions too, as when an appeal is made to consistency in the course
of rhetoric. This may be particularly true of conflicts involving the
application of different rules to, objectively, the same social situation. Then the very structure of the system of rules may become
an object of social transactions.

With this general point of view, and taking a few leads from
Barnes' (1962) comments on the New Guinea Highlands and
Sahlins' (1963) on Melanesian political systems in general, we
can to a degree account for the nature of the Choiseulese ideology about their social structure, or at least some aspects of it,
and in a manner which can be, and has been, applied to other societies with different "structures." The degree to which I can do
so here is constricted by the lack of detailed economic and ecological data pertaining to the past.

As noted in Chapter 1, the Choiseulese depended primarily
upon small-scale and nonintensive taro horticulture for their subsistence. This permitted only a fairly low population density and
required general dispersal of the population too. Large nucleated
settlements could be only temporary. The only long-term durable
resource was the land itself, and it does not seem to have varied
greatly in economic potentiality or desirability in the context of
the taro economy. Furthermore, any small parcel of land could

not be continuously productive, and hence persons had to have access to a number of such areas within a fairly confined range. Some coöperation was necessary in subsistence pursuits, but there seem to have been no substantial economic reasons why these task groups should have endured as solidary units beyond the immediate tasks. Also, continuous planting year round and differential rates of consumption probably made it difficult for them to do so. Each residential unit, no matter how small, could be self-sufficient for subsistence purposes so long as it could from time to time count on the aid of other such units in clearing gardens.

A man's principal capital resources consisted in his labor and his allegiances. No one area or group of people was more attractive to him economically than any other *except* when he had crops in the land or had developed strong bonds of mutual obligation and allegiance with his fellow members of the group. The kinds of interests and the kinds of obligations and allegiances men could have in other groups and in their material and personnel resources were of the same sort as those they had in their own residential units. The kinds of services a man could render kinsmen in other groups were precisely the same as those he could render his own coresidents or as could be rendered to those others by their own coresidents. The differences were matters of degree, conditioned by proximity and the consequent differential interaction rates, and also highly dependent upon individual initiative. It was possible for men to divide their interests between several nucleated groupings that might arise without the material object of those interests becoming thereby less productive. Perhaps it was economically essential to do so, and there were good political reasons too.

The principal advantage to be gained by "sitting tight" in one place and among one group was in the elaboration and consolidation of mutual obligations and allegiances. But it was also useful to expand those allegiances too, for only in this way could a broad security network become established and maintained. If the latter was done, it diminished the potential solidarity and stability of nucleated groupings. The solidarity of the group, its capability for concerted action, and its stability depended on the particular balance struck between concentration as opposed to dispersion of the mutual obligations and allegiances of its constituent members. The primary factor in counteracting the tendency towards expansion of allegiances seems to have been the necessity for the co-operation of many in defense of the interests of one or a few. As conflicts arose over failure to fulfill obligations or to sustain allegiances, or over women, sorcery, and so on, the only source of security was one's ability to make use of the obligations and allegiances of others to form a faction which could oppose the factions formed or used by others. Not all men were equally adept at building or managing factions, and some had to seek the protection of those who were and give them their allegiances in return for services rendered.

Particular factions, at many levels, could become stabilized around such men who consolidated their positions just as other men did, though on a larger scale. They dealt not only in their own allegiances but also in those of groups of men. Land, as the only durable resource, figured prominently in their dealings. But it was not so much the land itself or its productivity that mattered in these dealings as it was the stewardship of land and its use as a means of tying men to factions and their managers. The stability of factions depended, among other things, upon the skills of their managers in manipulating cohesive and divisive tendencies, but it was impossible for a manager ever to garner completely, for all times and under all conditions, the total allegiances of all faction members (see Sahlins 1963: 289–94).

The enlargement and contraction of factions, which were residentially concentrated but only relatively discrete in respect of the allegiances of their constituents, was the major dramatic social and political process in Choiseulese society. It is obvious, however, that in the long run the factions were stable enough for the Choiseulese to come to conceptualize them as permanent units within a larger social field. There might be some small justification for assuming that this was at least partly wishful thinking, but the conceptualization of these factions as descent groups within a field of descent groups did have some basis.

Factions were not necessarily composed solely of nuclear families nor did they fractionate along nuclear family lines alone. Some men were more closely allied with others and their families, and these tended to form small "blocs" which could give their allegiances to other such blocs. Men tended to remain after marriage with other men among whom they had come to maturity and with whom they had therefore already developed strong reciprocal bonds. As their sons matured and did the same, the blocs tended towards patrilateral and perhaps even patrilineal composition. But factions did coalesce around big-men too, and it was only to be expected that when those men died (or were otherwise unable) the factions might have tended to disintegrate. Sometimes there was little to keep them from doing so, for if the group were small, just getting organized or relatively "poor" and without another capable man to take up and maintain the former manager's consolidated allegiances, the group was more likely to ally itself with other such groups, whether larger or of the same size. And if the group were large and already had several able and ambitious men within it, it probably tended to fractionate and to form two or more factions, perhaps still more or less allied. (One would like to be able to be more specific about sizes here, but these probably varied with external political conditions and the productive state of available lands.) However, a faction did not have to disintegrate upon the death of its manager and could promote another manager from among its own ranks. If the constituents of the faction were willing to continue to recognize any obligations their former manager had contracted, they might have been able to count upon the assured protection of other factions, especially those which were cognate descent groups, while they were reordering internally. It would have been to their advantage to remain together since they had vested interests in gardens, groves, and one another's services, and it would have been all the more possible if there were only slight external political pressures upon them. In such "crisis" situations the "core" of the group probably remained together, if possible, while many "attached" parties who had sought the support or protection of the eminent manager then looked elsewhere. If the group had been well organized under a manager who had been adept at keeping internal peace, then it probably had a better chance of maintaining its identity and promoting another manager from "inside."

The Choiseulese could conceptualize and make moral and political capital out of the inherent tendency towards patrilateral allegiances. An agnatic idiom was useful for expressing continuity of the groups around managers and useful to the managers for justifying their positions and demands for allegiance in moral and not simply self-interest terms. Such an idiom was also useful for them and their descendants in justifying assumption of or succession to the position. And it was useful, too, in expressing the bonds which remained after segmentation (or were perhaps created) between managers and their groups. But an agnatic idiom could not express, for moralistic and rhetorical purposes, the ways in which persons became members of factions and the interests of most members of those factions. Diverse as these were, if an abstract appeal to unity were to be effective it had to be general and ambiguous. Thus cognatic descent was the logical complement to agnatic descent, the latter expressing the continuity of the group through a manager and validating his right to the allegiances of the members of the group and his privilege to control its resources, the former the continuity and the solidarity of the whole group as a body of kinsmen, especially vis-à-vis other such groups. Cognatic descent also served as a logical expression of the fact that the bonds between members of the same group were of the same kind, although perhaps differing in intensity, as those between members of different groups. It served as a moral cover for the diversity and yet similarity of interests which bound people into groups, and some groups into a more or less orderly whole.

To put this briefly: On Choiseul, agnatic descent provided the moral basis for the privileges of men who were able to acquire and maintain such privileges. Cognatic descent expressed the common allegiances of men who comprised the groups and also the possible allegiances of those men to other groups. It could do both because the allegiances were of the same sort and because conflicts of allegiance were neither created nor sustained by the norms. Transactions, not norms, sorted out whatever conflicts of allegiance there might have been and did so only situationally and temporarily.[6]

Social structures similar to this one are frequently characterized by the "optative" nature of kin-group affiliation as opposed to the "definitive" mode of affiliation purportedly characteristic of unilineal descent systems (but cf. Forde 1963). But the "choices of affiliation" open to persons were in fact choices between factions to which one could render one's allegiances, and the choices that were or could be made can only be understood in terms of the

---

[6] Cf. Groves (1963: 289), who argues that "In Oceania, descent validates privilege [while] kinship validates collaboration." Although I cannot accept the categorical distinction between "descent" and "kinship" it should be apparent that I agree with his general argument.

structure of the factions, their operations, and their interrelations. Expression of the "choice" in terms of descent was only the logical consequence of construing the factions as descent groups. But it was more than that too, for it put "choice" and "refusal" in a moralistic rather than a purely self-interest context. Cognatic descent was not an expression of any underlying moral principles but rather a moralistic expression of the inevitable interdependence of men in society and more especially of the particular forms of interdependence characteristic of this society. A morality enjoining harmony was probably an essential, and perhaps inevitable, part of the social structure evolved under the specific historical and economic conditions of Choiseulese life (cf. Worsley 1956: 63).

It should be apparent, but it may be worth stating once more, that when I say these idioms or ideological components of conduct "expressed" various forms of privilege or interdependence I do not refer to any "rules," "structural principles," or "basic moral axioms" that were being "expressed" but rather to the fact that people needed such concepts to talk about their social relations and that "talk" was sometimes rhetorical.

I do not maintain that this was the only logical or meaningful structural possibility under the circumstances, but I do maintain that it was reasonable and workable under those circumstances, and "the system," including its ideology, persisted only as long as its larger economic and political context. This latter contention will be documented in a study of social change on Choiseul.

To argue that these "idioms" evolved by the Choiseulese were more logical and reasonable and perhaps more workable under the circumstances than some others might have been, or that they were in some sense inevitable, would demand a lengthy comparative exercise and require typological considerations. I would note here only that a typology useful in generating meaningful propositions (i.e., testable and capable of generating further problems and propositions) about social and ideological forms and their conditions of occurrence and change must of necessity be based primarily upon the operations groups perform. It is apparent that the basic differences between "optative" and "definitive" descent-group systems are not to be attributed to the fact that one permits some choice of affiliation whereas the other does not. This is a matter of degree, not a difference in kind, for it is well known that unilineal descent systems, especially where the "descent groups" are "separate and physically identifiable as such," also permit alternate affiliations under defined circumstances (see e.g., Forde 1963). The differences in group structure, with which the necessity for, the possibility of, and the rates of alternate affiliation are only correlated, lie in the kinds of operations these groups perform; and, in turn, these and their combinations are doubtlessly correlated with the nature of available resources, technology, and the forms of coöperation necessary to use them effectively. The Choiseulese formed the kinds of groups they did and those groups combined or failed to combine in the ways they did, and these were different from the ways of, say, the Tallensi, the Nuer, or the Trobriand Islanders, not because the Choiseulese permitted "choice of affiliation" between descent groups but because the multiple conditions under which these various peoples lived were different in many ways. Any useful typology must reflect those conditions more closely than any "holistic" typology based upon formal organizational concepts (the cultural constructs, norms or rules) is capable of doing.

The attempt to view the Choiseulese "kinship system" as idiomatic of social relations and not as a jural system with moral force in its own right began when the Choiseulese themselves forced the recognition of its idiomatic character upon me by insisting that "It is all just talk." They made it apparent that economic and political concerns, along with the necessity to accommodate oneself to others since most interests can be attained only through other people, were and are the major constraints upon their conduct. They did, indeed, teach me a few things about "kinship," for which I am grateful. Therefore, my apologies to them if they have suffered at my hands. They and I will have made our point if we have done something to lessen the lingering reification of the analytical distinction between "ideal" and "actual" conduct and shown that theory and practice cannot be isolated one from the other, for they are part and parcel of the social system.

BIBLIOGRAPHY

Allan, C. H.
  1957 Customary land tenure in the British Solomon Islands Pro-
        tectorate. Honiara, The Western Pacific High Commission.
Amherst of Hackney, Lord and B. Thomson (eds.)
  1901 *The Discovery of the Solomon Islands.* (Translated from the
        original Spanish manuscripts of Alvaro de Mendaña and
        others.) London, The Hakluyt Society.
Area Study, Allied Geographical Section
  1943 Terrain study No. 48, area study, Choiseul Island (revised
        12 Feb. 1943). (Australian National University Library,
        Canberra.)
Barnes, J. A.
  1955 Seven types of segmentation. Human Problems in British
        Central Africa 17: 1–22.
  1960 Marriage and residential continuity. American Anthropologist
        62: 850–866.
  1962 African models in the New Guinea Highlands. Man 62: 5–9.
Belshaw, C. S.
  1947 Native politics in the Solomon Islands. Pacific Affairs 20:
        187–193.
  1950 *Island Administration in the South West Pacific.* London,
        Royal Institute of International Affairs.
  1954 *Changing Melanesia: Social-Economics of Culture Contact.*
        Melbourne, Oxford University Press.
Berreman, G.
  1962 Behind many masks: ethnography and impression management
        in a Himalayan village. The Society for Applied Anthropology,
        Monograph No. 4. Ithaca, New York, The Society for Applied
        Anthropology.
Best, E.
  1924 *The Maori.* 2 vols. Wellington, The Polynesian Society.

Blumer, H.
　1962　Society as symbolic interaction. In: *Human Behavior and Social Processes*, ed. by A. Rose. Boston, Houghton Mifflin Co., pp. 179–192.

Bougainville, L. de
　1772　*A Voyage Around the World 1766–1769*. Trans. by J. R. Foster. Dublin, n.p.

British Solomon Islands Protectorate Annual Reports
　1914　Colonial annual reports: British Solomon Islands. London, H. M. Stationery Office.
　1918　Colonial annual reports: British Solomon Islands. London, H. M. Stationery Office.

Brown, G.
　1908　*Pioneer Missioner and Explorer: An Autobiography*. London, n.p.

Burke, K.
　1955a　*A Grammar of Motives*. New York, George Braziller, Inc.
　1955b　*A Rhetoric of Motives*. New York, George Braziller, Inc.

Burnett, F.
　1911　*Through Polynesia and Papua: Wanderings with a Camera in Southern Seas*. London, Francis Griffiths.

Burridge, K. O. L.
　1961　*Mambu: A Melanesian Millennium*. London, Methuen and Co.

Capell, A.
　1943　Notes on the islands of Choiseul and New Georgia, Solomon Islands. Oceania 14: 20–29.

Cheyne, A.
　1852　*A Description of Islands in the Western Pacific Ocean*. London, J. D. Potter.

Colson, E.
　1953　Social control and vengeance in Plateau Tonga society. Africa 23: 199–212.

Davis, K.
　1959　The myth of functional analysis. American Sociological Review 24: 757–772.

Easton, D.
　1959　Political anthropology. In: *Biennial Review of Anthropology 1959*, ed. by B. J. Siegel. Stanford, Stanford University Press, pp. 210–262.

Firth, R.
　1936　*We, The Tikopia*. London, Allen and Unwin.
　1949　Authority and public opinion in Tikopia. In: *Social Structure: Essays Presented to A. R. Radcliffe-Brown*, ed. by Fred Eggan

and M. Fortes. London, Oxford University Press, pp. 168–188.
1954   Social organization and social change. Journal of the Royal Anthropological Institute 84: 1–20.
1955   Some principles of social organization. Journal of the Royal Anthropological Institute 85: 1–18.
1957   A note on descent groups in Polynesia. Man 57: 4–8.
1963   Bilateral descent groups: an operational perspective. In: Studies in Kinship and Marriage, ed. by I. Schapera. Royal Anthropological Institute Occasional Paper No. 16, pp. 22–37.

Forde, C. D.
1963   Unilineal fact or fiction: an analysis of the composition of kin groups among the Yako. In: Studies in Kinship and Marriage, ed. by I. Schapera. Royal Anthropological Institute Occasional Paper No. 16, pp. 38–57.

Fortes, M.
1953   The structure of unilineal descent groups. American Anthropologist 55: 17–41.
1959   Descent, filiation and affinity: a rejoinder to Dr. Leach. Man 59: 193–197, 206–212.

Freeman, J. D.
1958   The family system of the Iban of Borneo. In: The Developmental Cycle in Domestic Groups, ed. by J. Goody. Cambridge Papers in Social Anthropology No. 1, pp. 15–52.
1961   On the concept of the kindred. Journal of the Royal Anthropological Institute 91: 192–220.

Gerth, H. and C. W. Mills
1954   *Character and Social Structure: The Psychology of Social Institutions.* London, Routledge and Kegan Paul Ltd.

Glasse, R.
1959   Revenge and redress among the Huli: a preliminary account. Mankind 5: 273–289.

Gluckman, M.
1955   *Custom and Conflict in Africa.* Glencoe, Ill., The Free Press.
1962   Les rites de passage. In: *Essays on the Ritual of Social Relations,* ed. by M. Gluckman. Manchester, Manchester University Press, pp. 1–52.

Goffman, E.
1958   *The Presentation of Self in Everyday Life.* Garden City, N.Y., Doubleday and Co.
1961   *Encounters: Two Studies in the Sociology of Interaction.* Indianapolis, Indiana, Bobbs-Merrill Co.

Goldie, J.
1909   The people of New Georgia, their manners and customs and

religious beliefs. Royal Society of Queensland, Proceedings 22: 23–30.

1914   The Solomon Islands. In: *A Century in the Pacific*, ed. by J. Cowell, Sydney, n.p.

Goodenough, W.

1955   A problem in Malayo-Polynesian social organization. American Anthropologist 57: 71–83.

1956   Componential analysis and the study of meaning. Language 32: 195–216.

Goody, J.

1958   The fission of domestic groups among the Lo Dagaba. In: The Developmental Cycle in Domestic Groups, J. Goody, ed. Cambridge Papers in Social Anthropology No. l, pp. 53–91.

Groves, M.

1963   The nature of Fijian society: a review. Journal of the Polynesian Society 72: 272–291.

Gulliver, P.

1963   *Social Control in an African Society*. London, Routledge and Kegan Paul Ltd.

Harré, R.

1961   *Theories and Things: A Brief Study in Descriptive Metaphysics*. London, Sheed and Ward.

Hogbin, H. I.

1939   *Experiments in Civilization*. London, Routledge.

Hogbin, H. I. and C. H. Wedgewood

1953   Local grouping in Melanesia. Oceania 23: 241–276.

Ivens, W. G.

1930   *Island Builders of the Pacific*. London, Seeley Service.

Kelly, G. and M. Rothschild

n.d.   Kinship as ideology. Unpublished manuscript.

Lands and Titles Ordinance

1959   Lands and titles ordinance of 1959, B.S.I.P. (mimeo., Honiara).

Lands Commission's Report

1925   Reports and proceedings of the first land's commissioner 1919–1924. Unpublished manuscript on deposit with the Secretariat of the British Solomon Islands Protectorate, Honiara.

Lawrence, P.

1954   Cargo cult and religious beliefs among the Garia. International Archives of Ethnography 47: 1–20.

Leach, E. R.

1958   Concerning Trobriand clans and the kinship category 'tabu.' In: The Developmental Cycle in Domestic Groups, ed. by

J. Goody. Cambridge Papers in Social Anthropology No. 1, pp. 120–145.

1960   The Sinhalese of the dry zone of Northern Ceylon. In: Social Structure in Southeast Asia, ed. by G. P. Murdock. Viking Fund Publications in Anthropology No. 29, pp. 116–126.

1961a   Rethinking Anthropology. London School of Economics Monographs in Social Anthropology No. 22. London, The Athlone Press.

1961b   *Pul Eliya: A Village in Ceylon.* Cambridge, Cambridge University Press.

1962   On certain unconsidered aspects of double descent. Man 62: 130–134.

Lévi-Strauss, C.
1953   Social structure. In: *Anthropology Today*, ed. by A. L. Kroeber. Chicago, University of Chicago Press, pp. 524–553.

Lounsbury, F. G.
1964   The structural analysis of kinship semantics. In: Proceedings of the Ninth International Congressof Linguists, H. G. Lunt, ed., pp. 1073–1093. The Hague, Mouton and Co.

Luxton, C. T. J.
1955   *The Isles of Solomon: A Tale of Missionary Adventure.* Auckland, Methodist Foreign Missionary Society of New Zealand.

Mills, C. W.
1940   Situated actions and vocabularies of motive. American Sociological Review 5: 904–913.

Morrell, W. P.
1960   *Britain in the Pacific Islands.* Oxford, Clarendon Press.

Murdock, G. P.
1964   Genetic classification of the Austronesian languages: a key to Oceanic culture history. Ethnology 3: 117–126.

Nadel, S. F.
1951   *The Foundations of Social Anthropology.* Glencoe, The Free Press.

1957   *The Theory of Social Structure.* Glencoe, The Free Press.

Oliver, D.
1955   *A Solomon Island Society.* Cambridge, Mass. Harvard University Press.

1961   *The Pacific Islands* (revised edition). Garden City, N.Y., Doubleday and Co.

Pacific Islands Year Book
1963   *Pacific Islands Year Book and Who's Who.* Sydney, Pacific Publications Pty. Ltd.

Pehrson, R.
1957   The bilateral network of social relations in Konkama Lapp district. Indiana University Publications, Slavic and East European Series No. 5.

Raulet, H. M.
1960   Social structure and ecology in northwest Melanesia. Unpublished doctoral dissertation, Columbia University.

Read, K.
1955   Morality and the concept of the person among the Gahuku-Gama. Oceania 25: 233–282.

Ribbe, C.
1903   *Zwei Jahre unter den Kannibalen der Salomo-Inseln.* Dresden, n.p.

Rivers, W. H. R.
1914   *The History of Melanesian Society.* 2 vols. Cambridge, Cambridge University Press.
1922   *Essays in the Depopulation of Melanesia.* Cambridge, Cambridge University Press.

Rose, A., Ed.
1962   *Human Behavior and Social Processes.* Boston, Houghton Mifflin Co.

Sahlins, M. D.
1961   The segmentary lineage: an organization of predatory expansion. American Anthropologist 63: 322–345.
1963   Poor man, rich man, big-man, chief: political types in Melanesia and Polynesia. Comparative Studies in Society and History 5: 285–303.

Scheffler, H. W.
1962   Kindred and kin groups in Simbo Island social structure. Ethnology 1: 135–157.
1963   Choiseul Island descent groups. Journal of the Polynesian Society 72: 177–187.
1964a Political finance in Melanesia. Natural History (in press).
1964b Descent concepts and descent groups: the Maori case. Journal of the Polynesian Society 73: 126–133.
1964c The genesis and repression of conflict on Choiseul Island. American Anthropologist 66: 789–804.
1964d The social consequences of peace on Choiseul Island. Ethnology 3: 398–403.

Schneider, D. M.
1961   Introduction: the distinctive features of matrilineal descent

groups. In: *Matrilineal Kinship*, ed. by D. M. Schneider and K. Gough. Berkeley and Los Angeles, University of California Press.

1963   Some muddles in the models: or "how the system really works." Mimeo. (Forthcoming in *The Relevance of Models for Social Anthropology*, M. Banton, ed. Association of Social Anthropologists Monograph No. 1.)

Service, E.
1962   *Primitive Social Organization: An Evolutionary Perspective.* New York, Random House.

Singh Uberoi, J. P.
1962   *Politics of the Kula Ring.* Manchester, Manchester University Press.

Sommerville, B. T.
1896   Ethnographic notes on New Georgia. Journal of the Royal Anthropological Institute 26: 357–412.

Stanner, W. E. H.
1959   Continuity and schism in an African tribe: a review. Oceania 29: 208–217.

1963   On aboriginal religion. Oceania 34: 56–58.

Thurnwald, R.
1912   *Forschungen auf den Salomo-Inseln und in dem Bismark-Archipel.* 3 vols. Berlin, n.p.

de Tolna, R. F.
1905   *Chez les Cannibales: Huit Ans de Croisière Dans l'Ocean Pacifique Abord du Yacht "Le Tolna."* Paris, Libraire Plon.

Turner, V. W.
1956   *Schism and Continuity in an African Society.* Manchester, Manchester University Press.

Wallace, A. F. C.
1961   *Culture and Personality.* New York, Random House.

Wallace, A. F. C. and J. Atkins
1960   The meaning of kinship terms. American Anthropologist 62: 58–80.

Watson, C. H.
1926   *Cannibals and Head-hunters: Victories of the Gospel in the South Seas.* Washington, D. C., n.p.

Woodford, C. M.
1909   The canoes of the British Solomon Islands Protectorate. Journal of the Royal Anthropological Institute 39: 506–516.

Worsley, P. M.
1956   The kinship system of the Tallensi: a revaluation. Journal of the Royal Anthropological Institute 86: 37–75.

INDEX

317

Cognatic-descent categories (*Continued*)
ture of, 55 ff.; size of, 54, 59 f.; number of, 49
Colson, E., 233
Compensation, 99, 106, 203, 235
Conflict: of allegiances, 153 f., 226, 233 ff., 288, 297 f.; between kin, 86; causes of, 216 ff., 234
Conflict, intergroup, 127, 153 ff.; constraints on, 216 ff., 233 ff., 288; effects on descent groups, 95; example of, 227 ff.; strategy of, 223 ff.; suppression of, 19–28 *passim*, 188
Conflict, intragroup, 124, 150 ff., 220 ff.
Contracts, 230 ff.; example of, 227 ff.
Conversion. *See* Missionization
Coöptative process, 116, 137 ff., 148, 158, 163; rarity of change of affiliation by, 161
Copra, 9, 18, 20, 31
Courts, native, 32 f., 120, 268, 270, 275, 276, 286
Cremation, 187, 248
Cumulative patrifiliation, 126

Davis, K., 299 n.
Debts, 94, 215 f.; inheritance of, 211
Descent, concepts, viii, 13 f., 42, 44, 46, 62
Descent groups, 42 ff., 92–109 *passim*, 286 ff.
agnatic status in, 46, 100 ff., 117; becoming a member, 97 ff., 114 ff.
branches of, 45, 50, 51, 61 f., 94; founding of, 58, 61 ff., *see also,* Segmentation; changes of status of, 192 f.; managers of, 119, 198 f.; rights of, 52, 119; through women, 60, 104 f.,
changes of affiliation, 96–99, 105, 137 ff., 144 ff., 151; constraints on changes of affiliation, 96, 115, 139 f., 142–152 *passim*, 262 ff.; frequency of changes of affiliation, 146 f., 152 ff., 162
choice of affiliation, 45–48, 62, 96, 99, 105, 108 f., 148
change of status in, 117 ff., 128
classes of membership, 100 ff., *see*

Descent groups (*Continued*)
also Primary, Secondary and Contingent members
competition for status in, 189, 192 f.
composition of, 159 ff.
consolidation of membership of, 114 ff., 125 ff., 151, 273, 284 f., 286
contingent membership, 103 ff., 129
"core" (*kapakapa*), 40, 46, 60, 92 f., 156, 159
criteria for affiliation, 44 ff., 62, 96 ff.
estates of, *see* Estates
factions in, 189, 191, 192 f.
founders of, 54 f.
guests of, 105 f., 133 f.
genealogies of, *see* Cognatic-descent categories
genealogical entitlement, 44 ff., 62, 96 ff., 108 f.; range of, 144, 145, 155, 175
ideology of, 45 ff., 61, 92 ff., 110–178 *passim*
ideology of openness of, 147, 149 f.
instability of, 95 f., 287
modes of affiliation, frequencies of, 158 ff.
membership, importance of securing, 113 f., 196 f.
membership, maintenance of, 151, 165
membership, multiple, 114 f., 255 ff., 286 f.
membership, nature of, 14, 147
major, 45, 94
minor, 45, 94
mobility between, 95, 106
non-residents, rights of, 106 ff.
primary members, 45, 47, 100 f., 117
as primary segments, 12 f., 40, 92
recognition as a member of, 62 f., 97
recruitment of outsiders, 137 ff.
relations between, 14, 179–239 *passim*, 287 f.
rights in, jural distribution of, 100 ff.
rights in, usage of, 116 ff., 156 f.
secondary members of, 47, 100 ff., 117 ff., 150